Universal Wisdom

Universal Wisdom

*Finding Answers to
Life's Ultimate Questions*

Brett Kelly

Author of the Bestseller *Collective Wisdom*

Published by Clown Publishing
PO Box 1764, North Sydney NSW 2059, Australia
www.brettkelly.com.au

Distributed by River Grove Books

Design and composition by Reno Design, Sydney (from original designs of Bowra & Bowra, Sydney)
Cover design by Reno Design, Sydney (from original designs of Bowra & Bowra, Sydney)

Publisher's Cataloging-in-Publication data is available.

Print ISBN: 978-1-7640485-3-8

eBook ISBN: 978-1-7640485-2-1

First Edition

For Rebecca, Thomas, Dad, Mark
and the 'Kelly Girls'.

'Wisdom is supreme; therefore get wisdom.

Though it cost you all you have, get understanding.'

Contents

PROFILES

Foreword

You meet some rather different people in life. You come across some interesting projects.

There is only one Brett Kelly. And our book, *Universal Wisdom* is very much a Brett Kelly vision and passion – and a project I feel immensely happy to have contributed to.

When Brett phoned me out of the blue to announce he wanted me to help him with this book project called *Universal Wisdom*, I thought to myself 'well, with a title like that, this will be a modest and unassuming little assignment – after all, not only are we writing about wisdom, but UNIVERSAL wisdom… piece of cake!'

Truth is, my facetious response probably resulted from a sense of profound shock – I hardly qualify as even a modest font of wisdom, let alone the universal variety.

When Brett began to explain his project, it became very quickly apparent that here was a young man on a mission – his very own mission to better understand… just about everything!

And he approached his quest with exceptional enthusiasm, exuberance, energy, good humour, endless curiosity… and compassion.

One good way of learning what life is about, is to explore the lives of the greats – you'll soon find that many of their lives contain contradictions, difficulties, challenges, and disappointments – as well as triumphs and achievements.

But in their life journeys, one can also begin to see what made them great – and therein are the lessons for us all.

Universal Wisdom is a book that features the lives of seven great people who obviously have special resonances for Brett. It is a book about how those seven lives have helped Brett learn more about life, and yes, become wiser.

His curiosity and enthusiasm have been more than just a little contagious – this has been one of the more enjoyable projects I have worked on. And in working with Brett on researching and assisting in writing the seven biographies, I have learned much more than I probably still realise.

And in working with Brett, I have made a firm friend of a young man whose search for truth and wisdom has taught me a few things, and has much to teach us all.

His is a journey well worth watching.

DAN STOJANOVICH
August 2005

Preface

This book wrote itself in a very real sense – the lives of the seven people featured have been well chronicled and lived in the full glare of the public.

Universal Wisdom is a series of seven profiles of prominent people that continues the conversation commenced with the 1998 publication of *Collective Wisdom*. It is Part II of a III book series.

The book features profiles of seven universally admired people – Warren Buffett, Martin Luther King, Nelson Mandela, Gandhi, Pope John Paul II, Helen Keller and Mother Teresa of Calcutta. Each profile contains:

- a biography of the person's life,

- an essay on how that person's example shed some light on one of life's ultimate questions for me; and finally

- some of the person's own words in the form of their own speeches and quotes.

The profiles demonstrate how each of these people discerned some "universal wisdom" – a commonly applicable principle – applied it in their own lives, improving themselves and the world inhabited by us all.

It is the book's aim to encourage people of all ages, stages and walks of life to consider the deepest "ultimate" questions of life.

Acknowledgements

Thank you to all those people throughout my life who have urged me to seek wisdom. Especially my late father, my mother, brothers, whole family, friends, teachers, current/former work colleagues and employers.

I would like to thank Mr Warren Buffett, Mr Nelson Mandela, Rev. Dr Martin Luther-King, Jr, Mr Mohandas Gandhi, His Holiness Pope John Paul II, Ms Helen Keller and Mother Teresa of Calcutta, for the good aspects of the lives that they have lived and for the example that they have given which has inspired me to seek the most from life.

Finally, I would like to thank Rebecca – it is a great privilege to be your husband.

Introduction

'Welcome back! Brett Kelly always did well at school and in sport, and at 22 he had already cracked a good job in merchant banking. But then his dream run ended. He was laid off, told his work was not good enough and that he didn't fit in with other people.

This setback spurred Brett Kelly to wonder what it was that made some people successful. He decided to try to find out from people who had achieved success. After thousands of phone calls and scores of interviews, here's the result – a book called *Collective Wisdom*.

Brett Kelly ignored all the doubters to write it, and to publish it himself. Howard Gipps has the story...'

It was Monday night, 3 August 1998, when Ray Martin on his top-rating television program *A Current Affair*, told his viewing audience of millions across Australia the story of my struggle from a tough spot, unemployed and searching for answers, to publishing a book. It was then that things started to get really frantic.

I had met Ray Martin at the opening of a performing arts centre in Crows Nest in Sydney, some months before. A friend of mine, knowing about my book project, had mentioned that he would be attending as the guest of honour and urged me to attend and try to speak with him. In the coffee break, I approached him and asked whether he would let me interview him for a book I was putting together of interviews with prominent Australians.

His interest aroused, he asked some questions which included, 'Who else have you interviewed?' (At this point I had gathered 33 people in all.) I pulled out the first draft of the cover of the book, which I had received that day from the graphic designer, and showed him the names that were listed on the back cover: Col Allen, Peter Brock, Professor Gavin Brown, Edmund Capon, Ken Done, Mark Ella, John Elliott, Peter Fitzsimons, Lindsay Fox, Peter Garrett, Sir John Gorton, Kathryn Greiner, Gerry Harvey, Bob Hawke, Kerry Jones, Jeff Kennett, Cheryl Kernot, Hugh Mackay, Rod McGeoch, H G Nelson, Pat O'Shane, Poppy King, Imelda Roche, Peter Ritchie, Bruce Ruxton, Siimon Reynolds, John Symond, Arthur Tunstall, Malcolm Turnbull, Robert Turner and Anthony Warlow.

Ray immediately asked 'How long did it take you to get the interviews?' My response 'four months to date' seemed to astonish him and he was happy to grant my request for an interview, passing me his contact details and urging me to contact his office on the following Monday morning.

This I did. My brother, who took the photographs in the book, and I presented ourselves at Channel Nine. Ray let me interview him and Nathan to photograph him – it was surreal and very kind of him.

Now for *A Current Affair* to feature the book all these months later was unbelievable. To put it mildly, I was absolutely amazed at the interest the book was generating – interviews on JJJ radio, *Good Morning Australia* with Bert Newton, FCTV on Channel 10, together with Bob Hawke... and so on.

By the time the book had been out less than a week, it had become a runaway national number one bestseller. At least I was not going to go bankrupt, which had been a distinct possibility, as I had had to borrow money to publish the book.

What followed was extraordinary. Let me relate just one example. While I was working on the book, and also unemployed, I used to watch the National Press Club addresses from Canberra on the ABC. All manner of incredible people spoke on a multitude of topics, and being someone who is interested in just about everything, I was always fascinated by the addressees. It came to my mind that when the book was eventually published I should see whether I could hold a book launch at the National Press Club. Perhaps I could speak about the book and the relevance of what I had learned for other young Australians.

Crazy idea: even crazier outcome. When the book was completed I phoned the National Press Club and asked how they select their speakers. I was put through to the relevant person who asked some questions, requested that I mail a copy of the book to them and assured me it would be considered. Just a couple of days later I received a phone call from the Press Club advising that, if I were able to arrange for Senator Natasha Stott Despoja, who had written the Foreword of the book, to speak with me, then they would welcome the opportunity to host the book launch live on national television.

On Tuesday 12 August 1998, together with my father, I arrived at the National Press Club in Canberra. On entry I was struck by two things: firstly the portraits on the wall of people who had previously addressed the Club (I remember particularly noting Sir Peter Ustinov and Greg Norman); secondly, I noted that Benjamin Netanyahu, the Israeli Prime Minister, had addressed the Club on the previous day, and on the next day it was to be the Prime Minister and Treasurer of Australia, Mr Howard and Mr Costello. Mind blowing company!

Senator Stott Despoja arrived and we ate lunch together. Then suddenly the lights in the room became very bright and we were asked to move onto the stage. A countdown occurred. (We were on live television to more than 60,000 viewers, I was later told.) Introductions were made and Senator Stott Despoja spoke on youth issues for 30 minutes. Then it was my turn. My stomach churned and my legs actually shook un-controllably. I clung to the podium that, thank goodness, was very solid and fixed to the stage. With a wave of emotional intensity I had never felt before, I commenced to address the audience. The story I related of being unemployed and the compilation of *Collective Wisdom* was very well received.

For two years following the publication of the book I was inundated with requests – from youth and community groups to conferences of large corporations and associations – to speak on how *Collective Wisdom* came into being. At the end of each presentation I would take questions and try, to the best of my ability, to provide answers.

These were incredible opportunities to meet people of all ages and from all walks and stages of life; more than twenty thousand people across Australia, aged from 12 to 90, giving me a tremendous insight into people and their questions about life.

As a young person I found it extremely confronting to be asked questions that were not the standard: 'Who did you like the best of the people you interviewed?', 'How did you find Mr X to be in real life?', 'What is Mrs so-and-so like?'. I was being asked the sorts of questions that, more than anything, pushed me to continue to seek and grow, 'What do you live for?', 'My son killed himself or my friend's son killed himself, why do you think our young men are killing themselves?', 'Who are your heroes – because not all of these people in your book are perfect?', 'My son or daughter or my parents will not listen to me. Why do you think that is?', 'How do you get the self-esteem to get up and do what you have done?', 'Are you a believer?', 'Are you married?', 'My parents take drugs/drink/gamble and don't care about me. What chance do I have with role models like them?'

What was very interesting was the consistent nature of the questions that I would be asked – no matter the age, geographical location or material circumstances of the group that I addressed. To the point where I would almost be able to name the questions that I would be asked and in what order!

The issue of youth suicide, particularly the suicide of young men, seemed to be everywhere. To be asked by a brother, sister, mother, father or grandparent – 'Why would a young person kill themselves?' troubled me very deeply. I did not have the answer, and yet I, too, had at times pondered what it would be like to no longer exist.

Given the serious nature of the questions I was being asked, I directed my habit of reading a minimum of one book per week towards literature addressing the issue of youth suicide, and began an intensely serious push to find answers to tough questions. I later read a book that raised questions such as, 'Why is there something and not nothing?', 'What am I here for?', 'How can I be happy?' – ultimate questions. I noted that they had not been considered in any of my schooling to date.

During the next five years I read something like six or seven hundred books and articles, essays, lecture notes and whatever I could get my hands on on all sorts of topics trying to find answers to the tough, ultimate, questions of life I had been asked repeatedly. These times also involved me in taking personal risks, being in relationships, starting a business, learning new skills, travelling and meeting new people.

In August 2003, after a long battle with cancer, my father died. He had been a great Dad, always there for me and my brothers and always encouraging me to 'have a go'. He had convinced me that I could achieve if I had a go, and even when I had the crazy idea of *Collective Wisdom* he supported my efforts.

Now death has an amazing ability to focus the mind and Dad's passing caused me to again look deeper at life. You see when he lay, entirely alone on his deathbed – in spite of the fact we were there, (he had eight sons) – no one else could take his place. And the stark fact that you come into this world by yourself and leave it the same way – that cars, houses and flat screen TVs do not visit you – were all too clear.

So what of life? What is it? What to do with it? This started again to have that deeply personal, searing interest for me.

Now, during and after the publication of *Collective Wisdom*, one of the most frequent questions I was continually asked was, 'Will you write another book?'. I had no idea and would simply respond, 'Yes, when I have something more to say.'

Then I received this letter in October 2004:

Dear Brett,

I recently had the pleasure of reading your book, 'Collective Wisdom' after coming across it in my local library. I was taken not only by the impressive and diverse group of people that you were able to gain a contribution from, I thought that the style, method and content of the interviews were useful, respectful and revealing. I was even more interested in the autobiographical introduction. The determination and vision displayed in conceiving and self-publishing such a book were really quite remarkable. Given that it is six years since the date of publication I am interested in what you have done since then and what impact the process you went through to bring the book to fruition and the ideas and experience that you gained from the interviews themselves have had on your life and career.

Yours sincerely, Young Australian

It was clear to me, as I regularly continued to receive such correspondence as well as plenty of invitations to present the story of *Collective Wisdom*, that I had started a conversation and that there were people out there who wanted to continue the discussion. And so I decided I should and would. Though I was filled with trepidation as to whether anyone would be interested and what they would think of what I thought!

Now this letter could not be simply answered, and on the day of writing this sentence I have not yet responded. Time was needed to sit down and write a thoughtful, honest and useful response.

Taking up this letter, I started to think through how best I could answer, some way that would adequately and helpfully respond. The writer is totally unknown to me and I did not want to offend, yet at the same time I wanted to share what I had discovered – which appeared to be what he wanted to know.

So I was thinking, 'I am too young, not qualified, etc' to write a book on what I really think. People will think I am full of myself, and wisdom anyway is humble and quiet. Still I am learning and want to do more study, yet the time was now and I am just continuing a conversation – perhaps that will be acceptable? And anyway, he asked the questions, they are not just my questions, what about all the people that asked me these questions?

Write a book Brett! I knew that was the answer. Just throw together where you are at, be honest, let people know that you are young, searching, just proposing where you are at for conversation and any use others may find. I knew that was what was needed to answer the letter and share with all those who had been good enough over the years to pose the questions – as well as those questions posed in day-to-day living.

It was while trying to study for my final exams in order to complete my Masters in Taxation degree that I jotted down the outline of the book as follows: ideas matter, so choose them carefully, same questions/different people – ultimate questions of life, universal principles, people who have lived the answers.

Now this gibberish may not look like much, but a book was to emerge from these rough notes. I went on that day and wrote a list of my heroes: Warren Buffett the man who took $50 and turned it into $US42 billion in his own lifetime – the greatest investor who ever has lived; Nelson Mandela who persisted and forgave his enemies; Mother Teresa of Calcutta who loved the unlovable; Helen Keller who, though deaf and blind, learned to read and encouraged others to hope in the possibilities of human life; Martin Luther King who would not let bigots win; Gandhi who conquered himself and showed others how to resist evil; and finally Pope John Paul II who stood for something even when hard!

With this outline, I simply thought through how I could best communicate what I had been shown, and concluded that many of us would like to read the biographies of these people and hear their words. Now this list is made up of real people, not saints (although one is!), who struggled with life and yet lived in accordance with a universal wisdom that they discovered and which made them universally admired.

And so this book was conceived to show what I have learned since the publication of *Collective Wisdom*, through the lives of my heroes. I have learned that ideas matter – and that some ideas apply as universal principles. They are more helpful for a fulfilling life in all times, places and cultures – so we should choose our ideas carefully – and heroes even more so!

In coming to know the heroes I have chosen over the years, I have read so much of their work and words. Each one of them, in their own words, had come to understand and live principles that they considered universal – always applicable – and this conclusion seemed to give them a certainty to pursue their unique course when the odds were against them. It appears to be what makes them the people the world most admires – their untiring dedication to Universal Wisdom in their lives. Consider the reflections of my heroes as follows:

'You're lucky in life if you have the right heroes. I advise all of you, to the extent that you can, pick out a few heroes. There's nothing like the right ones.' – WARREN BUFFETT

'For modern man, absolute right and absolute wrong are a matter of what the majority is doing. Right and wrong are relative to the likes and dislikes and the customs of a particular community. We have unconsciously applied Einstein's theory of relativity, which properly described the physical universe, to the moral and ethical realm.' – MARTIN LUTHER KING

'We must use time wisely and forever realize that the time is always ripe to do right.' – NELSON MANDELA

'Whether humanity will consciously follow the law of love, I do not know. But that need not disturb me. The law will work just as the law of gravitation works, whether we accept it or not. The person who discovered the law of love was a far greater scientist than any of our modern scientists. Only our explorations have not gone far enough and so it is not possible for everyone to see all its workings.' – MOHANDAS GANDHI

'When freedom does not have a purpose, when it does not wish to know anything about the rule of law engraved in the hearts of men and women, when it does not listen to the voice of conscience, it turns against humanity and society.' – POPE JOHN PAUL II

'It gives me a deep comforting sense that "things seen are temporal and things unseen are eternal."' – HELEN KELLER

'True love does not count the cost, it just loves.' – MOTHER TERESA

Collective Wisdom had taught me to work with people who had the skills and experience that I did not. So it was to be once again when I looked up the Yellow Pages and found an ad for a writer, 'Your story well told!'. Perhaps he could help me draft the biographies! Long enough to get the detail – not simply a magazine article, and short enough to be accessible to people who are busy.

I phoned Dan, told him the story of *Collective Wisdom*, pitched a proposal for his involvement in a new book project and arranged to meet him the next Saturday in Melbourne. We met. Dan agreed – liked the idea, agreed to a discounted rate for his involvement and we have worked together ever since on the project.

Now, Dan is over 50 years of age, has married, had children, gained degrees, held high-powered commercial positions and is a terrific thinking person. He would be a sounding board and representative during the process for the eventual readership.

The project was taking shape. Now just to finalise the ultimate questions I would seek to discuss in the book. Much to-ing and fro-ing went on in my head. My heart was challenged and I wondered whether I had the strength to really say it as I saw it. While people admired these heroes of mine, would they really want to hear their views when they didn't coincide with their own?

In the end I was tired and decided that I would just put it out there, propose not dictate, present clearly some – not all – of the questions I had been asked – what they were about for me – and a discussion of my understandings to date. The questions shaped up as follows:

1. What is the biggest lesson you learned from *Collective Wisdom*?
2. What are you doing for others?
3. What do you live for? What would you die for?
4. How did you decide to get up and write a book straight after getting sacked?
5. Are you a believer? (Is there a God?)
6. Why do you think my son killed himself?
7. Are you married? (What is love?)

So then it remained to write the seven essays, complete the intro-duction, preface, acknowledgements and later the epilogue, then have the book designed, typeset and see whether anyone wanted to publish it! The undertaking of a project like this is enormous and so many people have helped in various ways.

The adventure has yielded considerable results. The search has uncovered the little known source of the power that drives the truly extraordinary – it is a certainty that comes from Universal Wisdom. When these people unite(d) their unique gifts and talents with ideas that are true in all times, places and cultures – the self doubt disappears and they become unstoppable.

Should you be reading this introduction, I trust that Universal Wisdom encourages you in your own search for meaning.

BRETT KELLY
August 2005

PROFILES

Warren Buffett

INVESTOR

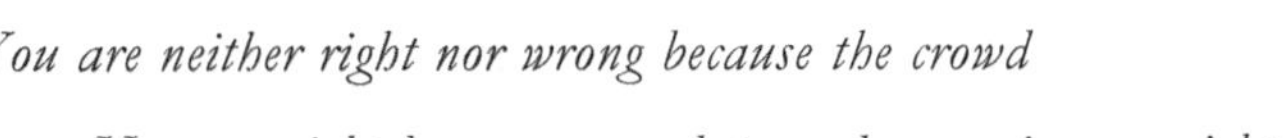

*'You are neither right nor wrong because the crowd
disagrees with you. You are right because your data and reasoning are right.'*

The Life of Warren Buffett

1930   30 August: Warren Edward Buffett born to Howard and Leila Buffett, in Nebraska.

1941   Buys first stock at age 11 at $38 per share. Falls to $27 then climbs to $40. Sells. Stock shoots over $200 per share.

1943   Warren declares he will be a millionaire by the time he turns 30.

1950   Turned down by Harvard Business School. Enrols at Columbia under Ben Graham, whom three years later offers him a job.

1952   Marries Susie, they have their first child, also called Susie.

1956   Ben Graham folds partnership. Since leaving college six years earlier, Warren's savings have grown from $9,800 to over $140,000.

1959   Meets Charlie Munger.

1962   Begins to buy stock in Berkshire Hathaway.

1964   Starts buying American Express shares.

1969   Following most successful year, Buffett closes the partnership, liquidates assets.

1973   Stock prices begin to drop, Buffett euphoric.

1987   October crash, Berkshire loses 25 percent of its value, Buffett loses $342 million personally.

1988   Buffett begins buying stock in Coca-Cola, eventually purchasing up to 7 percent of the company for $1.02 billion. It will turn out to be one of Berkshire's most lucrative investments.

1998   Berkshire posts a 48% increase in net earnings, to $2.8 billion, on revenues of $13.8 billion. Berkshire has amassed shareholder equity of $57 billion (well ahead of General Electric, Microsoft, and every other US corporation – ranking second in the world to Royal Dutch/Shell Group. Berkshire's book value per share has risen 24.7% a year since 1965.

2004   29 July: Wife Susie dies, aged 72. They were never divorced.

2005   Berkshire Hathaway average return since 1964 is 22.2%. Shares trade for $92,000 each. Buffett is the second wealthiest person in USA with personal wealth of $42 billion – from an initial investment of $100 in 1956. A $10,000 investment in Berkshire when Buffett bought control in 1965, would be worth over $50 million now, vs. $500,000 if invested in S&P 500 index. As CEO of Berkshire Buffett still pays himself a salary of $100,000 with no stock options.

biography

Lauded as the greatest stock market investor of all time, Warren Edward Buffett is one of the richest men in the world, and one of the few people who has amassed their fortune predominantly by investing directly in the stock market.

Yet, when you see this energised older man casually perched on the edge of a desk, speaking to a roomful of young business students, you realise that this is not the classic, ruthless Wall Street tycoon talking. When he engages them about money, investing, business principles and life in general, you realise that this is one very idiosyncratic man.

Here is a wisdom that resonates with "old style" values such as integrity, character, prudence and temperance. And it seems to work in one of the fiercest marketplaces on earth.

No wonder some 17,000 of the 275,000 shareholders in his company Berkshire Hathaway, turn up in Omaha for the Annual General Meeting (6 percent). It is like a religious convention where pilgrims come to pay homage to the guru. By comparison, an IBM annual general meeting might attract some 800 of its 640,000 shareholders (0.125 percent).

Needless to say, this annual event totally takes over the town of Omaha, Nebraska. And there in the middle of it all, as casual as ever, with his business partner Charlie Munger by his side, Warren Buffett presides.

As part of the festivities, "local boy" Warren, dressed in the uniform of the local baseball team, pitches the baseball to get things going down at the ball park, surrounded by adoring fans. But this is just a sideshow to the main event… the AGM, where Warren and Charlie hold court for their disciples, the many investors that they have made so wealthy.

There is a relaxed, country style, low-key demeanour about the man, who is very approachable, warm and friendly. What you see is what you get! A man who has formed a view of the world, who has found his voice, who knows who he is, has set his course in life, and has used his talents and interests to their best advantage.

No wonder people come in their thousands to listen to his approach to business and life in general. It is plain to see that under this friendly open style, there is a shrewd intelligence and a principled strength of character.

No one of course achieves such outstanding business success by being a naïve saint. Buffett is driven and disciplined, clever, cunning and tough. He has proven he can prosper in one of the toughest business environments in the world. But the underlying character of the man shines through – and it has been this constancy of character which has guided his course for decades.

It is not like he has been hiding his beliefs – they have always been out there in the open for all to see. Anybody who cares to listen is welcome to know…

Warren Edward Buffett was born in Omaha on 30 August 1930, the second child and only son of three children. His father was a securities salesman and for a while, a Republican congressman. His mother was the daughter of the newspaper publisher in the tiny town of West Point, Nebraska. They met while working on the local college newspaper.

The Buffetts had been in Nebraska since 1869, and were renowned as small business people who were not too keen on spending a dollar. Early life was very tough, and it was not until Warren was some 6 years old that the family fortunes began to look up a little.

But those times had their effect on Warren, and even at that age he was determined to be rich one day. It was a theme that dominated his thinking throughout his life.

Even at the age of six, during a family vacation, Warren bought a six-pack of Coca-Cola for 25 cents, selling them individually at five cents, thus showing a profit of 5 cents. Back in Omaha, he bought soda pop from his grandfather's grocery store and sold it door-to-door while the other children played.

Warren was committed to amassing capital. When he was seven he was hospitalised with a mysterious fever and doctors removed his appendix. While in recovery, he filled a page with numbers, telling the nurses that these represented his future capital, and that he would make money and have his picture in the paper!

His father Howard was very supportive and did not want his son to suffer the same privations of his own youth. Howard was a hard worker with an intellectual bent, interested in religion and politics. Strongly conservative, he was an independent thinker with firmly-held beliefs, and would often quote Emerson: "The great man is he who in the midst of the crowd keeps with perfect sweetness the independence of solitude." Warren must have been listening…

Warren was impressed and inspired by his father, and the independence to know his own mind and steer his own course stayed with him for the rest of his life. He was not afraid to be who he was – and still isn't.

As his father's business prospered, Warren became more interested in how the business worked, as well as the stock market in general. Some of the brokers allowed young Warren to chalk prices on the blackboard, and he also began to chart them, observing their fluctuations, bewitched by their patterns.

He was only eleven years old when in 1941 he made his first stock purchase: six shares of Cities Service preferred stock (three for himself, three for sister Doris), at $38 per share, only to see the price quickly plunge to $27. When it finally recovered to $40 dollars he sold, making his first $5 of profit, but having a very testing time of it. Even worse, the price soon surged to $200! It was the first lesson in patience and looking to the long term... a lesson he never forgot.

When his father was elected to Congress in 1942, the family moved to Washington DC. Warren did not like it, and after faking an illness, convinced his parents to send him back to Omaha for a year with his grandfather. However by the fall of 1943, he had to go back to Washington, and it was there that he took up a paper delivery round, distributing *The Washington Post*.

Making money was always an obsession – in 1943 he declared that he would be a millionaire by the time he turned thirty, or he would jump off the tallest building in Omaha!

Buffett was always a whiz with numbers, and was continually calculating the odds on various eventualities. Even when he went to Sunday School he sat there calculating life spans. There was a purpose to his calculations... he wanted to know whether faith would make him live longer! Practical Warren always liked measurable, visible, tangible results.

In 1945 he was making $175 a month delivering *The Washington Post*. During 1947, his senior year of high school, he and a friend bought a used pinball machine for $25. They placed it in a nearby barber shop to try and make some money. Within months, they had three machines in three locations. The business was sold later in the year to a war veteran for $1,200!

By the end of that year, Warren had earned over $5,000 delivering newspapers. His father urged him to attend college, but Warren was not too keen.

In his senior year he was already planning a career, not just in business, but specifically in investing. In his high-school graduation yearbook he was described as: "likes math... future stockbroker".

He enrolled at the Wharton School of Finance and Commerce at the University of Pennsylvania, but was soon complaining that he knew more than the teachers and so left.

He was developing a very strong faith in his own abilities and his own way of going about things... he was beginning to identify a way that the world worked for him, and a way that he could work in the world – but there was still a way to go.

When Howard was defeated in the 1948 Congressional race, Warren returned home to Omaha and transferred to the University of Nebraska-Lincoln. Working full-time, he managed to graduate in only three years by taking his last three credits over the summer. His savings by this time had amounted to $9,800.

He applied to Harvard Business School in 1950 but was turned down "too young", and eventually enrolled at Columbia after learning that the legendary stock market guru Ben Graham was a professor there. To Buffett, finding Graham was almost like finding God!

Graham had come up with the principle of the "intrinsic" value of a business – a measure of a business' true worth that was completely and totally independent of the stock price. This "intrinsic value" was based on the estimated owner earnings that could be expected in the future.

Using this "intrinsic value", investors could decide what a company was worth – and make investment decisions accordingly. Graham's book, entitled *The Intelligent Investor*, is still celebrated by Buffett as 'the greatest book on investing ever written'.

According to Graham, the prerequisites of good investing were 'first, good intelligence, second, sound principles of operation, and most important, firmness of character'. Buffett had all three.

Graham recommended investors disregard stock prices, and focus on the inherent value of the businesses "beneath". He suggested that the stock exchange was just a "voting machine" which registered people's opinions, but not a "weighing machine" that determined real value. The Graham approach was to invest at a price below the inherent value, and then wait for the market to catch up. Based on rigorous analysis, this approach appealed greatly to Buffett, and was fundamental to his own thinking.

This drive to understand completely occupied him extensively – it wasn't work – he absolutely enjoyed it! An insight into Buffett's thoroughness in getting the information he needed to make decisions his way, was provided by his interest in GEICO Insurance in 1951. Buffett discovered Graham was on the Board of GEICO, and he had to know more, so he took a train to the head office in Washington DC. It was closed. Determined to talk to someone, Buffett knocked on the door until a janitor let him in. Eventually they found a man on the sixth floor – the Financial Vice President, whom the eager Warren interrogated for hours, trying to really understand how the business worked. Many years later, Buffett bought GEICO outright.

Buffett was renowned for being mathematically gifted and having a prodigious memory for facts and figures. He knew almost every balance sheet on the New York Stock Exchange. This gave him a distinctive, if quirky, self confidence. He knew his stuff.

When Buffett graduated in 1951, both Graham and his father advised him not to get into the stock market, as each had memories of the Depression and stock market crashes. But Buffett had been awarded the only A+ Graham had ever given in some 20 years at Columbia, so Buffett made what he thought was an irresistible offer – to work for the Graham Newman firm for nothing! But Graham turned him down – he preferred to hold his spots for Jews, as Jews were locked out of gentile Wall Street firms in those days.

Buffett was not too interested in the rest of Wall Street, so he headed home to Omaha and his father's brokerage business, Buffett-Falk & Co where he became a securities salesman around Omaha, selling various stocks to clients. The young salesman's appetite for research was extraordinary, Buffett was full of facts.

He began dating local girl Susan Thompson, and also purchased a Texaco station and some real estate as a side investment, but neither worked out. He also took a Dale Carnegie public speaking course, and began teaching night class in "Investment Principles" at the University of Nebraska. Most of his students were twice his age.

The relationship with Susie progressed, and in April 1952 Warren and Susie were married, rented an apartment for $65 a month, and had their first child, also called Susie. In order to save money, they allegedly made a bed for her in a dresser drawer.

In 1954 Ben Graham phoned Warren to offer him a job at his partnership – the employment climate had changed – non-Jews were being hired – and Buffett's starting salary was to be $12,000 a year. He was on the next plane and Warren and Susie soon made a home in New York.

Graham Newman was a mutual fund that bought stocks according to particular techniques championed by Graham. Everything was done by the numbers. Buffett blossomed in this environment; it was soon apparent that he knew more about stocks than most. As his prowess grew, he developed a reputation – people would sit on the floor around him and listen to him talk. He was developing a real appetite for comprehensive information. But as well as studying balance sheets, he also wanted to talk to the people actually managing companies. He really wanted to get to understand the values of the people who drove these businesses, to get to grips with their characters. Differences between the Graham and Buffett philosophies began to emerge. Warren wanted to understand all the factors relevant to how a company actually worked and how it became superior in its field. He wanted both quantitative and qualitative data.

However, he retained Graham's principles of "buying value, keeping a margin of safety, and maintaining a detachment from daily market gyrations". Today, Buffett still abides by those principles.

Many years later, Buffett would still pay homage to Graham's influence when he said: 'The best thing I did was to choose the right heroes. It all comes from Graham.'

In 1956 Graham decided to retire from the partnership, bringing to an end Buffett's involvement. Buffett was now keen to get back to Omaha and see what he could do there, so he and his family returned there. Although Graham Newman's performance had been very good, it was not spectacular. In the meantime, investing on his own, Buffett had done better than the firm. In the six years since 1950, Buffett had increased his personal capital from $9,800 to $140,000.

On 1 May that year, at the age of 25, Warren created Buffett Associates Ltd. Seven family members and friends put in a total of $105,000 with Buffett himself investing only $100. He would never again work for anyone else. Before the end of the year, he was managing around $300,000 in capital. The boy had plans.

He had no track record as an independent operator and nothing on paper to show he was worthy of people's trust. He also wanted absolute control over the money entrusted to him as he was convinced that he could see things that others would miss. Exceptionally analytical and consistent, he absolutely hated losing money, looking upon it as a great waste of future compounding opportunities. Whether playing cards, golf or anything else, he was always assessing risk and always calculating the odds.

But his dedication and self-assurance impressed people, and the overall history of good results gradually increased the partnerships. Over the year, two additional partnerships were commenced, followed in 1957 by two more, making a total of five, all of which were managed from home.

In 1957, with their third child on the way, the Buffetts purchased a five-bedroom, stucco house on Farnam Street for $31,500. Affectionately nicknamed "Buffett's Folly", Buffett still lives there today.

Having established this comfort zone, Buffett resolutely remained in it. This also was only too apparent in his predictable personal habits, his crumpled clothing and simple meals (often just hamburgers, french fries and Coke). He liked to stay comfortable and focus on his work.

After all, life was looking good – he had three children, a beautiful wife, and a very successful business.

Although he had an encyclopedic knowledge of the market, his philosophy was not to chase everything, but rather choose a few stocks and really get to know them in depth. His emphasis was on fundamental, long term value and he avoided trying to forecast the stock market in general. It was not just the money at the end of the day, it was the process of actually creating it that he enjoyed so much.

He certainly would never buy stocks just on the basis of other people's opinions. He had to analyse the "businesses underneath" himself – the people, the products, the market and the longer term prospects. And only when the time was right, would he buy.

A cornerstone of his approach was never to rely on eventually making a good sale. The trick was to buy cheap – that way, even a mediocre sale would make money.

By the end of the third year of the partnerships, Buffett had doubled their money.

It was soon after, in 1959, that Warren met Charlie Munger, a highly erudite lawyer. The two of them "clicked" immediately. Munger would eventually become Vice Chairman of Berkshire Hathaway.

Buffett was keen to build his business and expand the partnerships, so in 1960 he asked one of his partners, a doctor, to find ten other doctors willing to invest $10,000 each into the partnership. Eventually, eleven doctors agreed to invest.

By 1961 the partnerships were worth millions, and Buffett made his first $1 million dollar investment in Dempster – a windmill manufacturing company.

In 1962 the partnerships that started out with an investment of $105,100 had grown to $7.2 million (of which $1 million was Buffett's personal stake).

Over the course of five years, the Buffett partnerships achieved a 251.0 percent profit, while the Dow was up 74.3 percent. Even so, despite constant requests, Buffett never gave stock tips.

He did not charge a fee for managing the partnerships – rather he generally took one-quarter of the profits above 4 percent. Soon he had more than 90 limited partners across the United States. It was getting complicated, so in a sweeping rationalisation, he merged the partnerships into a single entity called "Buffett Partnership Ltd", increased the minimum investment from $25,000 to $100,000 and opened an office in Kiewit Plaza on Farnam (just down the road from his house). Plain and unpretentious, Buffett's office is still there.

In 1962 Buffett consulted Charlie Munger on the Dempster business. It had good prospects, but someone was needed to run it properly to achieve the performance Buffett was looking for. Munger recommended an executive who cut costs, laid off workers and improved efficiencies and, most importantly, boosted profits – profits for Buffett to invest.

Buffett paid a lot of attention to getting management right. Once he had appointed them, he let them get on with it, as long as results were achieved. He had his own way of assessing people, making his decision largely on his judgment of character and temperament. To him, good character was absolutely essential. He also liked to have his managers visible and accountable to the shareholders. A good work ethic was mandatory, with Buffett making the comment: "the chains of habits are too light until they are too heavy to be broken".

He was fond of illustrating this point in a little exercise he would try with students. He asked them to imagine they would be guaranteed 10 percent of one of their classmate's future incomes. The question then was which classmate would they choose? As they assessed each other, he would ask them to consider whether they were looking for the smartest person, or a person with the right mix of qualities like integrity, energy, instinct and discipline.

Also in 1962, a textile manufacturing firm in New Bedford, Massachusetts, called Berkshire Hathaway, attracted Buffett's interest, with stock selling for under $8 per share, he began to buy up stock.

In 1963 Buffett sold Dempster for three times the amount invested, and also became the largest shareholder of Berkshire Hathaway. This was a major turning point.

The textile mill's return on capital was poor, so Buffett put the small amount of accessible funds to work in investments like insurance and banking, while starting a gradual move out of textiles. It would be Buffett's signature achievement.

Meanwhile, when in 1964 American Express shares fell to $35 as a result of a fraud scandal, Buffett, who was doing his homework, observed that people were still using the card quite freely. So he backed his own judgment and began buying shares.

When his father Howard died in 1965, Warren felt that he had lost his best friend. He hung a picture of his dad in his office facing his desk. Although he kept a lot to himself, it was apparent that he was devastated by his father's death.

By this time, the Buffett name was becoming very well known, and he had an extremely wide and influential network. He could telephone almost anyone he wanted to, when he wanted to. After meeting Walt Disney in 1965, Buffett invested $4 million in the Disney Company. At that time too, his shares in American Express were selling for more than double the price he'd paid for them.

1965 was a busy year, with Buffett also taking control of Berkshire Hathaway in a boardroom coup and naming a new CEO to run the company. The Berkshire legend was on its way.

Meanwhile, the value of Buffett's personal investment in the partnerships in 1966 reached some $6.85 million.

In October 1967, he advised his astonished partners that he could no longer find any bargains in the booming stock market! The Buffett Partnerships was now worth $65 million; his own share worth more than $10 million. For a while he considered giving up investing and pursuing other interests. But the going was too good.

In the same year, American Express shares surged to over $180, making the partnerships $20 million in profit on its $13 million investment.

Also in 1967, Berkshire Hathaway acquired National Indemnity Insurance for $8.6 million, and in 1968 the partnerships earned more than $40 million, bringing its total value to $104 million.

It had been a most successful run, so in 1969, following his most successful year ever, Buffett closed the partnerships, liquidated the assets, and paid out the partners. It was Warren's way!

Among the assets paid out were shares of Berkshire Hathaway. At 39 years old, Buffett's personal fortune was now $25 million.

The new decade saw a new beginning. The Buffett Partnerships was no more. Buffett owned 29 percent of Berkshire Hathaway and now, as Chairman, he began writing the first of his idiosyncratic annual letters to shareholders.

In that year of 1970, Berkshire made $45,000 from textile operations, and $4.7 million in insurance, banking and investments. Buffett's side investments were making more than the actual company itself!

About a year later, there was an opportunity to buy the See's Candy Company, a gourmet chocolate maker that sold its own brands at a premium. Customers appeared to believe the difference was worth it. Berkshire offered $25 million in cash, but the owners wanted $30 million. The deal was done at $25 million – the largest purchase by Buffett or Berkshire at the time, and became one of the best deals Berkshire ever made.

Buffett's wife Susie was a very different character from Warren. Bright, engaging and concerned for others, she forged her own career as a singer and campaigner for social reform, including the pro-abortion movement. She ran the house and lived an active social life, leaving Buffett to operate in his own universe. Buffett was notoriously frugal, however in 1971 she prevailed upon him to buy the family a summer house at Laguna Beach for $150,000. Once purchased, he quite enjoyed it, although he was never one for the beach.

When in 1973 the share market began to fall, Buffett was not concerned – on the contrary, he could see buying opportunities appearing... including *The Washington Post* Company.

Due to dramatically reducing share prices, the value of Berkshire's holdings fell, and in 1974 Buffett's personal wealth was cut by over 50 percent. His advice was "If you can't watch your stockholding decline by 50% without becoming panic stricken, you should not be in the stock market."

In October of that year he made his first ever public announcement on the general future of the stock during an interview with *Forbes* business magazine. When asked: "How do you feel?" Buffett's extraordinary reply was: "Like an oversexed guy in a whorehouse. This is the time to start investing. Now is the time to invest and get rich!" Pure Warren!

It was never all smooth sailing however. He may have made it look easy – he may even have made light of a few difficulties, but Wall Street has never been a picnic – at least not for very long. It was more often than not extremely challenging, rough, tough and ruthless. It was the mark of the man however, that in his own modest and self deprecating way, he did manage to make it look easy. What's more, he could explain it simply, and in a way that made sense. He could identify the principles that made the difference, and then actually tell people in a way that they could relate to.

Of course Buffett made mistakes, and perhaps his worst investment ever was US Air, which lost money from the day he bought it. But at least he was free and open with his confessions – when he screwed up, he generally told you about it.

Because of his growing profile, he became a target for officialdom as well as the unscrupulous. In 1974 The Securities & Exchange Commission (SEC) opened a formal investigation into one of Buffett's and Berkshire's mergers, but nothing of any consequence ensued. In 1977 Berkshire had indirectly purchased the *Buffalo Evening News*, and this later resulted in antitrust charges driven by a rival newspaper. There were no really major consequences. Business was business – just more hazards to negotiate.

After many years, the insurance company GEICO once again came to Buffett's notice. It was making huge losses; in 1976 its share price plummeted to $2 per share. Realising the basic business was still sound, Berkshire moved in. As management problems were resolved, Berkshire kept building its stake – and made millions. Some years later, Berkshire bought GEICO outright.

While he was used to the vicissitudes of the share market, Buffett had relied upon Susie to maintain a constancy and steadiness on the home front. When, in 1977 at the age of forty-five, Susan moved out, Buffett was devastated. It appeared that this was one "fluctuation" he hadn't anticipated – and it was a big one.

Suddenly, according to Buffett, it was like a huge cloud occluding the sun. Susie had been "the sunshine and rain in my garden". But there was no changing her mind – she had her own life to live and she went off to live it.

Although she remained married to Buffett, she moved into an apartment in San Francisco. Oddly enough, Warren and Susie remained friends, speaking every day, taking their annual two-week New York trip together, and meeting the kids at Laguna. It was a major change after so many regular years, but there was no going back.

Eventually Buffett became accustomed to the new arrangement. Susie even called several women in Omaha, and asked them to go out with her husband. She eventually set Buffett up with a local waitress called Astrid Menks, and in 1978 Astrid moved in with Buffett – all with Susie's blessing. Warren was comfortable again.

On 29 July 2004, Susie died of a stroke at the age of 72. They were never divorced.

But some things didn't change too much. In 1979 he still made do with a salary of $50,000 per year when Berkshire was trading at $290 per share and he was worth some $140 million.

Susie had had an effect on Buffett over the years. He had been introduced to charitable works by her, and Charlie Munger also had a philanthropic streak. So they created the Berkshire Charitable Contribution plan, allowing each shareholder to donate a proportion of their share of the company's profits to their individual selection of personal charities. This was in line with Buffett's thinking about corporate largesse, his opinion being that it was not for the CEO or board to dispense shareholders' funds to charities they liked, rather, it was the shareholders' money, and they should be able to distribute it to the charities they preferred.

In 1983 Berkshire began the year at $775 per share, but with $1.3 billion in its corporate stock portfolio by year end, it was then worth $1,310. Buffett's net worth was then $620 million. He made *Forbes Rich List* for the first time.

Although Buffett and Munger were predominantly interested in the stock exchange, they did look further afield, and were only too ready to buy good privately owned businesses outright as well.

A good example was the 1983 purchase of Nebraska Furniture Mart. Warren Buffett walked into this multi-million dollar furniture retailer in Omaha that had been built from scratch by an elderly but still very feisty Russian-born immigrant Rose Blumpkin. Buffett simply asked Mrs B if she would be interested in selling the store to Berkshire Hathaway. Her answer was a simple 'yes' followed by a simple '$60 million'. The deal was sealed with a handshake and a one-page contract was drawn up. When she received the cheque a few days later, she folded it up without looking at it and just kept working. There had been no long drawn-out due diligence process with armies of consultants and advisors – the deal with old Mrs B had been done on the spot!

Scott & Fetzer (Kirby Vacuum Cleaners and World Book Encyclopedia) was another 100 percent acquisition in 1985 – the target of a hostile takeover at $60 a share (original tender was $50, a premium of $5 above market value). Other predators were circling as well when Buffett, who owned a quarter of a million shares, asked if they were interested in $60 cash per share. The deal was done within a week with no investment bankers or other fancy-priced advisors. Berkshire just added a new $315 million cash-generator to its stable. That small trickle of cash from the Berkshire of old, was now compounding into an investment powerhouse.

It was that same year that Buffett finally shut down the Berkshire textile mills after years of nursing them along, refusing to allow them to drain shareholders' capital further.

In 1986 Berkshire broke through $3,000 per share, and by the mid 1990s it would hit $80,000.

In 1986, Buffett bought an $850,000 used Falcon business jet, which he called "The Indefensible". It was no longer comfortable for him to fly commercially as he was too well known. He did make out that he was uncomfortable with this conspicuous luxury, but he came to love the jet so much that he then also bought the Executive Jet Company in the 1990s.

He had driven a Volkswagen for many, many years and it was only when it became embarrassing to pick up business colleagues in it, that he agreed his wife should buy him another car – he professed not to care what, and she bought him a wide-finned Cadillac.

In the aftermath of the October 1987 market crash, Berkshire dropped in value by around 25 percent, (from $4,230 to around $3,170 per share). Buffett lost $342 million personally on the day. But he appeared to be not unduly upset. He just checked the prices and kept working. Obviously this was just one of "Mr Market's" temporary "aberrations" albeit a rather robust one. Warren went on…

1988 was a good year… Buffett started buying Coca-Cola shares, eventually purchasing up to 7 percent of the company for $1.02 billion. It became one of Berkshire's most lucrative investments. Within three years, Buffett's Coca-Cola stock would be worth more than the entire value of Berkshire when he made the investment.

In 1989 Berkshire was over $8,000 per share. Buffett's personal fortune was now $3.8 billion and within the next ten years, he would be worth ten times that amount.

From a share price of $12 in 1965, over the 30 years to 1995, Berkshire Hathaway was worth $25,000 per share! In 1994, *Forbes* business magazine declared Buffett the second richest man in the USA.

But there would always be bumps (and perhaps even a few ditches) along the road, and in the early 1990s, Buffett's reputation was under serious threat by a renegade trader at Salomon Brothers, the well-known Wall Street firm and major government bond trader, where Buffett was on the board. The firm was losing money, even while many employees were making over a million dollars a year. This was not normally what Buffett liked to see.

The head of Salomon's government bond desk, Paul Mozer, had illegally used customer accounts to purchase Treasury bonds. When found out, Mozer promised not to do it again... but he did, and the SEC became involved. Many top executives were shown the door. Salomon needed a saviour. If the firm failed, the repercussions throughout Wall Street and possibly the wider economy could have been massive. Buffett flew to New York and by the end of the day was CEO. His partner Charlie Munger, probably wisely, was totally opposed. But Buffett's reputation was at stake – and that was a lot to lose.

As in his other operating companies, Buffett wanted good leadership and wanted it under the spotlight, clearly identified. So it was important to clarify who would be sitting in the big chair after Buffett's "interim corporate quick fix". And fast.

Buffett called senior managers into a room individually and just asked them, one by one, who they thought should run the company. When he had their suggestions he was ready to decide. Human resources consultants and expensive headhunters were not asked for their opinions.

Just a few days later, the Treasury Department banned Salomon from trading. This was not part of the plan. Buffett had to make one of those special phone calls and plead with the Federal Reserve, including the Governor of the Federal Reserve Board, Alan Greenspan himself. The situation remained unresolved. Meanwhile, Buffett gave Salomon's top managers his home phone number, and told them to call him immediately if any one of them found any further evidence of dishonest behaviour. No one called. It had been a shrewd move. It appeared that by then everything was OK. Eventually Salomon gained its trading privileges again and Buffett went home, having saved the company. Buffett's emphasis on probity was reminiscent of JP Morgan's observation that character is the basis of credit, not money.

During the 1990s, Berkshire reached $80,000 per share. When during the dot.com era, Buffett was accused of being left behind by the new world, Buffett just went on being Buffett, allocating capital to undervalued businesses. When the markets finally came to their senses, Buffett became even more of a legend.

Buffett still has a very particular and principled attitude to corporate responsibility. To his way of thinking, the employees are there in the service of the shareholders and provided they are treated fairly, their task is to maximise return on capital, not to indulge in corporate excesses. Buffett's dislike of corporate fat cats, consultants and advisors etc is legend-ary. He is renowned for running organisations leanly and without super-fluous organisational trappings. 'A compact organisation' he says, 'lets all of us spend more time managing the business, rather than managing each other'. Berkshire Hathaway has some twelve full-time employees.

Buffett is a man who has lived his life according to a set of principles based on prudence, caution, honesty, patience, temperance, discipline and rationality. He would appear to be the epitome of the American ideal of an honest, self-made man from the mid-West.

Some would say that this Oracle from Omaha has made a career out of just being Warren, and that he is much, much more cunning than his easy-going, self-deprecating and modest style would indicate. He makes it look just too easy, just too simple.

But despite the critics, there has been a constancy and steadiness of purpose and direction that has served him well for decades. And he does not hide his principles.

Buffett's son Peter, a musician, recounted the story of how Buffett liked to relate to the Hollywood film *The Glenn Miller Story*, where the band leader was looking for his own distinctive "sound". He said that for his father, the right "sound" was not just making money, but superior reason-ing. Buffett is a man who has found his own voice and is comfortable with it. What you see is what you get!

He has always been suspicious of "inside information" preferring to stick to the principles rather than gossip, and has said: 'with enough inside information and a million dollars, you can go broke in a year'.

His has not been one of the thousands of cacophonous voices offering a multiplicity (and duplicity) of opinions. He has preferred to stick with the proven fundamentals as he sees them – and then stay the course. No wonder he has the reputation of having a down-to-earth decency and commonsense that triumphs over slick cosmopolitan guile. Warren is the sort of guy who says what he means, and means what he says. If you ask him for a loan or donation and he says no, don't bother asking again.

It is a modus operandi he enjoys and is very comfortable with. Critics have accused him of mythologising his past to fit the image. So rather than exaggerating and building things up, he has done the reverse, seemingly "cleansing his past" of characteristics such as cunning, cleverness, ambition, calculation, political adroitness, toughness, ruthlessness, etc.

While on the outside he may appear a straightforward country guy, no one gets as rich as he is without being very shrewd. Very shrewd! Although he tries to operate in a principled manner, he is aware that some others do not. His advice about playing cards is telling: 'you know when you go into a poker game, you look around, there is always one patsy. If you look around and you can't tell who the patsy is, that's because it's you.' Be warned.

It was inevitable that his wealth would not affect some changes in Buffett's lifestyle. Although still resident in the same house in Omaha, and still eating simple foods and drinking lots of Coke, his network regularly includes many of the rich, famous and powerful around the world. He dines regularly with presidents, politicians, media people, industrialists and other very, very rich folk. But he still affects a very down-to-earth humble demeanour, and apart from the jet and extensive travel, seems to live simply, especially by comparison with many other wealthy people around the world.

Another of Buffett's idiosyncrasies has been his endeavour to build a group of shareholders who think like he does, or at least trust him to think for them. He wants his investors to feel like business partners, with a really long-term perspective. Buffett's refusal to split his stock was indeed another mechanism for holding his shareholders for the longer term, to emphasise his conviction that his principles were tried and true and would indeed work over time.

He continues to write his newsletter in the same "Warren" way. Buffett used to write his 7,500 word newsletter in that particular down-to-earth style, as if he were writing to his sister, summarising the year's events for her benefit. Even though he had professional editorial input from time to time, the newsletters have been very much pure Buffett. No wonder he has been called "the Great Explainer of American Capitalism".

Rather than a fancy piece of PR spin, these have been very much "memos from Warren" – very unadorned affairs, not a lot of pictures of the businesses, or Buffett or Charlie Munger; no slick graphics, just a lot of typography. And often with commonsense exhortations to stick to the business you are good at, reminding people of Johnson's horse: 'A horse that can count to ten is a remarkable horse – not a remarkable mathematician.'

As he himself said, 'Your chairman has a firm belief that owners are entitled to hear directly from the CEO as to what is going on and how he evaluates the business, currently and prospectively. You would demand that in a private company; you should expect no less in a public company.'

He has long been a champion of proper reporting standards, complaining about the tendency of some to use "more flexible measurement systems" and described the approach of some of them as: 'They shoot the arrow of business performance into a blank canvas and then carefully draw the bullseye around the implanted arrow.' No, no, no says Warren. He has always been critical of window dressing company accounts, summarising the likely consequences: 'In the long run, managements stressing accounting appearances over economic substance usually achieve little of either.'

Very few of us are saints, each of us has our imperfections. The Oracle has not been without his percentage, but he has managed to maintain an idiosyncratic forthrightness because there are strong underlying principles which have been the foundation of his approach.

Buffett has been successfully operating for nearly 50 years, seeking out underpriced value and backing his judgment. Against a history of changing circumstances and opportunities, Buffett has managed to create one of the most outstanding track records ever.

What makes him such an item of fascination, however, is not that he is another rich old guy (a really rich old guy), but the way in which it has been done and the manner of man that he is. His insistence upon a long-term strategy based on clearly set-out principles has considerable appeal. And the manner in which he manages to deliver his insights also engages people. His down-to-earth style and approachability has endeared him to millions.

While on the one hand he can go and play a casual game of golf with the likes of Bill Gates of Microsoft, Michael Eisner of Disney and other political and business heavyweights, there is a wisdom there that enables him to talk to ordinary folk like he is one of them.

And so they in turn, can see that there is a lot of them in him.

wisdom

What is the biggest lesson you learned from your experiences with *Collective Wisdom*?

As you would appreciate there were many lessons learned from the project from conception to completion – back yourself, work with others, don't give up, ask and you shall receive!

It became apparent though that in the intervening years since the completion of *Collective Wisdom* one idea has most fundamentally impacted my life. That idea is so well expressed and has been so comprehensively demonstrated in the life of Warren Buffett.

> *I consider there to be three basic ideas, ideas that if they are really ground into your intellectual framework, I don't see how you could help but do reasonably well in stocks. None of them are complicated. None of them takes mathematical talent or anything of the sort. (Graham) said:*
>
> *1. you should look at the stocks as small pieces of the business.*
> *2. look at (market) fluctuations as your friend rather than your enemy – profit from folly rather than participate in it; and*
> *3. he said the three most important words of investing: "margin of safety".*
>
> *I think those ideas, 100 years from now, will still be regarded as the three cornerstones of sound investing.*

Buffett goes on to summarise Graham this way: 'When proper temperament joins with proper intellectual framework, then you get rational behavior. *If principles can become dated, they're not principles.*'

Here it was for me so clearly. A hero of mine putting forward very clearly that there are Universal Wisdoms, or Principles that he has operated to such incredible effect in his own life. Principles that never date, are always valid in all times and places. Laws that operate in spite of our acknowledging them or otherwise – they are ways that just are!

Now Warren Buffett is no saint, yet at the same time he is certainly not the rapacious swindler so common on Wall Street, raping and pillaging the corporate landscape to no other benefit than their own short term narrow self interest.

So often people would say to me, 'You are too idealistic. It is a mean world out there and you need to get real.' Yet I find a hero working amidst the toughest market environment on earth following tried and tested principles, and he is successful and happy.

Listen to Warren Buffett. 'It baffles us how many people know of Ben Graham. But so few follow. We tell our principles freely and write them extensively in our annual reports. They are easy to learn. They should be easy to follow. But the only thing anyone wants to know is, "what are you buying today?" Like Graham, we are widely recognized but least followed.'

He goes on to say, '…The business schools reward complex behavior more than simple behavior, but simple behavior is more effective.'

And this is where it is at with Universal Wisdom generally. There are no principles put forward in this book that, as the term suggests, have not been around and applicable forever. But they are not taught at school (for whatever reason) and we are not encouraged to seek them. To many people today, wisdom does not even exist. As a result it is of little surprise that so few of us know these principles or live them, even when we are provided with people who are great examples of their benefits.

In this case, we are listening to the words of the undisputed greatest investor that has ever lived – someone who started with nothing and turned it into a $US100,000,000,000 (billion) fortune – not some down home hack.

When the Internet boom started in the late 1990s, Buffett stayed true to his principles. His critics promoted a Brave New World where time-tested principles no longer applied and derided him for being out of step. Yet since his earliest years Buffett had practised being out of step. He is quoted as saying, 'You are neither right nor wrong because the crowd disagrees with you. You are right because your data and reasoning are right.'

And so it turned out to be, yet again. There was no Brave New World – his principles still applied.

We do live in times where money is so central to people's thoughts and attitudes and the economics invoked to justify actions that would once have seemed unjustifiable, where everyone we know wants more and more money – but, who can name any students of Buffett or Graham?

When considering writing this book, I worried what people would think of a young person such as me putting forward what is a different world-view than that prevailing for many people in our times. Ultimately, I considered the words of Buffett, 'but so few follow' and thought that for those who do not want to hear, no amount of proof is enough.

Buffett is a tremendous example to me of 'seek wisdom, get understanding', and the wise choices that can follow.

words

An Owner's Manual

First published in June 1996, Chairman Warren E Buffett issued a booklet entitled 'An Owner's Manual' to Berkshire's Class A and Class B shareholders. The purpose of the manual was to explain Berkshire's broad economic principles of operation.

OWNER-RELATED BUSINESS PRINCIPLES

At the time of the Blue Chip merger in 1983, I set down 13 owner-related business principles that I thought would help new shareholders understand our managerial approach. As is appropriate for "principles", all 13 remain alive and well today, and they are stated here in italics.

1. Although our form is corporate, our attitude is partnership.
Charlie Munger and I think of our shareholders as owner-partners, and of ourselves as managing partners. (Because of the size of our shareholdings we are also, for better or worse, controlling partners.) We do not view the company itself as the ultimate owner of our business assets but instead view the company as a conduit through which our shareholders own the assets.

Charlie and I hope that you do not think of yourself as merely owning a piece of paper whose price wiggles around daily and that is a candidate for sale when some economic or political event makes you nervous.

We hope you instead visualize yourself as a part owner of a business that you expect to stay with indefinitely, much as you might if you owned a farm or apartment house in partnership with members of your family. For our part, we do not view Berkshire shareholders as faceless members of an ever-shifting crowd, but rather as co-venturers who have entrusted their funds to us for what may well turn out to be the remainder of their lives.

The evidence suggests that most Berkshire shareholders have indeed embraced this long-term partnership concept. The annual percentage turnover in Berkshire's shares is a small fraction of that occurring in the stocks of other major American corporations, even when the shares I own are excluded from the calculation.

In effect, our shareholders behave in respect to their Berkshire stock much as Berkshire itself behaves in respect to companies in which it has an investment. As owners of, say, Coca-Cola or Gillette shares, we think of Berkshire as being a non-managing partner in two extraordinary businesses, in which we measure our success by the long-term progress of the companies rather than by the month-to-month movements of their stocks. In fact, we would not care in the least if several years went by in which there was no trading, or quotation of prices, in the stocks of those companies. If we have good long-term expectations, short term price changes are meaningless for us except to the extent they offer us an opportunity to increase our ownership at an attractive price.

2. *In line with Berkshire's owner-orientation, most of our directors have a major portion of their net worth invested in the company. We eat our own cooking.*

Charlie's family has 90% or more of its net worth in Berkshire shares; my wife, Susie, and I have more than 99%. In addition, many of my relatives – my sisters and cousins, for example – keep a huge portion of their net worth in Berkshire stock.

Charlie and I feel totally comfortable with this eggs-in-one-basket situation because Berkshire itself owns a wide variety of truly extraordinary businesses. Indeed, we believe that Berkshire is close to being unique in the quality and diversity of the businesses in which it owns either a controlling interest or a minority interest of significance.

Charlie and I cannot promise you results. But we can guarantee that your financial fortunes will move in lockstep with ours for whatever period of time you elect to be our partner. We have no interest in large salaries or options or other means of gaining an "edge" over you. We want to make money only when our partners do and in exactly the same proportion. Moreover, when I do something dumb, I want you to be able to derive some solace from the fact that my financial suffering is proportional to yours.

3. *Our long-term economic goal (subject to some qualifications mentioned later) is to maximize Berkshire's average annual rate of gain in intrinsic business value on a per-share basis.*

We do not measure the economic significance or performance of Berkshire by its size; we measure by per-share progress. We are certain that the rate of per-share progress will diminish in the future – a greatly enlarged capital base will see to that. But we will be disappointed if our rate does not exceed that of the average large American corporation.

4. *Our preference would be to reach our goal by directly owning a diversified group of businesses that generate cash and consistently earn above-average returns on capital.*

5. *Because of our two-pronged approach to business ownership and because of the limitations of conventional accounting, consolidated reported earnings may reveal relatively little about our true economic performance.*

6. *Accounting consequences do not influence our operating or capital-allocation decisions.*

7. *We use debt sparingly and, when we do borrow, we attempt to structure our loans on a long-term fixed rate basis.*

8. *A managerial "wish list" will not be filled at shareholder expense.*

9. *We feel noble intentions should be checked periodically against results.*

10. *We will issue common stock only when we receive as much in business value as we give.*

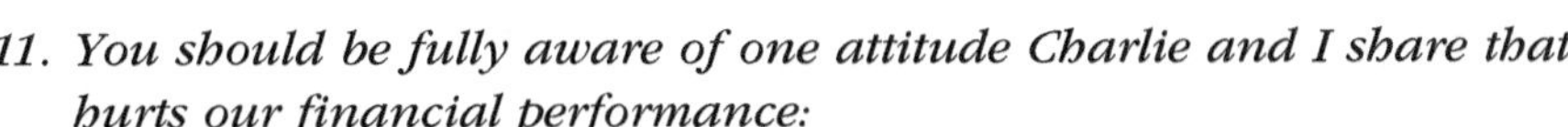

11. *You should be fully aware of one attitude Charlie and I share that hurts our financial performance:*

12. *We will be candid in our reporting to you, emphasizing the pluses and minuses important in appraising business value.*

13. *Despite our policy of candor, we will discuss our activities in marketable securities only to the extent legally required.*

WARREN E BUFFETT
Chairman

For the full text of this document please refer to
www.berkshirehathaway.com

BERKSHIRE HATHAWAY INC.
1440 KIEWIT PLAZA
OMAHA, NEBRASKA 68131
TELEPHONE (402) 346-1400
FAX (402) 346-0476

WARREN E. BUFFETT, CHAIRMAN

July 26, 2005

Mr. Brett Kelly
102/47 Carabella Street
Kirribilli NSW 2061
Sydney
AUSTRALIA

Dear Mr. Kelly:

Thanks for your nice letter and the books. I'm returning the book you requested to be autographed.

However, I can't help you on your other requests. I'm cooperating with Alice Schroeder who is working on a book about me and therefore regularly decline interviews from other authors.

It would be fine with me if you simply reference the Owner's Manual as being available to anyone who goes to our website. But I can't allow reprinting of an extended amount of copyrighted material. The reason for the copyright was to control reproduction. Since the Internet makes access free for anyone in the world, it would be a mistake to have major portions of my writings appear in other books, even if a portion of the proceeds were going to charity.

Good luck to you in your endeavors.

Sincerely,

Warren E. Buffett

WEB/db
Enclosure

quotes

'One of the things that attracted me to working with securities was the fact that you could live your own life. You don't have to dress for success.'

'Money, to some extent, sometimes lets you be in more interesting environments. But it can't change how many people love you or how healthy you are.'

'Chains of habit are too light to be felt until they are too heavy to be broken.'

'You're lucky in life if you have the right heroes. I advise all of you, to the extent that you can, pick out a few heroes. There's nothing like the right ones.'

'He said, 'If you let yourself be undisciplined on the small things, you'd probably be undisciplined on the large things too.'
– JACK BYRNE, *Chairman of GEICO*

quotes

'I enjoy the process far more than the proceeds, though I have learned to live with those also.'

'I choose to work with every single person that I work with. That ends up being the most important factor. I don't interact with people that I don't like or admire. That's the key. It's like marrying.'

'Before reading the book', Buffett says, 'I went the whole gamut. I collected charts and I read all the technical stuff. I listened to tips. And then I picked up Graham's *The Intelligent Investor*. That was like seeing the light.'

'I believe in going to work for a business you admire and people you admire. Anytime you're around somebody that you're getting something out of and you feel good about the organization, you just have to get a good result. I advise you never to do anything because you think it's miserable now, but it's going to be great in 10 years from now, but I'll have 10X. If you're not enjoying it today, you're probably not going to enjoy it 10 years from now.'

'An atmosphere encouraging exemplary behavior is probably more important than rules, necessary though they are. During my tenure as chairman, I will consider myself the firm's chief compliance officer, and I have asked all 9,000 of Salomon's employees to assist me in that effort. I have also urged them to be guided by a test that goes beyond rules. Contemplating any business act, an employee should ask himself whether he would be willing to see it immediately described by an informed and critical reporter on the front page of his local paper, there to be read by his spouse, children and friends. At Salomon, we simply want no part of any activities that pass legal tests but that we, as citizens, would find offensive.'

'Buffett says his employment form has one question: "Are you a fanatic?" The best investors are.'

'Rule No. 1: Never lose money. Rule No. 2: Never forget Rule No. 1.'

'I consider there to be three basic ideas, ideas that if they are really ground into your intellectual framework, I don't see how you could help but do reasonably well in stocks. None of them is complicated. None of them takes mathematical talent or anything of the sort. (Graham) said you should look at the stocks as small pieces of the business. Look at (market) fluctuations as your friend rather than your enemy – profit from folly rather than participate in it. And he said the three most important words of investing: "margin of safety". I think those ideas, 100 years from now, will still be regarded as the three cornerstones of sound investing.'

Buffett was 19 years old and a senior at The University of Nebraska when he read Graham's classic *The Intelligent Investor*. He likens the experience to that of Paul on the road to Damascus, and one in which he 'learned the philosophy of buying $1 for 40 cents.'

'I don't want to sound like a religious fanatic or anything, but it really did get me.'

'Somebody once said that in looking for people to hire, you look for three qualities: integrity, intelligence, and energy. And if they don't have the first, the other two will kill you. You think about it; it's true. If you hire somebody without the first, you really want them to be dumb and lazy.'

'Most people get interested in stocks when everyone else is. The time to get interested is when no one else is. You can't buy what is popular and do well.'

'We have no idea how long the excess will last, nor do we know what will change the attitudes of the government, lender and buyer that fuel them. But we know that the less prudence with which others conduct their affairs, the greater the prudence with which we should conduct our own affairs.'

Buffett summarizes Graham this way: 'When proper temperament joins with proper intellectual framework, then you get rational behavior.'

'If principles can become dated, they're not principles.'

'Risk comes from not knowing what you are doing.'

'People would rather be promised a (presumably) winning lottery ticket next week than an opportunity to get rich slowly.'

'Our riches are our curse in our attempts to attain trade balance. If we are less well-off, commercial realities would constrain our trade deficit. Because we are rich, however, we can continue to trade earning properties for consumable trinkets. We are much like a wealthy farm family that annually sells acreages so that it can sustain a lifestyle unwarranted by its current output. Until the plantation is gone, it's all pleasure and no pain. In the end, however, the family will have traded the life of an owner for the life of a tenant farmer.'

'You have to think for yourself. It always amazes me how high-IQ people mindlessly imitate. I never get good ideas talking to other people.'

'The larger investments always did better than the smaller investments.'

'You should invest in a business that even a fool can run, because someday a fool will.'

'We like to buy businesses. We don't like to sell, and we expect the relationships to last a lifetime.'

'Stocks are simple. All you do is buy shares in a great business for less than the business is intrinsically worth, with managers of the highest integrity and ability. Then you own those shares forever.'

'Buy companies with strong histories of profitability and with a dominant business franchise.'

'You are neither right nor wrong because the crowd disagrees with you. You are right because your data and reasoning are right.'

'Be fearful when others are greedy and greedy only when others are fearful.'

'Do not take yearly results too seriously. Instead, focus on four or five-year averages.'

'Always invest for the long term.'

'Does the business have favorable long term prospects?'

'An investor should ordinarily hold a small piece of an outstanding business with the same tenacity that an owner would exhibit if he owned all of that business.'

The Reverend
Dr Martin Luther King, Jr

PASTOR AND CIVIL RIGHTS LEADER

'Our scientific power has outrun our spiritual power.

We have guided missiles and misguided men.'

The Life of Rev. Dr Martin Luther King, Jr

1929   15 January: Born in Atlanta, Georgia.

1944   Graduates from Booker T Washington High School.

1948   Ordained to Baptist ministry at age 19.

1951   Enters Boston University Graduate School.

1953   Marries Coretta Scott and settles in Montgomery, Alabama.

1955   PhD in Theology from Boston University.
5 December: Elected president of the Montgomery Improvement Association, and spokesman for Bus Boycott.

1956   Montgomery Bus Boycott continues all year.

1957   Founds Southern Christian Leadership Conference for non-violent struggle against racism. First book published, *Stride Toward Freedom*.

1958   Stabbed by demented Black woman in New York.

1959   Visits India to study Gandhi's methods.
Resigns as pastor of Dexter Avenue Baptist Church to concentrate on civil rights.

1961   First Congress on Racial Equality (CORE).
Freedom Ride through the South.

1963   Birmingham campaign launched – turning point in ending segregation in the South.
Writes *Letter from Birmingham Jail*.
23 June: Leads Freedom Walk in Detroit.
28 August: March on Washington. *I Have a Dream* speech.
22 November: President Kennedy assassinated.

1964   *Time Magazine* Man of the Year.
Attends signing ceremony of the Civil Rights Act of 1964 at the White House.
10 December: Nobel Peace Prize.

1965   2 February: Arrested in Selma, Alabama during voting rights demonstration.
President Johnson signs Voting Rights Act.

1967   27 November: Announces *Poor People's Campaign* for poor of all races.

1968   28 March. Leads first march that turns violent.
I've Been to the Mountaintop speech.
4 April, sunset: Fatally shot in Memphis at age 39.

1983   Birthday declared a national holiday.

biography

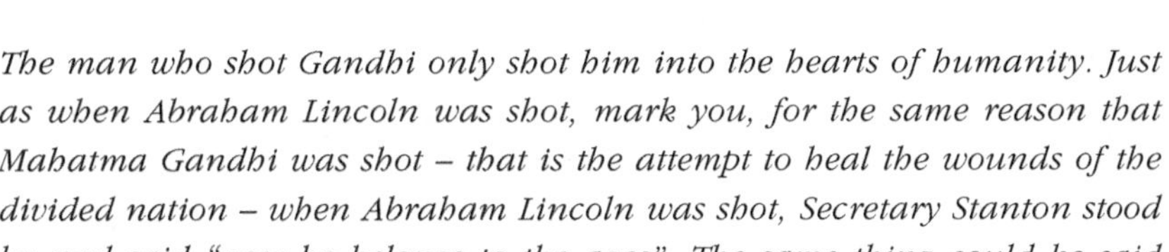

biography

The man who shot Gandhi only shot him into the hearts of humanity. Just as when Abraham Lincoln was shot, mark you, for the same reason that Mahatma Gandhi was shot – that is the attempt to heal the wounds of the divided nation – when Abraham Lincoln was shot, Secretary Stanton stood by and said "now he belongs to the ages". The same thing could be said about Mahatma Gandhi now. He belongs to the ages.

– MARTIN LUTHER KING, JR, *Sermon on Mohandas Gandhi. Montgomery, 22 March 1959*

Martin Luther King remains an inspiration and a symbol of hope around the world. He too belongs to the ages.

Driven by his strong Christian faith and belief in the ideals and promise of the American Constitution, he used his considerable intellect, courage and talent as a charismatic public speaker to engage a whole nation in a major transformation.

In less than 13 years, from the Montgomery Bus Boycott in December 1955, to his assassination in 1968 at the age of 39, he left a nation changed forever. His violent death was stark evidence that even more change was needed, but he had moved the most powerful nation on the planet a good deal further towards greater racial equality and justice for all.

One of the youngest-ever winners of the Nobel Peace Prize at the age of 35, he used his oratorical skills in dramatic theatrical speeches rich with biblical allusions, to inspire and energise Black congregations in particular. His repeated references to the spirit of Christianity, love, justice, temperance and the principles of the US Constitution made his message relevant to all across the land.

No wonder many major towns across the USA have streets named after him, for during those 13 brief years he was the right man with the wisdom for the times.

That wisdom is found not only in the character, approach and actions of King himself, but also in the many around him who helped him, and a whole nation, along the way.

Atlanta, Georgia. At noon on 15 January 1929, Martin Luther King was born to the Reverend and Mrs Martin Luther King, Sr. The family was part of a quite well-established and well-to-do Black society in Alabama. Their home at 501 Auburn Avenue was a large and comfortable one.

The culture of this home emphasised learning, integrity and religious observance, and the young Martin Luther was inquisitive, energetic, clever and articulate. He was also blessed with a happy disposition and a very healthy constitution, for he was rarely if ever ill.

Both of his parents were very supportive and wanted him to be positive, successful and respected. His mother often said to him, 'You are as good as anyone.' The self-confidence this engendered was to be crucial during the many trials and tribulations of his life. As he wrote in his autobiography: 'I have a marvelous mother and father. It is quite easy for me to think of a God of Love mainly because I grew up in a family where love was central and lovely relationships were ever present. It is quite easy for me to think of the universe as basically friendly, mainly because of my uplifting hereditary and environmental circumstances. It is quite easy for me to lean more toward optimism than pessimism about human nature, mainly because of my childhood experiences.'

His father was renowned as a leader of the Black Baptist Church – an influential man of integrity who was committed to maintaining moral and ethical principles, as well as some discipline, as the young Martin Luther experienced.

For a young person who was so able, well-loved and positive about life, it was oppressive in the extreme to be subjected to racial discrimination day after day, and he came to abhor segregation, considering it both rationally inexplicable and morally unjustifiable. It was an everyday fact of life in education, transportation, employment and most public places, including restaurants. In some towns in the south, a Black person would have to get off the sidewalk to allow a White person to go by. While Washington DC railed against the evils of communism and the Iron Curtain, the apartheid of the "Cotton Curtain" was a fact of life, especially across the southern United States.

Martin Luther King Jr excelled in many of the things White society considered important, such as educational achievement, civil politeness, neat personal habits, belief in the church, patriotic commitment, and respect for the law and the Constitution. But no matter how good he may have been, he was never quite good enough... he was *Black*.

But he was Martin Luther King Jr, and as well as his exceptional abilities and civil demeanour, there was also dignity, courage and a steely resolve.

In his autobiography he wrote:

In my own life and the person who is seeking to be strong, you combine in your character antitheses strongly marked. You are both militant and moderate; you are both idealistic and realistic. And I think that my stronger determination for justice comes from the very strong, and dynamic personality of my father, and I would hope that the gentle aspect comes in from a mother who is very gentle and sweet.

An essay he wrote when 14 years old in 1943, provides a prophetic insight into the formation of a young mind. He won an oratorical contest with the following speech. Even at that time there was plenty of evidence of the flamboyant biblical language and the theatrical delivery that was so characteristic of his speeches. But there was also the shrewdly targeted appeal to his audience, in this case emphasising both the principles of Christianity and the greater national interest of America (the speech was made during World War II):

We cannot have an enlightened democracy with one great group living in ignorance. We cannot have a healthy nation with one tenth of the people so ill nourished, sick, harboring germs of disease which recognise no colour lines – obey no Jim Crow laws. We cannot have a nation orderly and sound with one group so ground down and thwarted that it is almost forced into unsocial attitudes and crime. We cannot be truly Christian people so long as we flout the central teaching of Jesus: brotherly love and the Golden rule. We cannot come to full prosperity with one great group so ill delayed that it cannot buy goods. So as we gird ourselves to defend democracy from foreign attack let us see to it that increasingly at home we can give fair play and free opportunity for people.

Today 13 million Black sons and daughters of our forefathers continue the fight for the translation of the 13th 14th and 15th Amendments from writing on the printed page, to an actuality.

We believe with them that 'if freedom is good for any it is good for all', that we may conquer Southern armies by the sword, but it is another thing to conquer Southern hate, that if the franchise is given to Negroes, they will be vigilant and defend, even with their arms, the ark of federal liberty from treason and destruction by her enemies.

Having won the competition, the very young Martin Luther and Mrs. Bradley, his teacher, were in good spirits that evening, and were on their way back from Dublin to Atlanta by bus. When some White passengers boarded the bus a little later, the driver ordered King and his teacher to give up their seats. Then, because they had not been quick enough, he began to abuse them. The young King was furious and wanted to keep his seat, but Mrs Bradley urged him to stand up, arguing that as law-abiding citizens of the nation, they had to obey the law. They stood for the ninety miles back to Atlanta.

As King later recalled 'That night will never leave my memory. It was the angriest I have ever been in my life.' But his civility, temperance and Christian upbringing had enabled him to control his anger and retain his dignity.

His conviction that love was the key was the legacy of an extensive Christian heritage. As he would later say: 'Love is the only force capable of transforming an enemy into a friend.'

King's grandfather was a Baptist preacher and his father was pastor of Atlanta's Ebenezer Baptist Church. As Martin Luther King Jr himself would say: 'Of course I was religious. I grew up in the church. My father is a preacher, my grandfather was a preacher, my great grandfather was a preacher, my only brother is a preacher, my daddy's brother is a preacher. So I didn't have much choice.'

In 1944 King graduated from Booker T Washington High School and was admitted to the leading Black educational institution, Morehouse College, at the age of 15. Even then his concerns for racial and economic justice were developing.

It was at Morehouse that he first read the American writer, Henry David Thoreau's essay "Civil Disobedience", and it was his work that first introduced him to the possibilities of morally justifiable, non-violent resistance. Indeed, it had such a powerful effect on him that he re-read it several times. He became convinced that non-cooperation with evil was as much a moral obligation as cooperation with good. 'No person has been more eloquent and passionate in getting this idea across than Henry David Thoreau,' King wrote.

It was also around this time that King came into contact with White people who were not racists and were against segregation, and his earlier anger at White people in general began to mellow. As he later said, his 'resentment (of White folk) was softened', but his determination to do something about segregation and racists grew daily. Even so, he was a spirited young man, being a member of a gang called "the Wreckers" and enjoying an active social life. He even had a White girlfriend called Betty, but they decided to end the relationship, as having a White wife in Alabama would not have been acceptable and possibly even physically dangerous.

In his final year of college, he decided to enter the ministry, even though he had been a particularly questioning student. It was at this time that he began to feel 'a sense of responsibility that I could not escape', and he was ordained into the Baptist ministry on 25 February 1948, at the age of just 19. Having finished college he was off to Crozer Seminary.

Crozer was a new experience for him, as it was a non-segregated institution. When he first arrived there, he was embarrassed by the stereotype of the Negro, as he himself described it: 'always late, loud, laughing, dirty and messy'. King initially went to great pains to be very serious, punctual, polite, well spoken, clean and immaculately dressed.

Photographs from this period show him as a bit of a dandy, quite concerned about his appearance – a snappy dresser with an eye for the girls. He was not very tall and quite dark, and he did not think of himself as particularly handsome. So he had something to prove with the girls, and often tried his luck with the girlfriends of those to whom he felt a little inferior.

He wrote to his mother at the time: 'I never go anywhere but in these books' but then in the same letter: 'Do you know the girl?... I have been to see her twice. Also I met a fine chick in Phila who has gone wild over the old boy... since... told the members of his church that my family was rich, the girls are running me down.' And immediately thereafter: 'Of course I don't even think of them. I am too busy studying.'

What his mother really thought of such letters we can only surmise.

But in the midst of such understandable youthful preoccupations, the more serious side was building. He was fascinated by the history of ideas, philosophy and social development. His interest in the power of ideas, language, morality and social action was growing steadily. He wrote about becoming a minister of religion: 'It is my conviction that the minister must somehow take profound theological and philosophical views and place them in a concrete framework, I must forever make the complex the simple... I must attempt to change the souls of individuals so that their societies may be changed.'

It was at Crozer that he was first exposed to Gandhi, and he was so taken by him that he rushed out and bought several books about him.

As well as being intelligent and articulate, King as a young man was proud and even cocky. Even though he may have thought he was not the best looking guy on campus, he did think he had a bit of charm, and he was a good talker. The love and support he had experienced at home was manifest in his confident and engaged approach to life. He knew he was equal to most challenges, but the most testing part of his life was still ahead of him.

In 1951 he graduated with the degree of Bachelor of Divinity, but because he was considering teaching in a college or school of religion he thought he needed some graduate qualifications as well.

So in 1951 he commenced his PhD at Boston University. This was, among other things, a period of "rediscovering lost values," looking for insights into the human condition that were relevant across the ages and across cultures... he was looking for universal values, universal wisdoms.

'The thing we need in the world today is a group of men and women who will stand up for right and be opposed to wrong' he wrote at the time. 'If we are to go forward, we must go back and rediscover these precious values.' He knew that there were ideas that mattered, ideas that made a difference, ideas that had consequences. It was a time of important and consequential discoveries.

One of these Boston discoveries was a certain Miss Coretta Scott. She was a singer, a couple of years his senior, and hours into their first date, during which they talked excitedly about racial and economic injustice, King suggested that they 'should get married some day.' That day would be 18 June 1953 and would be celebrated in Marion, Alabama. Then they went back to begin married life in Boston.

Having satisfied the residential requirement for his PhD, King then had only the thesis to do, so he decided to get a job, and in January 1954 gave a trial sermon at Dexter Avenue Baptist Church in Montgomery, Alabama.

His Christian upbringing and theological education, together with his gift for language, resulted in a style of preaching which was full of biblical allusion and phraseology, theatrical delivery and a certain rhythm and musicality. He knew his audience. He had a unique and engaging style that appealed to Black parishioners in particular. However, as an educated man, he was not at all keen on the emotionally charged style of Negro religion in the south: the 'emotionalism of much Negro religion, the shouting and the stamping. I didn't understand it and it embarrassed me'.

In October 1954 he became pastor of the Dexter Avenue church, and they settled down to life in Montgomery, their first child Yolanda being born there in November 1955. He worked hard at finishing his thesis, fulfilling his many duties as pastor and getting involved in resolving social problems in the region. Life was proving to be full and interesting.

On 5 June that year he received his Doctorate of Philosophy in Systematic Theology from Boston University. His Dissertation Title was: *A Comparison of God in the Thinking of Paul Tillich and Henry Wiseman.*

And then in December 1955, came the bus boycott.

His life was changed forever by Rosa Parks, a Black seamstress who refused to give up her seat to a White man on an Alabama bus and was arrested on 1 December 1955.

Buses were a major mode of transport for the Black population, but they were subject to extreme discrimination. Black passengers had to ride in the back, not sit in the seats reserved for Whites at the front of the bus, and had to give up their seats for Whites if there were no more White seats available. Furthermore, if there were front and back doors on a bus, the Black person would often buy the ticket at the front door, then have to get out of the bus and enter via the back door. Some Black athletes who competed at the 1936 Berlin Olympics in Nazi Germany claim to have had greater freedom to socialise and mix with other people in Berlin than they did when they went back behind the "Cotton Curtain" in the "home of the free" and had to go to the back of the bus.

King was relatively new in town, but being a highly articulate and respectable preacher with genuine social justice concerns, he had been approached to become president of the local branch of the National Association for the Advancement of Colored People (NAACP). However he had declined because he felt he was too new in the community and he was also very committed to his work as a pastor.

When Rosa Parks was arrested, a boycott of the bus company was hastily organised, and a new organisation, the Montgomery Improvement Association (MIA) was formed. King was again called upon, and invited to simply be present at the foundation meeting. The meeting proceeded to the stage of election of office bearers, and to his astonishment, King was elected unanimously! Once that point had been reached, King took his commitment very seriously and he set to work.

It was characteristic of King's intellect and morality that he agonised over whether a boycott was the correct thing to do, what the consequences could be, and whether it could be used to unethical and unchristian ends. Boycotts had previously been used by Whites to deprive Negroes, but after much consideration he was convinced by Thoreau's essay "Civil Disobedience" and concluded that they were right in saying to the White community 'we can no longer lend our cooperation to an evil system'. It was characteristic of King that his passion for justice was to be achieved through temperate means. Their aim was not to put the bus company out of business, but as King declared: 'to put the justice in business'.

Organising a major boycott and taking the possible repercussions into account was a daunting task. This was more than a stirring sermon – there were some very real and immediate consequences and complexities. The Ku Klux Klan was active in the south and violence was ever threatening. They reviewed strategies… how overt or covert should they be? What were the possible consequences? How far did they dare go? After much concerned debate, one of the organisers, E D Nixon spoke up and asked the gathering: 'We'd better decide now if we are going to be fearless men or scared boys.' That was it. The tide had turned, and the course was set. It would be a major undertaking, very visible and assertive, but strictly non-violent. The Negro population's networks were engaged to organise as much support as possible, and to ensure life could go on around the boycott. The next day would tell just how much support there really was in the Black community for such a bold step, and just how significant – or otherwise not – the boycott would be.

On that first Monday morning of the boycott, King and Coretta were up and dressed at 5.30 am. There was a bus stop right outside their house, and hoping for a 60 percent level of cooperation, they eagerly watched from their front window to see how well the boycott would be supported by the Black population. The bus stop was on the South Jackson line, and normally carried more Negro passengers than any other in Montgomery.

The first bus rolled past... empty. Then another. Empty. Then another. Empty except for two White passengers... the protest would be a success!

Something significant happened to King at that time. He could feel the power of ideas and their consequences, and the power of social action and its possibilities.

The very strong support by the Black population took everyone, including the organisers, by surprise, and they were faced with the question of "what now?". An urgent meeting to plan the next moves was called by the organisers.

A major bus boycott had real and complex social and economic consequences. It was crucial to get the tone of the response and the strategy right. It was unanimously declared the protest should continue until their demands were met, and King set about writing what he called 'the most decisive speech of my life'.

Here then was a very real test of being a responsible leader. 'How' he asked himself, 'could I make a speech that would be militant enough to keep my people aroused to positive action and yet moderate enough to keep this fervor within controllable and Christian bounds?'

With great apprehension he started writing that speech... and it was decisive.

A new life course had begun.

The Holt Street church was packed and the television cameras were in action by the time King addressed the audience.

He recounted what had happened to Rosa Parks, and then summarised the long and ugly history of discrimination and injustice suffered by the Negro citizens of America.

His soaring oratory was in the classic Martin Luther King style – grand and biblical, metaphorical and musical, strong on repetition and memorable phrasing. And he had the stagecraft and timing to deliver it as only he could.

But he was also always careful to put his argument as being in accordance with the highest ideals of Christianity, the Constitution and the American dream, and to make it inclusive.

'We are here this evening for a serious business. We are here... because first and foremost we are American citizens and we are determined to apply our citizenship to the fullness of its meaning. We are here also because of our love for democracy, because of our deep-seated belief that democracy transformed from thin paper to thick action is the greatest form of government on Earth…

You know, my friends, there comes a time when people get tired of being trampled over by the iron feet of oppression. There comes a time, my friends, when people get tired of being plunged across the abyss of humiliation, where they experience the bleakness of nagging despair. There comes a time when people get tired of being pushed out of the glittering sunlight of life's July, and left standing amid the piercing chill of an Alpine November…

…We are not wrong in what we are doing. If we are wrong, the Supreme Court of this nation is wrong. If we are wrong, the Constitution of the United States is wrong. If we are wrong, God Almighty is wrong. If we are wrong, Jesus of Nazareth was merely a utopian dreamer that never came down to earth. And we are determined here in Montgomery to work and fight until justice runs down like water and righteousness like a mighty stream…

…We are going to work together. Right here in Montgomery, when the history books are written in the future, somebody will have to say, 'There lived a race of people, a Black people… a people who had the moral courage to stand up for their rights. And thereby they injected a new meaning into the veins of history and civilization.'

As King said about that night of 5 December 1955, 'That night was Montgomery's moment in history'.

And it was a turning point for King.

The authorities responded with a diversity of legal, quasi legal and downright devious means, including spreading rumours and encouraging conflict with the Black community. And there were those within the Black community who wanted to respond with violence, but King's exhortations for non-violent protest prevailed. Even so, King and others were arrested and spent some time in jail. It was an experience that made him even more committed to the cause of social reform.

Some of his opponents favoured more brutal responses. In the very early days of the boycott, he received a phone call at around midnight: 'Nigger, we are tired of you and your mess now. And if you aren't out of this town in three days, we're going to blow your brains out and blow up your house.'

King was shaken, and went to his kitchen to pray. 'I could hear an inner voice' he said, 'saying to me, "Martin Luther, stand up for right-eousness. Stand up for justice. Stand up for truth. And lo I will be with you, even until the end of the world."'

The front porch of his Montgomery home was indeed bombed while his wife and children were inside, but they were not injured. Even after this, King reaffirmed his non-violent approach. 'Christ furnished the spirit and motivation, Gandhi furnished the method,' he would write.

As the boycott dragged on, King was gaining a national reputation. On 13 November 1956 the Supreme Court ruled that bus segregation was illegal, ensuring victory for the boycott. The ultimate success of the year-long Montgomery bus boycott made King a hero to many across the nation – but there were also still many to whom he was anything but a hero.

Throughout his career, King faced many hundreds of death threats. As his visibility and importance increased, he became a marked man. Security was an ever-present issue, and he often talked about the very real possibility of being assassinated at any time.

But as he said, 'A man who won't die for something is not fit to live.' He was carrying the torch of hope for a tortured nation, and had the courage of his convictions: 'If you are cut down in a movement that is designed to save the soul of a nation, then no other death could be more redemptive.'

King was well aware of the nature of the huge, complex and powerful social forces swirling about him – both for and against him. And it was not a simple dividing line between Blacks and Whites – there were many Whites who were against segregation, and there were many Blacks who were against King and his approach.

His strategy of emphasising the teaching of Christianity, respect for the law and the ideals of the Constitution, as well as including Whites and others in the overall movement, was all part of a comprehensive non-violent approach designed to bring people together rather than tear them apart. He had to be wise enough to be a pragmatic, yet a principled politician.

He was only too well aware that a strategy based on violence and con-frontation along racial lines in a country like America, could lead to vicious conflagration and swift disaster. Appealing to the more civilised, principled and compassionate side of people across society was a strategy far shrewder than head-on confrontation. Asking America to act in accordance with its Christian principles and national ideals was a powerful argument.

In his campaigning for the ballot for Blacks, he also put the government's fear of communism to work for the cause. The thrust of the May 1957 Prayer Pilgrimage to Washington DC was, in King's words, 'to say to the men in the forefront of our government that the civil rights issue was not an ephemeral, evanescent domestic issue… rather it was an eternal moral issue which may well determine the destiny of our nation in the ideological struggle with Communism.'

King had now tasted the success (and trials) of large-scale civil action and was even more committed to righting a greater diversity of social wrongs across the country.

In 1957 he founded the Southern Christian Leadership Conference for non-violent struggle against racism and segregation and to achieve civil rights. Increasingly he was gaining a national and even international reputation as a major civil rights figure. He was frequently talking to Presidents, politicians and civic leaders. On 17 May he addressed a crowd of 15,000 in Washington DC. The fight was beginning to bear fruit... but there was much more to be done.

In 1957 the US Congress passed the first Civil Rights Act since reconstruction. A sequence of Civil Rights Acts followed over the next decade – it was one thing for Acts to be passed in Washington DC, another entirely to have them obeyed throughout the nation.

In 1958 King's first book, *Stride Toward Freedom – The Montgomery Story*, was published, and while on a speaking tour in New York he was stabbed in the chest by a deranged Black woman. He was lucky to survive when the knife narrowly missed his aorta.

He took the opportunity in 1959 to go to India to meet with followers of Gandhi to find out more about the philosophy, strategies and tactics of non-violent protest. He came away even more convinced than ever that non-violent resistance was the most potent weapon available in the circumstances. He was also impressed that the Indian media had provided a greater continuity of coverage of the bus boycott than had the media in the USA.

It was at this time that he decided that the fight for civil rights was his principal vocation, and he resigned as pastor of the Dexter Avenue Baptist Church. So in 1960, King and family moved to Atlanta to direct the activities of the Southern Christian Leadership Conference (SCLC) and concentrate on civil rights full time. He was also appointed co-pastor with his father at the Ebenezer Baptist Church in Atlanta, Georgia.

The nation was catching the mood. Sit-ins against segregated lunch counters broke out in Greensboro, North Carolina in 1960 and spread far and wide. King was not initially involved, but after some criticism he participated in a sit-in waiting to be served at a restaurant in Atlanta, and was duly arrested.

Sentenced to four months in jail, he was immediately transported to a high security prison. He was in fear of his life on that journey and at the prison, but was quickly released after intervention by John and Robert Kennedy, who were advised of the situation by King's supporters, which now increasingly included more Whites. King was learning how to play a dangerous game at a national and very serious level.

At this time, both Black and White students across the country were increasingly rallying to the cause, and in the Spring of 1961, The Congress on Racial Equality (CORE) began its first Freedom Ride through the South. The brutally violent reception they received in the south made national headlines. Many Freedom Rides followed, and in November 1961, the Interstate Commerce Commission banned segregation in interstate travel. King supported the rides, even to the extent of harbouring some of the riders in his church, which was then surrounded by a violent mob. It was only after a phone call to President Kennedy that the National Guard was mobilised to rescue them!

Serious violence was an everyday consideration – and very often a reality. While there was progress overall, there were many setbacks along the way. In July 1962 during the unsuccessful Albany, Georgia movement, King was arrested and jailed several times over several months. But the movement had taken the "moral offensive" and although only a partial victory was won, it was a positive and encouraging beginning. King summarised the result: 'The people of Albany had straightened their backs, and, as Gandhi had said, no one can ride on the back of man unless it is bent.'

One of his greatest challenges was Birmingham, Alabama, the largest industrialised city in the south and probably the most segregated city in America, and his legendary opponent Police Commissioner Eugene "Bull" Connor.

On Good Friday, 12 April 1963, King was arrested for demonstrating without a permit, and on 13 April, the Birmingham campaign was launched. The objective in Birmingham was to completely end the system of segregation in every aspect of public life, and this campaign would prove to be the turning point in ending segregation in the south. It consumed the city and made news across the nation and around the world.

Among other activities, protesters had organised a "Children's Crusade" with thousands of children joining the protests. The savagery of the response of the authorities resulted in huge national media coverage... especially when the Birmingham police used fire hoses and dogs against the demonstrators, and arrested over 1,000 youngsters. King was only one of the many in the overflowing jails of Birmingham.

Written during his 11 days in jail, King's *Letter from Birmingham Jail* inspired an even greater national civil rights movement. It was a long treatise that boldly sent out a call for total desegregation and justice across the country – and soon! America was being called to live up to the standards and promises of the Constitution and the Christian message.

Eventually a peace pact was negotiated, but even after this, the motel where King was supposed to be staying (he was in Atlanta) was bombed. His brother's house was also bombed, fortunately without any deaths.

biography

It was a national crisis, and even President Kennedy was reporting to the nation on the situation. Eventually the agreement was observed. The stores, restaurants and schools would be desegregated, hiring of Blacks implemented, and charges dropped. Although the situation was far from ideal, a major step forward had been achieved. The fight would continue.

King had an uneasy relationship with Kennedy, and King had to push Kennedy hard to expedite action on civil rights issues, as Kennedy tried to run the country at a very challenging time. They were both strong-willed, and were capable politicians, and each had his weaknesses, some of which were hidden from the public view. Both smoked cigarettes, but not in public, and both had a reputation for romantic involvements for example.

The Kennedy administration had announced that the civil rights legislation would be shelved for 1963, but the explosion of unrest in Birmingham meant that civil rights was now on the top of the congressional calendar. The call for Black emancipation was now being well and truly heard in the north as well as the south. One hundred years after a vacillating Abraham Lincoln had signed the Emancipation Declaration, Black people in America were still not free and equal, and they were getting angrier by the day… 'This is no time for the tranquilizing drug of gradualism,' thundered King.

On 23 June, King led 125,000 people on a Freedom Walk in Detroit.

And then on 28 August 1963 the "March on Washington" was a breakthrough on a truly national scale. This was a march that changed the face of America, and was the largest civil rights demonstration in the nation's history, involving some 300,000 people.

It was at this march that King made his famous *I Have a Dream* speech.

But it was much more than outlining a dream somewhere out there in the future… That speech also demanded what King thought was due right then and there:

We have come to our nation's capital to cash a check. When the architects of our republic wrote the magnificent words of the Constitution and the Declaration of Independence, they were signing a promissory note to which every American was to fall heir. Instead of honoring this sacred obligation, America has given the Negro people a bad check; a check which has come back marked "insufficient funds".

It was time to come to deliver NOW!

The "I have a dream" part of the speech was a vision of an ideal future – the "bite" in the speech was about demanding civil rights right then and there.

The "I have a dream" theme was suggested to King by one of his inner circle, Dorothy Cotton, who overhead a White woman in the local church congregation talking about having a dream that her children and little Black children would be able to live together in harmony one day. Taken up and delivered in the inimitable King way, that theme became the stuff of legend.

But the demand for immediate civil rights was where the immediate action was. There was a new consciousness and urgency across the land. The Black voice was getting bolder in the north as well as the south. One such was militant Black leader and Muslim, Malcolm X (who had many differences with Martin Luther King) and called for revolution and a separate Black nation. The pressure was on.

King continued in his more conciliatory and inclusive way: 'But we refuse to believe that the Bank of Justice is bankrupt.' The people had come to 'cash that check that will give us upon demand, the richness of freedom and the security of justice!'.

It was a time of increasing turmoil… and even more so when on 22 November 1963, President Kennedy was assassinated. But the momentum kept building and King and millions of others kept fighting on a multitude of fronts right across the country.

It was another mark of just how far he had come when in early 1964, Martin Luther King's achievements as a civil rights leader were recognised when he appeared on the cover of *Time Magazine* as Man of the Year.

Perhaps lacking the popular charisma of President Kennedy, President Lyndon Johnson was nevertheless a positive force in establishing greater civil rights (although Kennedy and Johnson had voted against Eisenhower's Civil Rights Bill of 1957), and the Civil Rights Bill of 1964 was a major step forward. The wheel was really turning now, and on 2 July 1964, King attended the signing ceremony of the Civil Rights Act of 1964 at the White House.

But even then nothing was ever clear and straightforward – that summer, King experienced a particularly intense and hurtful rejection by Black people, when he was stoned by Black Muslims. And Attorney General Robert Kennedy had authorised the FBI to place King under surveillance.

Despite the setbacks and inevitable complexities, his fame was now international. On 18 September he had an audience with Pope Paul VI at the Vatican, and was then awarded the Nobel Peace Prize on 10 December 1964 at the age of 35, the youngest person ever to have been awarded it at the time.

Even so the battle had not been totally won… he continued to be hounded by J Edgar Hoover's FBI – his telephone and hotel rooms were bugged, and malicious gossip about him was circulated. It was alleged that the FBI even tried to force him into committing suicide after he won the Nobel Peace Prize.

The struggle continued… on 2 February 1965, King was again arrested in Selma, Alabama during a voting rights demonstration.

When President Lyndon Johnson signed the Voting Rights Act into law in 1965, another significant battle in the ongoing war had been won – at least at an official level. King turned to addressing wider socioeconomic problems across the country.

In January 1966 he moved into a Chicago slum tenement to attract attention to the living conditions of the poor. In June, there was the March Against Fear through the South. Then in July, a campaign to end discrimination in housing, employment and schools in Chicago.

He was vehemently against American involvement in Vietnam, and in May 1966 argued strongly that America was being morally compromised by her involvement.

In 1967 King was back in jail in Birmingham for four days when the Supreme Court upheld an earlier conviction for demonstrating without a permit.

In the scale of things, that seemed to be just a minor irritation… there was always more to be done… and in the last months of 1967 he announced the Poor People's Campaign, an initiative to address issues of employment and liberty among the poor of all races.

In 1968 King announced that the Poor People's Campaign would make its presence manifest at another March on Washington to demand an Economic Bill of Rights to guarantee employment to the able-bodied, support incomes to those unable to work, and an end to housing discrimination.

The pressure was enormous, but his energy and determination were seemingly indefatigable. In one week in March 1968 he made 35 speeches, starting in Grosse Point, Michigan, then four speeches in Detroit on the Friday, Saturday in Los Angeles speaking five times, then on Sunday preaching in three churches in Los Angeles, and then on to Memphis to speak to the sanitation workers – and so it went on.

In a speech in Memphis it was apparent that the pressure was taking its toll as he said:

Having to live under the threat of death every day, sometimes I feel discouraged. Having to take so much abuse and criticism, sometimes from my own people, sometimes I feel discouraged… But then the Holy Spirit revives my soul again… and brings about the day when every valley will be exalted. Every mountain and hill will be made low. The rough places will be made plain, and the crooked places straight. And the glory of the Lord shall be revealed, and all flesh shall see it together.

And then on 3 April 1968 in Memphis, on the day before he died, he made his famous *I've Been to the Mountaintop* speech, which included the recognition that the struggle would continue to be long and hard, and that he may well be a casualty along the way: 'I just want to do God's will. And He's allowed me to go up to the mountain. And I've looked over, and I've seen the promised land. I may not get there with you. But I want you to know tonight, that we, as a people, will get to the promised land. And I am happy tonight, I'm not worried about anything. I'm not fearing any man. Mine own eyes have seen the glory of the coming of the Lord.' And he turned away and left the microphones...

The following day he was dead.

At sunset on 4 April 1968 he was fatally shot by James Earl Ray, a White man, while standing on the balcony of the Lorraine Motel in Memphis, Tennessee. He was only 39 years old. The 13 years since the Montgomery Bus Boycott had passed quickly and tumultuously. But the fires of freedom had been lit and were burning strongly.

Riots erupted in at least 130 American cities and there were some 20,000 arrests across the nation. King's funeral on 19 April was an international event. On 5 June Presidential candidate Senator Robert Kennedy was shot in Los Angeles and died the next day.

Within a week of the assassination, the Open Housing Act was passed by Congress.

In 1983 King's birthday was declared a national holiday.

Martin Luther King, Jr now also belonged to the ages.

wisdom

What are you doing for others?

Martin Luther King, a hero of mine, once observed. *'Every man must decide whether he will walk in the light of creative altruism or the darkness of destructive selfishness.* This is the judgment. Life's most persistent and urgent question is, "What are you doing for others?" '

The publication of *Collective Wisdom* I like to think of as an act of creative altruism – something that could benefit other young people, as well as me, by accessing and then sharing the experiences of the prominent people interviewed. The opportunity of passing on the help I was given for others has been very rewarding.

When you are young and finding your way input from others that have walked further in life can be invaluable. It can serve as a good example or a warning of how not to live. Time makes clear many things that are not immediately obvious and older people offer younger people a chance to observe the outcomes from each person's approach to living.

In his book *Stride Toward Freedom: The Montgomery Story* published in 1958 Luther King wrote about the need for love as part of one's approach to life:

A fifth point concerning nonviolent resistance is that it avoids not only external physical violence but also internal violence of spirit. The nonviolent resister not only refuses to shoot his opponent but he also refuses to hate him. At the center of nonviolence stands the principle of love. The nonviolent resister would contend that in the struggle for human dignity, the oppressed people of the world must not succumb to the temptation of becoming bitter or indulging in hate campaigns. To retaliate in kind would do nothing but intensify the existence of hate in the universe. Along the way of life, someone must have sense enough and morality enough to cut off the chain of hate. This can only be done by projecting the ethic of love to the center of our lives...

Another basic point about agape is that it springs from the need of the other person – his need for belonging to the best in the human family. The Samaritan who helped the Jew on the Jericho Road was 'good' because he responded to the human need that he was presented with. God's love is eternal and fails not because man needs his love. Saint Paul assures us that the loving act of redemption was done "while we were yet sinners" – that is, at the point of our greatest need for love. Since the white man's personality is greatly distorted by segregation, and his soul is greatly scarred, he needs the love of the Negro. The Negro must love the white man, because the white man needs his love to remove his tensions, insecurities, and fears.

When something in life is not quite as it should be or we are not getting what we want it is a temptation to focus on our own problems. If we take a minute to consider the person who is just burying their own child, who is struggling with illness, someone who is lost – we get a better appreciation of the scale of our problems. And we shift the focus from our own individualistic obsession: ourselves.

The power that comes from having a purpose is what life is about. To suffer through meaningless days attending to nothing of substance is crippling to the human spirit. When one takes up a project that can help others, or simply takes to treating others better a new energy is experienced.

And so it was, in this long-handed way, that I saw the response of Luther King:

When I went to Montgomery, Alabama, as a pastor in 1954, I had not the slightest idea that I would later become involved in a crisis in which non-violent resistance would be applicable. After I had lived in the community about a year, the bus boycott began. The Negro people of Montgomery, exhausted by the humiliating experiences that they had constantly faced on the buses, expressed in a massive act of non-cooperation their determination to be free. They came to see that it was ultimately more honorable to walk the streets in dignity than to ride the buses in humiliation. At the beginning of the protest the people called on me to serve as their spokesman. In accepting this responsibility my mind, consciously or unconsciously, was driven back to the Sermon on the Mount and the Gandhian method of nonviolent resistance. This principle became the guiding light of our movement. Christ furnished the spirit and motivation while Gandhi furnished the method.

Martin Luther King answered the question 'What are you doing for others?' in his life because there was no just alternative for him – with the talents he had, the need he could see and the wisdom to help he could not ignore the calls of his own conscience. In so doing he acquired the authority to ask others to act with justice in their own lives and in the conduct of their public office. And he helped change the world for millions of people.

So the question for us all, during the entirety of our lives, remains, "What are you doing for others?".

words

I Have A Dream

*Delivered on the steps at the Lincoln Memorial in Washington DC
– 28 August 1963.*

Five score years ago, a great American, in whose symbolic shadow we stand, signed the Emancipation Proclamation. This momentous decree came as a great beacon light of hope to millions of Negro slaves who had been seared in the flames of withering injustice. It came as a joyous daybreak to end the long night of captivity. But one hundred years later, we must face the tragic fact that the Negro is still not free.

One hundred years later, the life of the Negro is still sadly crippled by the manacles of segregation and the chains of discrimination. One hundred years later, the Negro lives on a lonely island of poverty in the midst of a vast ocean of material prosperity. One hundred years later, the Negro is still languishing in the corners of American society and finds himself an exile in his own land.

So we have come here today to dramatize an appalling condition. In a sense we have come to our nation's capital to cash a check. When the architects of our republic wrote the magnificent words of the Constitution and the Declaration of Independence, they were signing a promissory note to which every American was to fall heir.

This note was a promise that all men would be guaranteed the inalienable rights of life, liberty, and the pursuit of happiness. It is obvious today that America has defaulted on this promissory note insofar as her citizens of color are concerned. Instead of honoring this sacred obligation, America has given the Negro people a bad check which has come back marked "insufficient funds." But we refuse to believe that the bank of justice is bankrupt. We refuse to believe that there are insufficient funds in the great vaults of opportunity of this nation.

So we have come to cash this check – a check that will give us upon demand the riches of freedom and the security of justice. We have also come to this hallowed spot to remind America of the fierce urgency of now. This is no time to engage in the luxury of cooling off or to take the tranquilizing drug of gradualism. Now is the time to rise from the dark and desolate valley of segregation to the sunlit path of racial justice. Now is the time to open the doors of opportunity to all of God's children. Now is the time to lift our nation from the quicksands of racial injustice to the solid rock of brotherhood.

It would be fatal for the nation to overlook the urgency of the moment and to underestimate the determination of the Negro. This sweltering summer of the Negro's legitimate discontent will not pass until there is an invigorating autumn of freedom and equality. Nineteen sixty-three is not an end, but a beginning. Those who hope that the Negro needed to blow off steam and will now be content will have a rude awakening if the nation returns to business as usual. There will be neither rest nor tranquility in America until the Negro is granted his citizenship rights.

The whirlwinds of revolt will continue to shake the foundations of our nation until the bright day of justice emerges. But there is something that I must say to my people who stand on the warm threshold which leads into the palace of justice. In the process of gaining our rightful place we must not be guilty of wrongful deeds. Let us not seek to satisfy our thirst for freedom by drinking from the cup of bitterness and hatred.

We must forever conduct our struggle on the high plane of dignity and discipline. We must not allow our creative protest to degenerate into physical violence. Again and again we must rise to the majestic heights of meeting physical force with soul force.

The marvelous new militancy which has engulfed the Negro community must not lead us to distrust all white people, for many of our white brothers, as evidenced by their presence here today, have come to realize that their destiny is tied up with our destiny and their freedom is inextricably bound to our freedom.

We cannot walk alone. And as we walk, we must make the pledge that we shall march ahead. We cannot turn back. There are those who are asking the devotees of civil rights, 'When will you be satisfied?' We can never be satisfied as long as our bodies, heavy with the fatigue of travel, cannot gain lodging in the motels of the highways and the hotels of the cities. We cannot be satisfied as long as the Negro's basic mobility is from a smaller ghetto to a larger one. We can never be satisfied as long as a Negro in Mississippi cannot vote and a Negro in New York believes he has nothing for which to vote. No, no, we are not satisfied, and we will not be satisfied until justice rolls down like waters and righteousness like a mighty stream.

I am not unmindful that some of you have come here out of great trials and tribulations. Some of you have come fresh from narrow cells. Some of you have come from areas where your quest for freedom left you battered by the storms of persecution and staggered by the winds of police brutality. You have been the veterans of creative suffering. Continue to work with the faith that unearned suffering is redemptive.

Go back to Mississippi, go back to Alabama, go back to Georgia, go back to Louisiana, go back to the slums and ghettos of our northern cities, knowing that somehow this situation can and will be changed. Let us not wallow in the valley of despair. I say to you today, my friends, that in spite of the difficulties and frustrations of the moment, I still have a dream. It is a dream deeply rooted in the American dream.

I have a dream that one day this nation will rise up and live out the true meaning of its creed: 'We hold these truths to be self-evident: that all men are created equal.' I have a dream that one day on the red hills of Georgia the sons of former slaves and the sons of former slaveowners will be able to sit down together at a table of brotherhood. I have a dream that one day even the state of Mississippi, a state sweltering with the heat of injustice and oppression, will be transformed into an oasis of freedom and justice. I have a dream that my four children will one day live in a nation where they will not be judged by the color of their skin but by the content of their character. I have a dream today.

I have a dream that one day the state of Alabama, whose governor's lips are presently dripping with the words of interposition and nullification, will be transformed into a situation where little black boys and black girls will be able to join hands with little white boys and white girls and walk together as sisters and brothers. I have a dream today. I have a dream that one day every valley shall be exalted, every hill and mountain shall be made low, the rough places will be made plain, and the crooked places will be made straight, and the glory of the Lord shall be revealed, and all flesh shall see it together. This is our hope. This is the faith with which I return to the South. With this faith we will be able to hew out of the mountain of despair a stone of hope. With this faith we will be able to transform the jangling discords of our nation into a beautiful symphony of brotherhood. With this faith we will be able to work together, to pray together, to struggle together, to go to jail together, to stand up for freedom together, knowing that we will be free one day.

This will be the day when all of God's children will be able to sing with a new meaning, 'My country, 'tis of thee, sweet land of liberty, of thee I sing. Land where my fathers died, land of the pilgrim's pride, from every mountainside, let freedom ring.' And if America is to be a great nation, this must become true. So let freedom ring from the prodigious hilltops of New Hampshire. Let freedom ring from the mighty mountains of New York. Let freedom ring from the heightening Alleghenies of Pennsylvania! Let freedom ring from the snowcapped Rockies of Colorado! Let freedom ring from the curvaceous peaks of California! But not only that; let freedom ring from Stone Mountain of Georgia! Let freedom ring from Lookout Mountain of Tennessee! Let freedom ring from every hill and every molehill of Mississippi. From every mountainside, let freedom ring.

When we let freedom ring, when we let it ring from every village and every hamlet, from every state and every city, we will be able to speed up that day when all of God's children, black men and white men, Jews and Gentiles, Protestants and Catholics, will be able to join hands and sing in the words of the old Negro spiritual, 'Free at last! free at last! thank God Almighty, we are free at last!'

I've Been to the Mountaintop

Dr Martin Luther King, Jr delivered this speech in support of the striking sanitation workers at Mason Temple in Memphis, Tennessee on 3 April 1968 – the day before he was assassinated.

Thank you very kindly, my friends. As I listened to Ralph Abernathy in his eloquent and generous introduction and then thought about myself, I wondered who he was talking about. It's always good to have your closest friend and associate say something good about you. And Ralph is the best friend that I have in the world.

I'm delighted to see each of you here tonight in spite of a storm warning. You reveal that you are determined to go on anyhow. Something is happening in Memphis, something is happening in our world.

As you know, if I were standing at the beginning of time, with the possibility of general and panoramic view of the whole human history up to now, and the Almighty said to me, 'Martin Luther King, which age would you like to live in?' – I would take my mental flight by Egypt through, or rather across the Red Sea, through the wilderness on toward the promised land. And in spite of its magnificence, I wouldn't stop there. I would move on by Greece, and take my mind to Mount Olympus. And I would see Plato, Aristotle, Socrates, Euripides and Aristophanes assembled around the Parthenon as they discussed the great and eternal issues of reality.

But I wouldn't stop there. I would go on, even to the great heyday of the Roman Empire. And I would see developments around there, through various emperors and leaders. But I wouldn't stop there. I would even come up to the day of the Renaissance, and get a quick picture of all that the Renaissance did for the cultural and aesthetic life of man. But I wouldn't stop there. I would even go by the way that the man for whom I'm named had his habitat. And I would watch Martin Luther as he tacked his ninety-five theses on the door at the church in Wittenberg.

But I wouldn't stop there. I would come on up even to 1863, and watch a vacillating president by the name of Abraham Lincoln finally come to the conclusion that he had to sign the Emancipation Proclamation. But I wouldn't stop there. I would even come up to the early thirties, and see a man grappling with the problems of the bankruptcy of his nation. And come with an eloquent cry that we have nothing to fear but fear itself.

But I wouldn't stop there. Strangely enough, I would turn to the Almighty, and say, 'If you allow me to live just a few years in the second half of the twentieth century, I will be happy.' Now that's a strange statement to make, because the world is all messed up. The nation is sick. Trouble is in the land. Confusion all around. That's a strange statement. But I know, somehow, that only when it is dark enough, can you see the stars. And I see God working in this period of the twentieth century in a way that men, in some strange way, are responding – something is happening in our world. The masses of people are rising up. And wherever they are assembled today, whether they are in Johannesburg, South Africa; Nairobi, Kenya; Accra, Ghana; New York City; Atlanta, Georgia; Jackson, Mississippi; or Memphis, Tennessee – the cry is always the same – 'We want to be free.'

And another reason that I'm happy to live in this period is that we have been forced to a point where we're going to have to grapple with the problems that men have been trying to grapple with through history, but the demand didn't force them to do it. Survival demands that we grapple with them. Men, for years now, have been talking about war and peace. But now, no longer can they just talk about it. It is no longer a choice between violence and nonviolence in this world; it's nonviolence or nonexistence.

That is where we are today. And also in the human rights revolution, if something isn't done, and in a hurry, to bring the colored peoples of the world out of their long years of poverty, their long years of hurt and neglect, the whole world is doomed. Now, I'm just happy that God has allowed me to live in this period, to see what is unfolding. And I'm happy that He's allowed me to be in Memphis.

I can remember, I can remember when Negroes were just going around as Ralph has said, so often, scratching where they didn't itch, and laughing when they were not tickled. But that day is all over. We mean business now, and we are determined to gain our rightful place in God's world.

And that's all this whole thing is about. We aren't engaged in any negative protest and in any negative arguments with anybody. We are saying that we are determined to be men. We are determined to be people. We are saying that we are God's children. And that we don't have to live like we are forced to live.

Now, what does all of this mean in this great period of history? It means that we've got to stay together. We've got to stay together and maintain unity. You know, whenever Pharaoh wanted to prolong the period of slavery in Egypt, he had a favorite, favorite formula for doing it. What was that? He kept the slaves fighting among themselves. But whenever the slaves get together, something happens in Pharaoh's court, and he cannot hold the slaves in slavery. When the slaves get together, that's the beginning of getting out of slavery. Now let us maintain unity.

Secondly, let us keep the issues where they are. The issue is injustice. The issue is the refusal of Memphis to be fair and honest in its dealings with its public servants, who happen to be sanitation workers. Now, we've got to keep attention on that. That's always the problem with a little violence. You know what happened the other day, and the press dealt only with the window-breaking. I read the articles. They very seldom got around to mentioning the fact that one thousand, three hundred sanitation workers were on strike, and that Memphis is not being fair to them, and that Mayor Loeb is in dire need of a doctor. They didn't get around to that.

Now we're going to march again, and we've got to march again, in order to put the issue where it is supposed to be. And force everybody to see that there are thirteen hundred of God's children here suffering, sometimes going hungry, going through dark and dreary nights wondering how this thing is going to come out. That's the issue. And we've got to say to the nation: we know it's coming out. For when people get caught up with that which is right and they are willing to sacrifice for it, there is no stopping point short of victory.

We aren't going to let any mace stop us. We are masters in our nonviolent movement in disarming police forces; they don't know what to do, I've seen them so often. I remember in Birmingham, Alabama, when we were in that majestic struggle there we would move out of the 16th Street Baptist Church day after day; by the hundreds we would move out. And Bull Connor would tell them to send the dogs forth and they did come; but we just went before the dogs singing, 'Ain't gonna let nobody turn me round.' Bull Connor next would say, 'Turn the fire hoses on.' And as I said to you the other night, Bull Connor didn't know history. He knew a kind of physics that somehow didn't relate to the transphysics that we knew about. And that was the fact that there was a certain kind of fire that no water could put out. And we went before the fire hoses; we had known water. If we were Baptist or some other denomination, we had been immersed. If we were Methodist, and some others, we had been sprinkled, but we knew water.

That couldn't stop us. And we just went on before the dogs and we would look at them; and we'd go on before the water hoses and we would look at them, and we'd just go on singing 'Over my head I see freedom in the air.' And then we would be thrown in the paddy wagons, and sometimes we were stacked in there like sardines in a can. And they would throw us in, and old Bull would say, 'Take them off', and they did; and we would just go in the paddy wagon singing, *We Shall Overcome*. And every now and then we'd get in the jail, and we'd see the jailers looking through the windows being moved by our prayers, and being moved by our words and our songs. And there was a power there which Bull Connor couldn't adjust to; and so we ended up transforming Bull into a steer, and we won our struggle in Birmingham.

Now we've got to go on to Memphis just like that. I call upon you to be with us Monday. Now about injunctions: We have an injunction and we're going into court tomorrow morning to fight this illegal, unconstitutional injunction. All we say to America is, 'Be true to what you said on paper.' If I lived in China or even Russia, or any totalitarian country, maybe I could understand the denial of certain basic First Amendment privileges, because they hadn't committed themselves to that over there. But some-where I read of the freedom of assembly. Somewhere I read of the free-dom of speech. Somewhere I read of the freedom of the press. Some-where I read that the greatness of America is the right to protest for right. And so just as I say, we aren't going to let any injunction turn us around. We are going on.

We need all of you. And you know what's beautiful to me, is to see all of these ministers of the Gospel. It's a marvelous picture. Who is it that is supposed to articulate the longings and aspirations of the people more than the preacher? Somehow the preacher must be an Amos, and say, 'Let justice roll down like waters and righteousness like a mighty stream.' Somehow, the preacher must say with Jesus, 'The spirit of the Lord is upon me, because he hath anointed me to deal with the problems of the poor.'

And I want to commend the preachers, under the leadership of these noble men: James Lawson, one who has been in this struggle for many years; he's been to jail for struggling; but he's still going on, fighting for the rights of his people. Rev. Ralph Jackson, Billy Kiles; I could just go right on down the list, but time will not permit. But I want to thank them all. And I want you to thank them, because so often, preachers aren't concerned about anything but themselves. And I'm always happy to see a relevant ministry.

It's all right to talk about "long white robes over yonder," in all of its symbolism. But ultimately people want some suits and dresses and shoes to wear down here. It's all right to talk about "streets flowing with milk and honey," but God has commanded us to be concerned about the slums down here, and his children who can't eat three square meals a day. It's all right to talk about the new Jerusalem, but one day, God's preachers must talk about the New York, the new Atlanta, the new Philadelphia, the new Los Angeles, the new Memphis, Tennessee. This is what we have to do.

Now the other thing we'll have to do is this: Always anchor our external direct action with the power of economic withdrawal. Now, we are poor people, individually, we are poor when you compare us with white society in America. We are poor. Never stop and forget that collectively, that means all of us together, collectively we are richer than all the nations in the world, with the exception of nine. Did you ever think about that? After you leave the United States, Soviet Russia, Great Britain, West Germany, France, and I could name the others, the Negro collectively is richer than most nations of the world. We have an annual income of more than thirty billion dollars a year, which is more than all of the exports of the United States, and more than the national budget of Canada. Did you know that? That's power right there, if we know how to pool it.

We don't have to argue with anybody. We don't have to curse and go around acting bad with our words. We don't need any bricks and bottles, we don't need any Molotov cocktails, we just need to go around to these stores, and to these massive industries in our country, and say, 'God sent us by here, to say to you that you're not treating his children right. And we've come by here to ask you to make the first item on your agenda fair treatment, where God's children are concerned. Now, if you are not prepared to do that, we do have an agenda that we must follow. And our agenda calls for withdrawing economic support from you.'

And so, as a result of this, we are asking you tonight, to go out and tell your neighbors not to buy Coca-Cola in Memphis. Go by and tell them not to buy Sealtest milk. Tell them not to buy – what is the other bread? – Wonder Bread. And what is the other bread company, Jesse? Tell them not to buy Hart's bread. As Jesse Jackson has said, up to now, only the garbage men have been feeling pain; now we must kind of redistribute the pain. We are choosing these companies because they haven't been fair in their hiring policies; and we are choosing them because they can begin the process of saying, they are going to support the needs and the rights of these men who are on strike. And then they can move on downtown and tell Mayor Loeb to do what is right.

But not only that, we've got to strengthen black institutions. I call upon you to take your money out of the banks downtown and deposit your money in Tri-State Bank – we want a "bank-in" movement in Memphis. So go by the savings and loan association. I'm not asking you something we don't do ourselves at SCLC. Judge Hooks and others will tell you that we have an account here in the savings and loan association from the Southern Christian Leadership Conference. We're just telling you to follow what we're doing. Put your money there. You have six or seven black insurance companies in Memphis. Take out your insurance there. We want to have an "insurance-in".

Now these are some practical things we can do. We begin the process of building a greater economic base. And at the same time, we are putting pressure where it really hurts. I ask you to follow through here.

Now, let me say as I move to my conclusion that we've got to give ourselves to this struggle until the end. Nothing would be more tragic than to stop at this point, in Memphis. We've got to see it through. And when we have our march, you need to be there. Be concerned about your brother. You may not be on strike. But either we go up together, or we go down together.

Let us develop a kind of dangerous unselfishness. One day a man came to Jesus; and he wanted to raise some questions about some vital matters in life. At points, he wanted to trick Jesus, and show him that he knew a little more than Jesus knew, and through this, throw him off base. Now that question could have easily ended up in a philosophical and theological debate. But Jesus immediately pulled that question from mid-air, and placed it on a dangerous curve between Jerusalem and Jericho. And he talked about a certain man, who fell among thieves. You remember that a Levite and a priest passed by on the other side. They didn't stop to help him. And finally a man of another race came by. He got down from his beast, decided not to be compassionate by proxy. But with him, administering first aid, and helped the man in need. Jesus ended up saying, this was the good man, this was the great man, because he had the capacity to project the "I" into the "thou", and to be concerned about his brother. Now you know, we use our imagination a great deal to try to determine why the priest and the Levite didn't stop. At times we say they were busy going to church meetings – an ecclesiastical gathering – and they had to get on down to Jerusalem so they wouldn't be late for their meeting. At other times we would speculate that there was a religious law that 'One who was engaged in religious ceremonials was not to touch a human body twenty-four hours before the ceremony.' And every now and then we begin to wonder whether maybe they were not going down to Jerusalem, or down to Jericho, rather to organize a "Jericho Road Improvement Association". That's a possibility. Maybe they felt that it was better to deal with the problem from the causal root, rather than to get bogged down with an individual effort.

But I'm going to tell you what my imagination tells me. It's possible that these men were afraid. You see, the Jericho road is a dangerous road. I remember when Mrs King and I were first in Jerusalem. We rented a car and drove from Jerusalem down to Jericho. And as soon as we got on that road, I said to my wife, 'I can see why Jesus used this as a setting for his parable.' It's a winding, meandering road. It's really conducive for ambushing. You start out in Jerusalem, which is about 1,200 miles, or rather 1200 feet above sea level. And by the time you get down to Jericho, fifteen or twenty minutes later, you're about 2,200 feet below sea level.

That's a dangerous road. In the days of Jesus it came to be known as the "Bloody Pass". And you know, it's possible that the priest and the Levite looked over that man on the ground and wondered if the robbers were still around. Or it's possible that they felt that the man on the ground was merely faking. And he was acting like he had been robbed and hurt, in order to seize them over there, lure them there for quick and easy seizure. And so the first question that the Levite asked was, 'If I stop to help this man, what will happen to me?' But then the Good Samaritan came by. And he reversed the question: 'If I do not stop to help this man, what will happen to him?'

That's the question before you tonight. Not, 'If I stop to help the sanitation workers, what will happen to all of the hours that I usually spend in my office every day and every week as a pastor?' The question is not, 'If I stop to help this man in need, what will happen to me?' 'If I do not stop to help the sanitation workers, what will happen to them?' That's the question.

Let us rise up tonight with a greater readiness. Let us stand with a greater determination. And let us move on in these powerful days, these days of challenge to make America what it ought to be. We have an opportunity to make America a better nation. And I want to thank God, once more, for allowing me to be here with you.

You know, several years ago, I was in New York City autographing the first book that I had written. And while sitting there autographing books, a demented black woman came up. The only question I heard from her was, 'Are you Martin Luther King?'

And I was looking down writing, and I said yes. And the next minute I felt something beating on my chest. Before I knew it I had been stabbed by this demented woman. I was rushed to Harlem Hospital. It was a dark Saturday afternoon. And that blade had gone through, and the X-rays revealed that the tip of the blade was on the edge of my aorta, the main artery. And once that's punctured, you drown in your own blood – that's the end of you.

It came out in *The New York Times* the next morning, that if I had sneezed, I would have died. Well, about four days later, they allowed me, after the operation, after my chest had been opened, and the blade had been taken out, to move around in the wheelchair in the hospital. They allowed me to read some of the mail that came in, and from all over the states, and the world, kind letters came in. I read a few, but one of them I will never forget. I had received one from the President and the Vice-President. I've forgotten what those telegrams said. I'd received a visit and a letter from the Governor of New York, but I've forgotten what the letter said. But there was another letter that came from a little girl, a young girl who was a student at the White Plains High School. And I looked at that letter, and I'll never forget it. It said simply, 'Dear Dr King: I am a ninth-grade student at the White Plains High School.' She said, 'While it should not matter, I would like to mention that I am a white girl. I read in the paper of your misfortune, and of your suffering. And I read that if you had sneezed, you would have died. And I'm simply writing you to say that I'm so happy that you didn't sneeze.'

And I want to say tonight, I want to say that I am happy that I didn't sneeze. Because if I had sneezed, I wouldn't have been around here in 1960, when students all over the South started sitting-in at lunch counters. And I knew that as they were sitting in, they were really standing up for the best in the American dream. And taking the whole nation back to those great wells of democracy which were dug deep by the Founding Fathers in the Declaration of Independence and the Constitution. If I had sneezed, I wouldn't have been around in 1962, when Negroes in Albany, Georgia, decided to straighten their backs up. And whenever men and women straighten their backs up, they are going somewhere, because a man can't ride your back unless it is bent. If I had sneezed, I wouldn't have been here in 1963, when the black people of Birmingham, Alabama, aroused the conscience of this nation, and brought into being the Civil Rights Bill. If I had sneezed, I wouldn't have had a chance later that year, in August, to try to tell America about a dream that I had had. If I had sneezed, I wouldn't have been down in Selma, Alabama, been in Memphis to see the community rally around those brothers and sisters who are suffering. I'm so happy that I didn't sneeze.

And they were telling me, now it doesn't matter now. It really doesn't matter what happens now. I left Atlanta this morning, and as we got started on the plane, there were six of us, the pilot said over the public address system, 'We are sorry for the delay, but we have Dr Martin Luther King on the plane. And to be sure that all of the bags were checked, and to be sure that nothing would be wrong with the plane, we had to check out everything carefully. And we've had the plane protected and guarded all night.'

And then I got to Memphis. And some began to say the threats, or talk about the threats that were out. What would happen to me from some of our sick white brothers?

Well, I don't know what will happen now. We've got some difficult days ahead. But it doesn't matter with me now. Because I've been to the mountaintop. And I don't mind. Like anybody, I would like to live a long life. Longevity has its place. But I'm not concerned about that now. I just want to do God's will. And He's allowed me to go up to the mountain. And I've looked over. And I've seen the promised land. I may not get there with you. But I want you to know tonight, that we, as a people, will get to the promised land. And I'm happy, tonight. I'm not worried about anything. I'm not fearing any man. Mine eyes have seen the glory of the coming of the Lord.

words

quotes

'An individual has not started living until he can rise above the narrow confines of his individualistic concerns to the broader concerns of all humanity.'

'Every man must decide whether he will walk in the light of creative altruism or the darkness of destructive selfishness. This is the judgment. Life's most persistent and urgent question is, What are you doing for others?'

'Love is the only force capable of transforming an enemy into a friend.'

'For modern man, absolute right and absolute wrong are a matter of what the majority is doing. Right and wrong are relative to the likes and dislikes and the customs of a particular community. We have unconsciously applied Einstein's theory of relativity, which properly described the physical universe, to the moral and ethical realm.'

'The ultimate measure of a man is not where he stands in moments of comfort and convenience, but where he stands at times of challenge and controversy. The true neighbour will risk his position, his prestige, and even his life for the welfare of others. In dangerous valleys and hazardous pathways, he will lift some bruised and beaten brother to a higher and more noble life.'

'Many people fear nothing more terribly than to take the position which stands out sharply and clearly from the prevailing opinion. The tendency of most is to adopt a view that is so ambiguous that it will include everything and so popular that it will include everybody. Not a few men who cherish lofty and noble ideas hide them under a bushel for fear of being called different.'

'When evil men plot, good men just plan. When evil men burn and bomb, good men just build and bind. When evil men shout ugly words of hatred, good men must commit themselves to the glories of love. Where evil men would seek to perpetuate an unjust status quo, good men must seek to bring into being a real order of justice.'

'I have the audacity to believe that peoples everywhere can have three meals a day for their bodies, education and culture for their minds, and dignity, equality, and freedom for their spirits. I believe that what self-centred men have torn down, other-centred men can build up.'

'The poor in our countries have been shut out of our minds and driven from the mainstream of our societies, because we have allowed them to become invisible.'

'A man who won't die for something is not fit to live.'

'There is so much frustration in the world because we have relied on gods rather than God. We have genuflected before the god of science only to find that it has given us the atomic bomb, producing fears and anxieties that science can never mitigate. We have worshipped the god of pleasure only to discover that thrills play out and sensations are short lived. We have bowed before the god of money only to learn that there are such things as love and friendship that money cannot buy and that in a world of possible depressions, stock market crashes, and bad business investments, money is a rather uncertain deity. These transitory gods are not able to save or bring happiness to the human heart. Only god is able. It is faith in Him that we must rediscover.'

'So I say to you, seek God and discover Him and make Him a power in your life. Without Him all our efforts turn to ashes and our sunrises into darkest nights. Without Him, life is a meaningless drama with the decisive scenes missing. But with Him we are able to rise from the fatigue of despair to the buoyancy of hope. With Him we are able to rise from the midnight of desperation to the daybreak of joy. St Augustine was right – we are made for God and will be restless until we find rest in Him.'

'He who is devoid of the power to forgive is devoid of the power to love.'

'I've decided that I'm going to do battle for my philosophy. You ought to believe something in life, believe that thing so fervently that you will stand up with it till the end of your days. I can't make myself believe that God wants me to hate. I'm tired of violence. And I'm not going to let my oppressor dictate to me what method I must use. We have a power, power that can't be found in Molotov cocktails, but we do have a power. Power that cannot be found in bullets and guns, but we have a power. It is a power as old as the insights of Jesus of Nazareth and as modern as the techniques of Mahatma Gandhi.'

'If there is to be peace on earth and goodwill toward men, we must finally believe in the ultimate morality of the universe, and believe that all reality hinges on moral foundations.'

'Admittedly, non-violence in the truest sense is not a strategy that one uses simply because it is expedient at the moment; non-violence is ultimately a way of life that men live by because of the sheer morality of its claim. But even granting this, the willingness to use non-violence as a technique is a step forward. For he who goes this far is more likely to adopt non-violence later as a way of life.'

'True peace is not merely the absence of tension; it is the presence of justice.'

'We will never have peace in the world until men everywhere recognise that ends are not cut off from the means, because the means represent the ideal in the making, and the end of the process. Ultimately you can't reach good ends through evil means, because the means represent the seed and the end represents the tree.'

'If you are cut down in a movement that is designed to save the soul of a nation, then no other death could be more redemptive.'

'Hatred and bitterness can never cure the disease of fear; only love can do that. Hatred paralyses life; love releases it. Hatred confuses life; love harmonises it. Hatred darkens life, love illuminates it.'

'It was argued that the Negro was inferior by nature because of Noah's curse upon the children of Ham... The greatest blasphemy of the whole ugly process was that the white man ended up making God his partner in the exploitation of the Negro.'

'One has not only a legal but a moral responsibility to obey just laws. Conversely, one has a moral responsibility to disobey unjust laws.'

'Probably no admonition has been more difficult to follow than Jesus' command to love your enemies. Some men have sincerely felt that this actual practice is not possible... Jesus, they say, was an impractical idealist.'

'The hard-hearted individual never sees people as people, but rather as mere objects or impersonal cogs in an ever-turning wheel. In the vast wheel of industry, he sees men as hands.'

'Power at its best is love implementing the demands of justice. Justice at its best is love correcting everything that stands against love.'

'If you are cut down in a movement that is designed to save the soul of a nation, then no other death could be more redemptive.'

'I submit that an individual who breaks a law that conscience tells him is unjust, and is willing to accept the penalty of imprisonment in order to arouse the conscience of the community over its injustice, is in reality expressing the highest respect for the law.'

'Every Negro comes face to face with this colour shock, and it constitutes a major emotional crisis... All prejudice is evil, but the prejudice that rejects a man because of the colour of his skin is the most despicable expression of man's inhumanity to man.'

'We are called to be people of conviction, not conformity; of moral nobility, not social respectability. We are commanded to live differently and according to higher loyalty.'

'Our scientific power has outrun our spiritual power. We have guided missiles and misguided man.'

quotes

Nelson Mandela

FIRST BLACK PRESIDENT, REPUBLIC OF SOUTH AFRICA

'For to be free is not merely to cast off one's chains,
but to live in a way that respects and enhances the freedom of others.'

The Life of Nelson Mandela

1918	18 July: Born in the Transkei.
1944	Joins the anti-apartheid African National Congress.
1960	Burns his passbook.
1956-61	Tried for treason and acquitted.
1961	Three-day national strike.
1961	ANC endorses armed resistance. Mandela appointed head of Umkhonto we Sizwe (The Spear of the Nation) or MK. Campaign of bombing government facilities and symbols of apartheid commences.
1964	Imprisoned for life at the age of 46.
1990	11 February: Released from prison after nearly 27 years.
1991	President of the ANC.
1993	Shares Nobel Peace Prize with F W de Klerk for abolishing apartheid in South Africa.
1994	President of South Africa.

biography

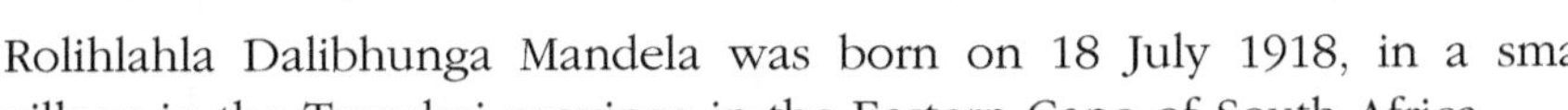

To receive a life sentence at the age of 46, then serve nearly 27 years in prison, only to emerge and take the leadership of a new nation at the age of 76 is truly a remarkable human story.

To live a life as full, as proud, passionate, disappointing and successful, is an extraordinary journey of gaining wisdom about oneself and the ways of the world.

Inspirational wisdom – and very practical wisdom; inspired wisdom to sustain the spirit that fuelled the fight over so many years, and considerable practical wisdom to negotiate the real world complexities of good and bad people of all colours and cultures both in South Africa and far beyond.

Here is a man who found his voice and used it to call out for justice in his country and around the world – a man with an iron will and the courage of his convictions.

He would learn much along his journey, and have much to teach many. Through extraordinary challenges and tribulations, his character and principles have enabled him to maintain a course that has set an example for millions everywhere.

His passion for justice and the courage to pursue it was dramatically expressed in his address to the court that sentenced him to life imprisonment:

> *I have fought against white domination and I have fought against black domination. I have cherished the ideal of a democratic and free society in which all persons live together in harmony and with equal opportunities. It is an ideal for which I hope to live for and achieve. But if needs be, it is an ideal for which I am prepared to die.*

The dignity, compassion and forgiveness he was able to demonstrate after his release showed yet more wisdom gained.

Rolihlahla Dalibhunga Mandela was born on 18 July 1918, in a small village in the Transkei province in the Eastern Cape of South Africa.

The Madiba, his tribal clan, was part of the Thembu people. His great-grandfather was a Thembu king and Mandela's father was a respected counsellor to the Thembu royal family. His father had four wives and

Mandela was one of thirteen children. The family lived in a traditional thatched hut and raised livestock, and as a young boy, he grew up in an African society, with little personal contact with Whites. On his first day of school, at the age of 7, Rolihlahla (which meant "troublemaker") was given the English name "Nelson" by an African teacher.

Mandela's father died in 1927, and at the age of nine Mandela became the ward of the acting regent of the Thembu people, Chief Jongintaba Dalindyebo. He was raised lovingly, but with discipline, by the chief and his wife in the Thembu royal household.

After receiving a good education at local boarding schools during 1939 to 1940, Mandela entered Fort Hare University and completed two years when he was elected to student office. But he considered the elections unfair, and refused to participate. It was an early demonstration of his stubborn determination. His reward was to find himself expelled. He then returned to his village, only to find that his guardian had arranged a marriage for him. This was not what he wanted and so he ran away to Johannesburg at the age of 21. There he found a new world that was nothing like his boyhood. There he experienced first-hand exposure to a society where there were things that Africans did and did not do, and other things that Whites did and did not do. It was one of his first experiences of seeing himself as a black man in a white dominated society.

In 1941 Mandela met Walter Sisulu, a businessman who became a mentor and lifelong friend. It was he who introduced Mandela to the law firm Witkin, Sidelsky and Eidelman, where he obtained a position as a clerk.

Mandela then studied to earn his BA degree, and subsequently enrolled in Law School. He joined the African National Congress (ANC) in 1944.

It was at this time that Mandela met and married Walter Sisulu's cousin, Evelyn Mase, a nursing student living in Johannesburg, who grew up in Mandela's home province.

The ANC had been founded in 1912 and its principal goal was to end white domination and create a multi-racial South Africa. Believing that the ANC leadership was too staid, Mandela, Oliver Tambo and Walter Sisulu formed the ANC Youth League. They planned to invigorate the organisation and generate mass support. Sisulu was impressed by Mandela whom he described as a 'bright and lively young man'.

At this time, in the latter part of World War II, many black Africans were working in the factories to support a fight for freedom that they were not able to enjoy in their own land.

But for Mandela, life in 1946 was pretty good – he had a reasonable job, his studies were progressing and his first son had been born.

But then in 1948 The National Party came to power under Dr Daniel Malan, and with him came the official policy of Apartheid. A variety of new laws were implemented to entrench racial discrimination and oppression, including the Separate Representation of Voters Act and the Prohibition of Mixed Marriages Act. For a proud and capable young man who had grown up loved and self-assured, this was a total affront to his sense of justice.

In response to the new policies, in 1949 the ANC Youth League drafted a Program of Action calling for mass strikes, boycotts, protests and passive resistance. Whereas when he joined the ANC, Mandela had been shy and lacking confidence in public and embarrassed by his poor command of English, now he became a lion for the cause. He was a good organiser and motivator and soon became a powerful speaker.

He became known across the country as the new militant face of rebellion, despite the emphasis on non-violent resistance.

In 1950 The National Party responded with a series of laws such as the Suppression of Communism Act, the Population and Registration Act, and the Group Areas Act, endeavouring to enforce apartheid policies and eliminate opposing mass movements.

Mandela's abilities and popularity saw him elected national president of the ANC Youth League in 1951, and when in June 1952, the government rejected the ANC's call for greater rights for Blacks, the ANC launched the campaign of non-violent mass resistance known as the Defiance Campaign.

Mandela was its leader and over the next five months, over 8,500 people took part in the campaign. As well as a leader, Mandela had now become a marked man.

In July 1952 he was arrested and charged for violating the Suppression of Communism Act. Although he and other ANC members were found guilty, the sentence of nine months imprisonment was suspended for two years.

Despite the demands of his ANC activities, Mandela opened his own law office in August 1952, and was joined by Oliver Tambo a few months later to form Mandela & Tambo. The practice was in an Indian-owned building across the road from the Magistrate's Court, in one of the few places Africans were able to rent offices. From day one, the office was 'besieged with clients', according to Mandela. 'To reach our offices each morning we had to move through a crowd of people in the hallways, on the stairs and in our small waiting room.'

The government had identified Mandela as a voice that had to be silenced. As well as hindering his legal practice, in September 1952, he was subjected to a Banning Order and was forbidden from attending meetings or gatherings for the next two years. This was just the beginning however, and such restrictions were to continue on and off for the next nine years. Despite having become, in Mandela's own words: 'A man of the city' who 'wore smart suits' and 'drove a colossal Oldsmobile', the pressure on him would only intensify…

At the annual ANC conference, Mandela was elected the Deputy President, and as part of his responsibilities he began to prepare plans to extend the activities of the ANC. This initiative was referred to as the M-Plan.

Mandela was a big, strong man who had trained as an amateur boxer, and the notion of fighting violence with violence was attractive to him. This led to differences with older and wiser members of the ANC – as Mandela himself wrote about some of his activities in 1953, 'I was a young man who attempted to make up for his ignorance with militancy.'

Even so, Mandela was suggesting that Sisulu, who had been invited as a guest of honour to a World Festival of Peace and Friendship in Bucharest, should, during his trip, visit China to see if they would supply the ANC with weapons for an armed struggle.

It was an intense and frenzied time – not only with regard to battling the government, but also in ongoing differences within the ANC as well as with other organisations that sought their own ways forward.

In an endeavour to gain greater influence by appearing to be more generally inclusive, the ANC created the Congress of the People in June 1955. Representing members of all races, the Congress was to develop a set of principles for a new South Africa. The Freedom Charter was also established to advance the abolition of racial discrimination and oppression for all.

But in December 1956, Mandela was arrested again, together with over 150 others and tried for high treason. The "Treason Trial" took up much of Mandela's time over the next several years.

In 1957 the pressure on his marriage became too much. Evelyn had also become more committed to her particular religious beliefs, and the couple was divorced. Their three children remained with her.

Not long after, Mandela met a spirited young social worker at a bus stop, still in her twenties. Her name was Winnie Madzikela, and in June 1958 they were married. The fiery Winnie became a committed political activist, and was a great support while Mandela was occupied with his trials. In between their various activities, two daughters, Zenani and Zindzi, were born over the next few years.

Later that same year, Hendrik Verwoerd, who had been responsible for much of the apartheid legislation, became Prime Minister and increased the pressure further.

The Promotion of Bantu Self-Government Act was passed in 1959, which had the objective of resettling Blacks into eight separate "tribal homelands". The ANC vigorously opposed this, but there were some tribal leaders who saw benefits for their own groups and adopted the Bantu policy and indeed worked with the government to try and achieve it. This sort of divisiveness among the black population was to be a significant and ever-present factor throughout Nelson Mandela's long struggle.

One of the major competitors to the ANC was the PAC, the Pan Africanist Congress, which was launched in April 1959 by a former ANC Youth League member, Robert Sobukwe. This new political group opposed the inclusion of Whites and Indians to help in the anti-apartheid struggle, and caused the ANC and Mandela frequent and ongoing grief.

And then came Sharpeville... on 21 March 1960, a group of protesters gathered in this township to challenge South Africa's pass laws that defined where Blacks could and could not go. When the police opened fire on the demonstrators, they killed 69 people – many received bullet wounds in their backs.

On 29 March 1961, a great victory was achieved when Mandela and the other defendants in the Treason Trial were found not guilty. It was a major triumph.

This was explosive, and the government responded with a State of Emergency that lasted until the end of August that year. Mandela was arrested and Oliver Tambo then left the country to work for the ANC from exile.

When a three day National strike was called later in 1961, the ANC responded to the government's banning by endorsing "armed struggle". Mandela went underground, and launched a militant campaign by forming Umkhonto we Sizwe (The Spear of the Nation), or MK. MK's policy was to sabotage and destroy government offices and symbols of apartheid, but not to target people. The government would now see it as a terrorist organisation.

Mandela then escaped the country and travelled widely in Africa and Europe for several months, studying guerrilla warfare, undergoing military training, organising munitions, personnel and funding, and building support for the ANC. He even got to London. While he 'abhorred the notion of British imperialism,' he 'never rejected the trappings of British style and manners!'.

While in Khartoum he had a pistol under his jacket, 200 rounds of ammunition wrapped around his waist under his trousers, and several thousand pounds in cash!

Upon his return to South Africa in mid 1962, Mandela was arrested, convicted and sentenced to five years. He was held on Robben Island, off the coast of Capetown.

Although already serving a sentence, in 1963 Mandela was brought to trial again along with other ANC leaders, and charged with sabotage and attempting to violently overthrow the government.

This was the landmark Rivonia Trial. The sentence was handed down in June 1964. The defendants were found guilty, and were fortunate to escape execution, the judge sentencing them to life imprisonment. So in the winter of 1964, Mandela and his comrades were transported to Robben

Island. Mandela was 46 years old.

For over a decade they endured heavy physical labour in a limestone quarry. There were no newspapers, no clocks, and the lights in the prison burned 24 hours a day.

In the first year he was allowed one visit from Winnie; the next one would be two years later. It would be some 20 years before he could touch his wife's hand.

In 1966 Verwoerd was assassinated by a deranged white farmer and John Vorster succeeded him as Prime Minister. Meanwhile, Mandela continued his activities as best he could from the prison, while Oliver Tambo worked from exile in London.

Within a one-year period during 1968-69, Mandela's mother died and his oldest son was killed in a car crash; however Mandela was not allowed to attend the funerals.

In 1976 Soweto students protested mandatory instruction in Afrikaans, the language of the white rulers, and the protests spread throughout Soweto. In crushing the protest, the government killed 575 people over an eight month period, a quarter of them under the age of 18.

The pressure was being applied to Winnie and in 1977 she was banished to Brandfort, a remote township where it would be difficult for her to continue her political activities. Her daughter Zindzi went with her. Over the following years, Winnie would spend over a year in jail (including solitary confinement) and face constant police harassment and humiliation. In response, she became more aggressive and militant in opposing white rule.

Vorster resigned in 1978 which saw the ascension of P W Botha to the Prime Ministership.

From their bases in exile, in 1980 Oliver Tambo and the ANC launched the "Release Mandela" campaign internationally. In the following years, numerous countries and international groups would sign petitions, pass resolutions and hold rallies for Mandela's release.

At last in March 1982 after 18 years on Robben Island, Mandela was transferred to Pollsmoor Prison on the mainland. Here the conditions were more conducive to reading and corresponding as he had a much higher degree of privacy and level of comfort.

From 1983 to 1984, angered by rent increases and Botha's plan for giving Indian and mixed-race voters token places in Parliament while still excluding Blacks, black residents of townships south of Johannesburg began an insurrection that spread across the country. The police response was brutal. In one township, Langa, 20 people were fatally shot at a funeral procession.

The resistance escalated and township operatives organised strikes and boycotts to make black townships "ungovernable". MK guerrillas began killing farmers, policemen and accused collaborators. The whole situation was escalating at a frightening rate.

In January 1985, United States Senator Edward Kennedy visited South Africa to show his anti-apartheid support. He was hosted by Bishop Desmond Tutu, the recipient of the 1984 Nobel Peace Prize. Kennedy would also visit Winnie Mandela.

Led by Bishop Tutu, the church leaders of South Africa took up the anti-apartheid cause, and sympathetic anti-apartheid rallies and protests took place in New York City, Atlanta and Washington.

World famous musicians, including Bruce Springsteen and Miles Davis, released the anti-apartheid disk Sun City and the song Free Nelson Mandela reached the Top Ten on rock-music charts in England.

Something had to be done. Botha offered to free Mandela if he would renounce violence. Mandela's daughter Zindzi read his response rejecting the deal to a packed stadium near Johannesburg.

The government was losing the battle internationally.

In November, Minister of Justice Kobie Coetsee made an unexpected visit to Mandela who had been hospitalised for prostate surgery. Although a social visit, it had political consequences and marked a turning point. On Mandela's return to prison, he was put in a separate cell from his comrades so the government could have private access to him and a process of gradual negotiation could be set in train. It was a process which continued for several years. While the government could not afford to make Mandela a martyr, it could not simply let him free immediately either… a prolonged period of negotiation and positioning that would determine the new South Africa was now under way.

While Mandela was trying to play the part of the statesman in his more frequent, delicate but robust negotiations with the government, Winnie's activities were becoming increasingly militant and controversial. These culminated in a speech at a funeral in April 1986, during which she endorsed "necklace murders" – death by burning tyres around the necks of those who collaborated with the government. Her speech was widely reported in the foreign press as a call to violence; and was denounced by the ANC.

But the situation was still unstable, and in June 1986 the government declared a State of Emergency in response to widespread unrest in the black townships.

In July 1986 secret talks, approved by Botha and led by Coetsee began between Mandela and the government. This was the time where Mandela decided that he had to make decisions on behalf of the ANC without first consulting the other leaders.

A few months after the Reagan administration reassessed its policy on South Africa, the US Senate Foreign Relations Committee voted overwhelmingly in August 1986 for strict economic sanctions against South Africa. Over the next few years, major US companies started curtailing their operations in South Africa and US banks stopped loaning money.

The momentum was building mightily, both across South Africa and the world with a well-coordinated international campaign for Mandela's release.

By 1987 talks with the government were proceeding in earnest, and Mandela told his ANC comrades such as Govan Mbeki and Ahmed Kathrada about the negotiations. This was an extremely perilous stage, as it was difficult to predict the reactions of his fellow ANC members. Their reactions varied considerably, ranging from outrage to strong support. Rumours soon started within the ANC that Mandela had "sold out" and the other players such as the PAC and the Zulu Inkatha organisation increasingly began to pursue their own game plans.

On the 24th anniversary of Mandela's imprisonment in June 1988, a rock concert called Freedomfest – Nelson Mandela's 70th Birthday Celebration was held outside London and televised in 60 countries.

In December 1988 after being treated for tuberculosis, Mandela was transferred to Victor Verster Prison. Here he was housed in an isolated cottage with a pool, a chef and gardens. He liked this house so much that when he was eventually released from prison, the design of his own new house was inspired by this one. His meetings with the government continued.

That same month, four young males, including 13-year-old Stompie Seipei, were abducted by members of the Mandela United Football Club (in fact a group of young men acting as Winnie Mandela's bodyguards) and beaten inside Winnie's home. The other youths escaped, but Stompie disappeared. His battered body was found weeks later and Winnie was eventually implicated in the whole affair. She was rapidly becoming somewhat of a political liability for Mandela.

After numerous delays, on 5 July 1989, Mandela and Botha met for tea at the President's residence. The meeting was cordial and positive, with Mandela pressing for the release of Walter Sisulu from prison.

When Botha resigned and F W de Klerk was elected President in September 1989, things began to move quickly, as de Klerk released most of the Rivonia Trial prisoners, including Sisulu, and began to dismantle the apartheid structure. He abandoned the long-term master plan of congregating Blacks into separate homelands, and accepted the principle of "power sharing" with them. De Klerk recognised that apartheid was not working, for despite millions of arrests for violations of the pass laws, Blacks continued to migrate into banned areas.

On 13 December 1989, Mandela and de Klerk had the first of three important meetings to try and find a way forward that would avoid the country descending into chaos and greater bloodshed.

On 2 February 1990, de Klerk announced to Parliament the lifting of the bans against the ANC and other political organisations.

And then on 11 February 1990, after nearly 27 years of imprisonment, Mandela was released. His new life was very busy immediately, visiting old friends and supporters, becoming Deputy President of the ANC, and travelling with Winnie to the US, Europe and North Africa. In Sweden, he visited his old friend Oliver Tambo.

In May 1990, the ANC and the National Party began negotiations on forming a new multi-racial democracy for South Africa. These talks were off and on for months, with delays due to the ANC's anger over the violence in the black townships. However, Mandela and de Klerk continued to hold their private meetings.

The situation was anything but straightforward as there were many competing interests and agendas. On 14 July 1990, Inkatha Freedom Party, a Zulu group led by Chief Buthelezi, was launched as a political party. They had long been at odds with the ANC, particularly over the issue of armed struggle. Although Mandela reached out to Buthelezi to resolve their differences, the Inkatha targeted ANC strongholds in the Natal province and widespread violence escalated, with some support from the white police force.

On 6 August 1990, the ANC and the government signed the Pretoria Minute, in which both parties agreed to end the armed struggle.

Mandela pressed de Klerk to investigate police brutality and government support of the violence in the Natal province. Their relation-ship was strained over the issue of violence, but both men could see the bigger picture of a new South Africa, and both were strong and capable negotiators. They would have to move forward.

In February 1991 Winnie's trial for the kidnapping and assault of four youths by the Mandela United Football Club started. Throughout the years of the controversy, Mandela stood by his wife; and he attended the trial. She was found guilty of kidnapping, but not assault, and sentenced to six years in prison. On appeal, she was given a suspended sentence and fined.

Then in July 1991, the ANC held its annual conference in South Africa for the first time. Mandela was elected ANC President.

Things were progressing on many fronts… on 20 December 1991 the first formal negotiations with the government took place at the Convention for a Democratic South Africa (CODESA 1). It was here that Mandela lashed out at de Klerk in his speech, after de Klerk berated the ANC in an earlier speech. They did not meet again for five months.

On 13 April 1992, Mandela announced his separation from Winnie. She resigned as head of Social Welfare for the ANC, but not from the National Executive Committee.

It was a complex and perilous political situation, with violence continuing in many townships, and with frequent clashes between police and residents. Mandela was outraged and accused the police of supporting the violence rather than stopping it. Mandela held de Klerk responsible, while de Klerk remained adamant that he did not have the power to control the violence.

In May 1992, another round of talks was held at CODESA 2 to construct a plan for a future democracy. The talks ended in a stalemate, but both sides agreed to continue to work towards a solution – a way through had to be found.

Then from June-September 1992, frustrated over the unsuccessful negotiations, the ANC decided on a policy of "rolling mass action" consisting of strikes, protests and boycotts, to show the government the extent of the support the ANC had across the country. Meanwhile, the violence continued with an Inkatha raid on ANC members that left 46 dead in Boipatong township.

The rolling mass action culminated in a general strike protesting against the violence and in September 1992 the increasing death toll forced Mandela and de Klerk to restart negotiations. They signed the Record of Understanding, which promised to establish formal investigations into the violence and police actions. It also established an elected constitutional assembly that would develop a new constitution for the country.

On 10 April 1993, when Chris Hani, a popular young ANC leader, was killed by a white extremist, Mandela appeared on television calling for restraint and successfully headed off a violent response.

In December 1993, Mandela and de Klerk were jointly awarded the Nobel Peace Prize, and in between 26-29 April 1994, for the first time in South Africa's history, all races were able to vote in democratic elections. Mandela was elected President, with the ANC winning 252 of the 400 seats in the National Assembly.

On 10 May 1994, Nelson Mandela was inaugurated as President of South Africa, with his daughter Zenani beside him. F W de Klerk was sworn in as Deputy President.

During March 1996, Mandela divorced Winnie, although she tried to prevent it to the end, and in 1997 he stepped down as President of the ANC.

On 18 July 1998, on his 80th birthday, Mandela married Graca Machel, the widow of a former President of Mozambique.

He retired from active politics at the 1999 general election.

wisdom

What do you live for? (What would you die for?)

As I complete my presentation to a group on *Collective Wisdom* and ask for questions. I get the usual and then someone chimes in with this showstopper, 'What do you live for?'

The first time the question was asked I was tremendously taken aback. This was what I would come to later know as an 'ultimate question', a question about the true nature of the purpose of human life itself.

In compiling *Collective Wisdom* I had met lots of great people and asked them for a motto, quote or thought that summarised their approach to life. And it was in these terms that I came to think of this question. 'To thine own self be true', 'Always remain capable of laughing at oneself', 'Be good citizens and help those less fortunate than yourself', 'Faith conquers the world', 'Be healthy and be happy'.

I had been asking the questions and had yet to conclude an answer to those same questions myself. One of my heroes however is Nelson Mandela and he was to show me, and give me the confidence to acknowledge my answer to the question.

We are asked this question whether in such radical circumstances as those confronted by Nelson Mandela in South Africa, or just when our life changes in an unexpected or profound way. Your father or, as has now just happened to me, my brother dies, somebody you know has a child die, a Tsunami wipes out hundreds of thousands of people, or you lose your job – the world becomes different from what it was before.

Mandela relates, 'We went to jail because it was impossible to sit still while the obscenity of the apartheid system was being imposed on our people. It would have been immoral to keep quiet while the racist tyranny sought to reduce an entire people into a status worse than the beasts of the forest'.

But many people did keep quiet.

When asked the question repeatedly, either privately or in the course of my presentations on *Collective Wisdom*, it was this question more than any other that had me stumped.

It seems easier in the case of Mandela. Let's face it there was an obvious injustice and cause to take up. But very few people, in percentage terms, did take up the cause.

Mandela said, 'It will forever remain an accusation and a challenge to all men and women of conscience that it took as long as it has before all of us stood up to say enough is enough. The United Nations was established primarily because of the determination of all humanity not to allow racism to again dragoon the world into the clutches of war. And yet, for all that, a racist tyranny established itself in our country.'

This question generally feels like an accusation when asked of anybody, 'What do you live for?' What matters to you so much that you would give your life for it or them?

Mandela again, 'Our message was that no sacrifice was too great in the struggle for freedom.'

And again, 'I was prepared to die secure in the knowledge that my death would be an inspiration to the cause for which I was giving my life.'

And again, 'I thought of the line from Shakespeare: "Be absolute for death; for either death or life shall be the sweeter." '

It is clear from observing the life of Mandela that this was someone who was committed to a cause – a right and just cause. One who made plenty of mistakes along the way – hurt two wives, terrorist acts, as examples – yet he continued to ask the hard question and answer it in his commitment to seeing not just his people, but all the people of South Africa set free. For he believed that the untruth of apartheid was, 'a poison that bred moral decay in all areas' and was, as a result, unjust to Whites as well as to Blacks.

Mandela spent more than 20 years in prison improving himself, committed to a cause. All his resources and energies were directed to that end. He became a hero to our times – his time, money, gifts, energies and talents were directed to a noble cause. He is a towering figure – precisely because of his courage to commit when others turned a blind eye; and having secured victory, he demonstrated the value of forgiveness – he answered the question in his life!

Yet despite his hero status and excellent example, the very, very personal question remains – what do you live for? The most straightforward way, it seemed to me, in order to answer this question was to consider, 'What do I spend my time and money on or in aid of?'.

'So I charted out my days and listed my expenditures. I actually took my bank statements for the previous year – a few months would do – had them entered into an accounting software package and produced a list of expenditures. It was clear what I had been spending my time and money on – more than $5,000 per year on books, three hours plus reading per week day and more on weekends.'

Mandela has shown me the answer to the question of what I should live for, '**Seek wisdom. Get understanding.**'

words

I am Prepared to Die

Statement from the dock at the opening of the defence case in the Rivonia Trial in the Pretoria Supreme Court – 20 April 1964

I am the First Accused.

I hold a Bachelor's Degree in Arts and practised as an attorney in Johannesburg for a number of years in partnership with Oliver Tambo. I am a convicted prisoner serving five years for leaving the country without a permit and for inciting people to go on strike at the end of May 1961.

At the outset, I want to say that the suggestion made by the State in its opening that the struggle in South Africa is under the influence of foreigners or communists is wholly incorrect. I have done whatever I did, both as an individual and as a leader of my people, because of my experience in South Africa and my own proudly felt African background, and not because of what any outsider might have said.

In my youth in the Transkei I listened to the elders of my tribe telling stories of the old days. Amongst the tales they related to me were those of wars fought by our ancestors in defence of the fatherland. The names of Dingane and Bambata, Hintsa and Makana, Squngthi and Dalasile, Moshoeshoe and Sekhukhuni, were praised as the glory of the entire African nation. I hoped then that life might offer me the opportunity to serve my people and make my own humble contribution to their freedom struggle. This is what has motivated me in all that I have done in relation to the charges made against me in this case.

Having said this, I must deal immediately and at some length with the question of violence. Some of the things so far told to the Court are true and some are untrue. I do not, however, deny that I planned sabotage. I did not plan it in a spirit of recklessness, nor because I have any love of violence. I planned it as a result of a calm and sober assessment of the political situation that had arisen after many years of tyranny, exploitation, and oppression of my people by the Whites.

I admit immediately that I was one of the persons who helped to form Umkhonto we Sizwe, and that I played a prominent role in its affairs until I was arrested in August 1962.

In the statement which I am about to make I shall correct certain false impressions which have been created by State witnesses. Amongst other things, I will demonstrate that certain of the acts referred to in the evidence were not and could not have been committed by Umkhonto. I will also deal with the relationship between the African National Congress and Umkhonto, and with the part which I personally have played in the affairs of both organizations. I shall deal also with the part played by the Communist Party. In order to explain these matters properly, I will have to explain what Umkhonto set out to achieve; what methods it prescribed for the achievement of these objects, and why these methods were chosen. I will also have to explain how I became involved in the activities of these organizations.

I deny that Umkhonto was responsible for a number of acts which clearly fell outside the policy of the organisation, and which have been charged in the indictment against us. I do not know what justification there was for these acts, but to demonstrate that they could not have been authorized by Umkhonto, I want to refer briefly to the roots and policy of the organization.

I have already mentioned that I was one of the persons who helped to form Umkhonto. I, and the others who started the organization, did so for two reasons. Firstly, we believed that as a result of Government policy, violence by the African people had become inevitable, and that unless responsible leadership was given to canalize and control the feelings of our people, there would be outbreaks of terrorism which would produce an intensity of bitterness and hostility between the various races of this country which is not produced even by war. Secondly, we felt that without violence there would be no way open to the African people to succeed in their struggle against the principle of white supremacy. All lawful modes of expressing opposition to this principle had been closed by legislation, and we were placed in a position in which we had either to accept a permanent state of inferiority, or to defy the Government. We chose to defy the law. We first broke the law in a way which avoided any recourse to violence; when this form was legislated against, and then the Government resorted to a show of force to crush opposition to its policies, only then did we decide to answer violence with violence.

But the violence which we chose to adopt was not terrorism. We who formed Umkhonto were all members of the African National Congress, and had behind us the ANC tradition of non-violence and negotiation as a means of solving political disputes. We believe that South Africa belongs to all the people who live in it, and not to one group, be it black or white. We did not want an interracial war, and tried to avoid it to the last minute. If the Court is in doubt about this, it will be seen that the whole history of our organization bears out what I have said, and what I will subsequently say, when I describe the tactics which Umkhonto decided to adopt. I want, therefore, to say something about the African National Congress.

The African National Congress was formed in 1912 to defend the rights of the African people which had been seriously curtailed by the South Africa Act, and which were then being threatened by the Native Land Act. For thirty-seven years – that is until 1949 – it adhered strictly to a constitutional struggle. It put forward demands and resolutions; it sent delegations to the Government in the belief that African grievances could be settled through peaceful discussion and that Africans could advance gradually to full political rights. But White Governments remained un-moved, and the rights of Africans became less instead of becoming greater. In the words of my leader, Chief Lutuli, who became President of the ANC in 1952, and who was later awarded the Nobel Peace Prize:

'Who will deny that thirty years of my life have been spent knocking in vain, patiently, moderately, and modestly at a closed and barred door? What have been the fruits of moderation? The past 30 years have seen the greatest number of laws restricting our rights and progress, until today we have reached a stage where we have almost no rights at all.'

Even after 1949, the ANC remained determined to avoid violence. At this time, however, there was a change from the strictly constitutional means of protest which had been employed in the past. The change was embodied in a decision which was taken to protest against apartheid legislation by peaceful, but unlawful, demonstrations against certain laws. Pursuant to this policy the ANC launched the Defiance Campaign, in which I was placed in charge of volunteers. This campaign was based on the principles of passive resistance. More than 8,500 people defied apart-heid laws and went to jail. Yet there was not a single instance of violence in the course of this campaign on the part of any defier. I and nineteen colleagues were convicted for the role which we played in organizing the campaign, but our sentences were suspended mainly because the Judge found that discipline and non-violence had been stressed throughout. This was the time when the volunteer section of the ANC was established, and when the word "Amadelakufa" was first used: this was the time when the volunteers were asked to take a pledge to uphold certain principles. Evidence dealing with volunteers and their pledges has been introduced into this case, but completely out of context. The volunteers were not, and are not, the soldiers of a black army pledged to fight a civil war against the whites. They were, and are dedicated workers who are prepared to lead campaigns initiated by the ANC to distribute leaflets, to organize strikes, or do whatever the particular campaign required. They are called volunteers because they volunteer to face the penalties of imprisonment and whipping which are now prescribed by the legislature for such acts.

During the Defiance Campaign, the Public Safety Act and the Criminal Law Amendment Act were passed. These Statutes provided harsher penalties for offences committed by way of protests against laws. Despite this, the protests continued and the ANC adhered to its policy of non-violence. In 1956, 156 leading members of the Congress Alliance, including myself, were arrested on a charge of high treason and charges under the Suppression of Communism Act. The non-violent policy of the ANC was put in issue by the State, but when the Court gave judgement some five years later, it found that the ANC did not have a policy of violence. We were acquitted on all counts, which included a count that the ANC sought to set up a communist state in place of the existing regime. The Government has always sought to label all its opponents as communists. This allegation has been repeated in the present case, but as I will show, the ANC is not, and never has been, a communist organization.

In 1960 there was the shooting at Sharpeville, which resulted in the proclamation of a state of emergency and the declaration of the ANC as an unlawful organization. My colleagues and I, after careful consideration, decided that we would not obey this decree. The African people were not part of the Government and did not make the laws by which they were governed. We believed in the words of the Universal Declaration of Human Rights, that 'the will of the people shall be the basis of authority of the Government', and for us to accept the banning was equivalent to accepting the silencing of the Africans for all time. The ANC refused to dissolve, but instead went underground. We believed it was our duty to preserve this organization which had been built up with almost fifty years of unremitting toil. I have no doubt that no self-respecting White political organization would disband itself if declared illegal by a government in which it had no say.

In 1960 the Government held a referendum which led to the establishment of the Republic. Africans, who constituted approximately 70 per cent of the population of South Africa, were not entitled to vote, and were not even consulted about the proposed constitutional change. All of us were apprehensive of our future under the proposed White Republic, and a resolution was taken to hold an All-In African Conference to call for a National Convention, and to organize mass demonstrations on the eve of the unwanted Republic, if the Government failed to call the Convention. The conference was attended by Africans of various political persuasions. I was the Secretary of the conference and undertook to be responsible for organizing the national stay-at-home which was subsequently called to coincide with the declaration of the Republic. As all strikes by Africans are illegal, the person organizing such a strike must avoid arrest. I was chosen to be this person, and consequently I had to leave my home and family and my practice and go into hiding to avoid arrest.

The stay-at-home, in accordance with ANC policy, was to be a peaceful demonstration. Careful instructions were given to organizers and members to avoid any recourse to violence. The Government's answer was to introduce new and harsher laws, to mobilize its armed forces, and to send Saracens, armed vehicles, and soldiers into the townships in a massive show of force designed to intimidate the people. This was an indication that the Government had decided to rule by force alone, and this decision was a milestone on the road to Umkhonto.

Some of this may appear irrelevant to this trial. In fact, I believe none of it is irrelevant because it will, I hope, enable the Court to appreciate the attitude eventually adopted by the various persons and bodies concerned in the National Liberation Movement. When I went to jail in 1962, the dominant idea was that loss of life should be avoided. I now know that this was still so in 1963.

I must return to June 1961. What were we, the leaders of our people, to do? Were we to give in to the show of force and the implied threat against future action, or were we to fight it and, if so, how?

We had no doubt that we had to continue the fight. Anything else would have been abject surrender. Our problem was not whether to fight, but was how to continue the fight. We of the ANC had always stood for a non-racial democracy, and we shrank from any action which might drive the races further apart than they already were. But the hard facts were that fifty years of non-violence had brought the African people nothing but more and more repressive legislation, and fewer and fewer rights. It may not be easy for this Court to understand, but it is a fact that for a long time the people had been talking of violence – of the day when they would fight the White man and win back their country – and we, the leaders of the ANC, had nevertheless always prevailed upon them to avoid violence and to pursue peaceful methods. When some of us discussed this in May and June of 1961, it could not be denied that our policy to achieve a nonracial State by non-violence had achieved nothing, and that our followers were beginning to lose confidence in this policy and were developing disturbing ideas of terrorism.

It must not be forgotten that by this time violence had, in fact, become a feature of the South African political scene. There had been violence in 1957 when the women of Zeerust were ordered to carry passes; there was violence in 1958 with the enforcement of cattle culling in Sekhukhuniland; there was violence in 1959 when the people of Cato Manor protested against pass raids; there was violence in 1960 when the Government attempted to impose Bantu Authorities in Pondoland. Thirty-nine Africans died in these disturbances. In 1961 there had been riots in Warmbaths, and all this time the Transkei had been a seething mass of unrest. Each disturbance pointed clearly to the inevitable growth among Africans of the belief that violence was the only way out – it showed that a Government which uses force to maintain its rule teaches the oppressed to use force to oppose it. Already small groups had arisen in the urban areas and were spontaneously making plans for violent forms of political struggle. There now arose a danger that these groups would adopt terrorism against Africans, as well as Whites, if not properly directed. Particularly disturbing was the type of violence engendered in places such as Zeerust, Sekhukhuniland, and Pondoland amongst Africans. It was increasingly taking the form, not of struggle against the Government – though this is what prompted it – but of civil strife amongst themselves, conducted in such a way that it could not hope to achieve anything other than a loss of life and bitterness.

At the beginning of June 1961, after a long and anxious assessment of the South African situation, I, and some colleagues, came to the conclusion that as violence in this country was inevitable, it would be unrealistic and wrong for African leaders to continue preaching peace and non-violence at a time when the Government met our peaceful demands with force.

This conclusion was not easily arrived at. It was only when all else had failed, when all channels of peaceful protest had been barred to us, that the decision was made to embark on violent forms of political struggle, and to form Umkhonto we Sizwe. We did so not because we desired such a course, but solely because the Government had left us with no other choice. In the Manifesto of Umkhonto published on 16 December 1961, which is Exhibit AD, we said:

'The time comes in the life of any nation when there remain only two choices - submit or fight. That time has now come to South Africa. We shall not submit and we have no choice but to hit back by all means in our power in defence of our people, our future, and our freedom.'

This was our feeling in June of 1961 when we decided to press for a change in the policy of the National Liberation Movement. I can only say that I felt morally obliged to do what I did.

We who had taken this decision started to consult leaders of various organizations, including the ANC. I will not say whom we spoke to, or what they said, but I wish to deal with the role of the African National Congress in this phase of the struggle, and with the policy and objectives of Umkhonto we Sizwe.

As far as the ANC was concerned, it formed a clear view which can be summarized as follows:

It was a mass political organization with a political function to fulfil. Its members had joined on the express policy of non-violence.

Because of all this, it could not and would not undertake violence. This must be stressed. One cannot turn such a body into the small, closely knit organization required for sabotage. Nor would this be politically correct, because it would result in members ceasing to carry out this essential activity: political propaganda and organization. Nor was it permissible to change the whole nature of the organization.

On the other hand, in view of this situation I have described, the ANC was prepared to depart from its 50-year-old policy of non-violence to this extent that it would no longer disapprove of properly controlled violence. Hence members who undertook such activity would not be subject to disciplinary action by the ANC.

I say "properly controlled violence" because I made it clear that if I formed the organization I would at all times subject it to the political guidance of the ANC and would not undertake any different form of activity from that contemplated without the consent of the ANC. And I shall now tell the Court how that form of violence came to be determined.

As a result of this decision, Umkhonto was formed in November 1961. When we took this decision, and subsequently formulated our plans, the ANC heritage of non-violence and racial harmony was very much with us. We felt that the country was drifting towards a civil war in which Blacks and Whites would fight each other. We viewed the situation with alarm. Civil war could mean the destruction of what the ANC stood for; with civil war, racial peace would be more difficult than ever to achieve. We already have examples in South African history of the results of war. It has taken more than fifty years for the scars of the South African War to disappear. How much longer would it take to eradicate the scars of inter-racial civil war, which could not be fought without a great loss of life on both sides?

The avoidance of civil war had dominated our thinking for many years, but when we decided to adopt violence as part of our policy, we realized that we might one day have to face the prospect of such a war. This had to be taken into account in formulating our plans. We required a plan which was flexible and which permitted us to act in accordance with the needs of the times; above all, the plan had to be one which recognized civil war as the last resort, and left the decision on this question to the future. We did not want to be committed to civil war, but we wanted to be ready if it became inevitable.

Four forms of violence were possible. There is sabotage, there is guerrilla warfare, there is terrorism, and there is open revolution. We chose to adopt the first method and to exhaust it before taking any other decision.

In the light of our political background the choice was a logical one. Sabotage did not involve loss of life, and it offered the best hope for future race relations. Bitterness would be kept to a minimum and, if the policy bore fruit, democratic government could become a reality. This is what we felt at the time, and this is what we said in our Manifesto (Exhibit AD):

> *'We of Umkhonto we Sizwe have always sought to achieve liberation without bloodshed and civil clash. We hope, even at this late hour, that our first actions will awaken everyone to a realization of the disastrous situ-ation to which the Nationalist policy is leading. We hope that we will bring the Government and its supporters to their senses before it is too late, so that both the Government and its policies can be changed before matters reach the desperate state of civil war.'*

The initial plan was based on a careful analysis of the political and economic situation of our country. We believed that South Africa depended to a large extent on foreign capital and foreign trade. We felt that planned destruction of power plants, and interference with rail and telephone communications, would tend to scare away capital from the country, make it more difficult for goods from the industrial areas to reach the seaports on schedule, and would in the long run be a heavy drain on the economic life of the country, thus compelling the voters of the country to reconsider their position.

Attacks on the economic life lines of the country were to be linked with sabotage on Government buildings and other symbols of apartheid. These attacks would serve as a source of inspiration to our people. In addition, they would provide an outlet for those people who were urging the adoption of violent methods and would enable us to give concrete proof to our followers that we had adopted a stronger line and were fighting back against Government violence.

In addition, if mass action were successfully organized, and mass reprisals taken, we felt that sympathy for our cause would be roused in other countries, and that greater pressure would be brought to bear on the South African Government.

This then was the plan. Umkhonto was to perform sabotage, and strict instructions were given to its members right from the start, that on no account were they to injure or kill people in planning or carrying out operations. These instructions have been referred to in the evidence of "Mr X" and "Mr Z".

The affairs of the Umkhonto were controlled and directed by a National High Command, which had powers of co-option and which could, and did, appoint Regional Commands. The High Command was the body which determined tactics and targets and was in charge of training and finance. Under the High Command there were Regional Commands which were responsible for the direction of the local sabotage groups. Within the framework of the policy laid down by the National High Command, the Regional Commands had authority to select the targets to be attacked. They had no authority to go beyond the prescribed frame-work and thus had no authority to embark upon acts which endangered life, or which did not fit into the overall plan of sabotage. For instance, Umkhonto members were forbidden ever to go armed into operation. Incidentally, the terms High Command and Regional Command were an importation from the Jewish national underground organization Irgun Zvai Leumi, which operated in Israel between 1944 and 1948.

Umkhonto had its first operation on 16 December 1961, when Government buildings in Johannesburg, Port Elizabeth and Durban were attacked. The selection of targets is proof of the policy to which I have referred. Had we intended to attack life we would have selected targets where people congregated and not empty buildings and power stations. The sabotage which was committed before 16 December 1961 was the work of isolated groups and had no connection whatever with Umkhonto. In fact, some of these and a number of later acts were claimed by other organizations.

The Manifesto of Umkhonto was issued on the day that operations commenced. The response to our actions and Manifesto among the white population was characteristically violent. The Government threatened to take strong action, and called upon its supporters to stand firm and to ignore the demands of the Africans. The Whites failed to respond by suggesting change; they responded to our call by suggesting the laager.

In contrast, the response of the Africans was one of encouragement. Suddenly there was hope again. Things were happening. People in the townships became eager for political news. A great deal of enthusiasm was generated by the initial successes, and people began to speculate on how soon freedom would be obtained.

But we in Umkhonto weighed up the white response with anxiety. The lines were being drawn. The whites and blacks were moving into separate camps, and the prospects of avoiding a civil war were made less. The white newspapers carried reports that sabotage would be punished by death. If this was so, how could we continue to keep Africans away from terrorism?

Already scores of Africans had died as a result of racial friction. In 1920 when the famous leader, Masabala, was held in Port Elizabeth jail, twenty-four of a group of Africans who had gathered to demand his release were killed by the police and white civilians. In 1921, more than one hundred Africans died in the Bulhoek affair. In 1924 over 200 Africans were killed when the Administrator of South-West Africa led a force against a group which had rebelled against the imposition of dog tax. On 1 May 1950, eighteen Africans died as a result of police shootings during the strike. On 21 March 1960, 69 unarmed Africans died at Sharpeville.

How many more Sharpevilles would there be in the history of our country? And how many more Sharpevilles could the country stand without violence and terror becoming the order of the day? And what would happen to our people when that stage was reached? In the long run we felt certain we must succeed, but at what cost to ourselves and the rest of the country? And if this happened, how could black and white ever live together again in peace and harmony? These were the problems that faced us, and these were our decisions.

Experience convinced us that rebellion would offer the Government limitless opportunities for the indiscriminate slaughter of our people. But it was precisely because the soil of South Africa is already drenched with the blood of innocent Africans that we felt it our duty to make prepa-rations as a long-term undertaking to use force in order to defend our-selves against force. If war were inevitable, we wanted the fight to be conducted on terms most favourable to our people. The fight which held out prospects best for us and the least risk of life to both sides was guerrilla warfare. We decided, therefore, in our preparations for the future, to make provision for the possibility of guerrilla warfare.

All whites undergo compulsory military training, but no such training was given to Africans. It was in our view essential to build up a nucleus of trained men who would be able to provide the leadership which would be required if guerrilla warfare started. We had to prepare for such a situation before it became too late to make proper preparations. It was also necessary to build up a nucleus of men trained in civil administration and other professions, so that Africans would be equipped to participate in the government of this country as soon as they were allowed to do so.

At this stage it was decided that I should attend the Conference of the Pan-African Freedom Movement for Central, East, and Southern Africa, which was to be held early in 1962 in Addis Ababa, and, because of our need for preparation, it was also decided that, after the conference, I would undertake a tour of the African States with a view to obtaining facilities for the training of soldiers, and that I would also solicit scholarships for the higher education of matriculated Africans. Training in both fields would be necessary, even if changes came about by peaceful means. Administrators would be necessary who would be willing and able to administer a non-racial State and so would men be necessary to control the army and police force of such a State.

It was on this note that I left South Africa to proceed to Addis Ababa as a delegate of the ANC. My tour was a success. Wherever I went I met sympathy for our cause and promises of help. All Africa was united against the stand of White South Africa, and even in London I was received with great sympathy by political leaders, such as Mr Gaitskell and Mr Grimond. In Africa I was promised support by such men as Julius Nyerere, now President of Tanganyika; Mr Kawawa, then Prime Minister of Tanganyika; Emperor Haile Selassie of Ethiopia; General Abboud, President of the Sudan; Habib Bourguiba, President of Tunisia; Ben Bella, now President of Algeria; Modibo Keita, President of Mali; Leopold Senghor, President of Senegal; Sekou Toure, President of Guinea; President Tubman of Liberia; and Milton Obote, Prime Minister of Uganda. It was Ben Bella who invited me to visit Oujda, the Headquarters of the Algerian Army of National Liberation, the visit which is described in my diary, one of the Exhibits.

I started to make a study of the art of war and revolution and, whilst abroad, underwent a course in military training. If there was to be guerrilla warfare, I wanted to be able to stand and fight with my people and to share the hazards of war with them. Notes of lectures which I received in Algeria are contained in Exhibit 16, produced in evidence. Summaries of books on guerrilla warfare and military strategy have also been produced. I have already admitted that these documents are in my writing, and I acknowledge that I made these studies to equip myself for the role which I might have to play if the struggle drifted into guerrilla warfare. I approached this question as every African Nationalist should do. I was completely objective. The Court will see that I attempted to examine all types of authority on the subject – from the East and from the West, going back to the classic work of Clausewitz, and covering such a variety as Mao Tse Tung and Che Guevara on the one hand, and the writings on the Anglo-Boer War on the other. Of course, these notes are merely summaries of the books I read and do not contain my personal views.

I also made arrangements for our recruits to undergo military training. But here it was impossible to organize any scheme without the co-operation of the ANC offices in Africa. I consequently obtained the permission of the ANC in South Africa to do this. To this extent then there was a departure from the original decision of the ANC, but it applied outside South Africa only. The first batch of recruits actually arrived in Tanganyika when I was passing through that country on my way back to South Africa.

I returned to South Africa and reported to my colleagues on the results of my trip. On my return I found that there had been little alteration in the political scene save that the threat of a death penalty for sabotage had now become a fact. The attitude of my colleagues in Umkhonto was much the same as it had been before I left. They were feeling their way cautiously and felt that it would be a long time before the possibilities of sabotage were exhausted. In fact, the view was expressed by some that the training of recruits was premature. This is recorded by me in the document which is Exhibit R.14. After a full discussion, however, it was decided to go ahead with the plans for military training because of the fact that it would take many years to build up a sufficient nucleus of trained soldiers to start a guerrilla campaign, and whatever happened the training would be of value.

I wish to turn now to certain general allegations made in this case by the State. But before doing so, I wish to revert to certain occurrences said by witnesses to have happened in Port Elizabeth and East London. I am referring to the bombing of private houses of pro-Government persons during September, October and November 1962. I do not know what justification there was for these acts, nor what provocation had been given. But if what I have said already is accepted, then it is clear that these acts had nothing to do with the carrying out of the policy of Umkhonto.

One of the chief allegations in the indictment is that the ANC was a party to a general conspiracy to commit sabotage. I have already explained why this is incorrect but how, externally, there was a departure from the original principle laid down by the ANC. There has, of course, been overlapping of functions internally as well, because there is a difference between a resolution adopted in the atmosphere of a committee room and the concrete difficulties that arise in the field of practical activity. At a later stage the position was further affected by bannings and house arrests, and by persons leaving the country to take up political work abroad. This led to individuals having to do work in different capacities. But though this may have blurred the distinction between Umkhonto and the ANC, it by no means abolished that distinction. Great care was taken to keep the activities of the two organizations in South Africa distinct. The ANC remained a mass political body of Africans only carrying on the type of political work they had conducted prior to 1961. Umkhonto remained a small organization recruiting its members from different races and organizations and trying to achieve its own particular object. The fact that members of Umkhonto were recruited from the ANC, and the fact that persons served both organizations, like Solomon Mbanjwa, did not, in our view, change the nature of the ANC or give it a policy of violence. This overlapping of officers, however, was more the exception than the rule. This is why persons such as "Mr X" and "Mr Z", who were on the Regional Command of their respective areas, did not participate in any of the ANC committees or activities, and why people such as Mr Bennett Mashiyana and Mr Reginald Ndubi did not hear of sabotage at their ANC meetings.

Another of the allegations in the indictment is that Rivonia was the headquarters of Umkhonto. This is not true of the time when I was there. I was told, of course, and knew that certain of the activities of the Communist Party were carried on there. But this is no reason (as I shall presently explain) why I should not use the place.

I came there in the following manner:

As already indicated, early in April 1961 I went underground to organize the May general strike. My work entailed travelling throughout the country, living now in African townships, then in country villages and again in cities.

During the second half of the year I started visiting the Parktown home of Arthur Goldreich, where I used to meet my family privately. Although I had no direct political association with him, I had known Arthur Goldreich socially since 1958.

In October, Arthur Goldreich informed me that he was moving out of town and offered me a hiding place there. A few days thereafter, he arranged for Michael Harmel to take me to Rivonia. I naturally found Rivonia an ideal place for the man who lived the life of an outlaw. Up to that time I had been compelled to live indoors during the daytime and could only venture out under cover of darkness. But at Liliesleaf [farm, Rivonia] I could live differently and work far more efficiently.

For obvious reasons, I had to disguise myself and I assumed the fictitious name of David. In December, Arthur Goldreich and his family moved in. I stayed there until I went abroad on 11 January 1962. As already indicated, I returned in July 1962 and was arrested in Natal on 5 August.

Up to the time of my arrest, Liliesleaf farm was the headquarters of neither the African National Congress nor Umkhonto. With the exception of myself, none of the officials or members of these bodies lived there, no meetings of the governing bodies were ever held there, and no activities connected with them were either organized or directed from there. On numerous occasions during my stay at Liliesleaf farm I met both the Executive Committee of the ANC, as well as the NHC, but such meetings were held elsewhere and not on the farm.

Whilst staying at Liliesleaf farm, I frequently visited Arthur Goldreich in the main house and he also paid me visits in my room. We had numer-ous political discussions covering a variety of subjects. We discussed ideological and practical questions, the Congress Alliance, Umkhonto and its activities generally, and his experiences as a soldier in the Palmach, the military wing of the Haganah. Haganah was the political authority of the Jewish National Movement in Palestine.

Because of what I had got to know of Goldreich, I recommended on my return to South Africa that he should be recruited to Umkhonto. I do not know of my personal knowledge whether this was done.

Another of the allegations made by the State is that the aims and objects of the ANC and the Communist Party are the same. I wish to deal with this and with my own political position, because I must assume that the State may try to argue from certain Exhibits that I tried to introduce

Marxism into the ANC. The allegation as to the ANC is false. This is an old allegation which was disproved at the Treason Trial and which has again reared its head. But since the allegation has been made again, I shall deal with it as well as with the relationship between the ANC and the Communist Party and Umkhonto and that party.

The ideological creed of the ANC is, and always has been, the creed of African Nationalism. It is not the concept of African Nationalism expressed in the cry, 'Drive the White man into the sea'. The African Nationalism for which the ANC stands is the concept of freedom and fulfilment for the African people in their own land. The most important political document ever adopted by the ANC is the "Freedom Charter". It is by no means a blueprint for a socialist state. It calls for redistribution, but not national-ization, of land; it provides for nationalization of mines, banks, and monopoly industry, because big monopolies are owned by one race only, and without such nationalization racial domination would be perpetuated despite the spread of political power. It would be a hollow gesture to repeal the Gold Law prohibitions against Africans when all gold mines are owned by European companies. In this respect the ANC's policy corre-sponds with the old policy of the present Nationalist Party which, for many years, had as part of its programme the nationalization of the gold mines which, at that time, were controlled by foreign capital. Under the Freedom Charter, nationalization would take place in an economy based on private enterprise. The realization of the Freedom Charter would open up fresh fields for a prosperous African population of all classes, including the middle class. The ANC has never at any period of its history advocated a revolutionary change in the economic structure of the country, nor has it, to the best of my recollection, ever condemned capitalist society.

As far as the Communist Party is concerned, and if I understand its policy correctly, it stands for the establishment of a State based on the principles of Marxism. Although it is prepared to work for the Freedom Charter, as a short term solution to the problems created by white supremacy, it regards the Freedom Charter as the beginning, and not the end, of its programme.

The ANC, unlike the Communist Party, admitted Africans only as members. Its chief goal was, and is, for the African people to win unity and full political rights. The Communist Party's main aim, on the other hand, was to remove the capitalists and to replace them with a working-class government. The Communist Party sought to emphasize class distinctions whilst the ANC seeks to harmonize them. This is a vital distinction.

It is true that there has often been close co-operation between the ANC and the Communist Party. But co-operation is merely proof of a common goal – in this case the removal of white supremacy – and is not proof of a complete community of interests.

The history of the world is full of similar examples. Perhaps the most striking illustration is to be found in the co-operation between Great Britain, the United States of America, and the Soviet Union in the fight against Hitler. Nobody but Hitler would have dared to suggest that such co-operation turned Churchill or Roosevelt into communists or communist tools, or that Britain and America were working to bring about a communist world.

Another instance of such co-operation is to be found precisely in Umkhonto. Shortly after Umkhonto was constituted, I was informed by some of its members that the Communist Party would support Umkhonto, and this then occurred. At a later stage the support was made openly.

I believe that communists have always played an active role in the fight by colonial countries for their freedom, because the short-term objects of communism would always correspond with the long-term objects of freedom movements. Thus communists have played an important role in the freedom struggles fought in countries such as Malaya, Algeria, and Indonesia, yet none of these States today are communist countries. Similarly in the underground resistance movements which sprung up in Europe during the last World War, communists played an important role. Even General Chiang Kai-Shek, today one of the bitterest enemies of communism, fought together with the communists against the ruling class in the struggle which led to his assumption of power in China in the 1930s.

This pattern of co-operation between communists and non-communists has been repeated in the National Liberation Movement of South Africa. Prior to the banning of the Communist Party, joint campaigns involving the Communist Party and the Congress movements were accepted practice. African communists could, and did, become members of the ANC, and some served on the National, Provincial, and local committees. Amongst those who served on the National Executive are Albert Nzula, a former Secretary of the Communist Party, Moses Kotane, another former Secretary, and J B Marks, a former member of the Central Committee.

I joined the ANC in 1944, and in my younger days I held the view that the policy of admitting communists to the ANC, and the close co-operation which existed at times on specific issues between the ANC and the Communist Party, would lead to a watering down of the concept of African Nationalism. At that stage I was a member of the African National Congress Youth League, and was one of a group which moved for the expulsion of communists from the ANC. This proposal was heavily defeated. Amongst those who voted against the proposal were some of the most conservative sections of African political opinion. They defended the policy on the ground that from its inception the ANC was formed and built up, not as a political party with one school of political thought, but as a Parliament of the African people, accommodating people of various political convictions, all united by the common goal of national liberation. I was eventually won over to this point of view and I have upheld it ever since.

It is perhaps difficult for white South Africans, with an ingrained prejudice against communism, to understand why experienced African politicians so readily accept communists as their friends. But to us the reason is obvious. Theoretical differences amongst those fighting against oppression is a luxury we cannot afford at this stage. What is more, for many decades communists were the only political group in South Africa who were prepared to treat Africans as human beings and their equals; who were prepared to eat with us; talk with us, live with us, and work with us. They were the only political group which was prepared to work with the Africans for the attainment of political rights and a stake in society. Because of this, there are many Africans who, today, tend to equate freedom with communism. They are supported in this belief by a legislature which brands all exponents of democratic government and African freedom as communists and bans many of them (who are not communists) under the Suppression of Communism Act. Although I have never been a member of the Communist Party, I myself have been named under that pernicious Act because of the role I played in the Defiance Campaign. I have also been banned and imprisoned under that Act.

It is not only in internal politics that we count communists as amongst those who support our cause. In the international field, communist countries have always come to our aid. In the United Nations and other Councils of the world the communist bloc has supported the Afro-Asian struggle against colonialism and often seems to be more sympathetic to our plight than some of the Western powers. Although there is a universal condemnation of apartheid, the communist bloc speaks out against it with a louder voice than most of the white world. In these circumstances, it would take a brash young politician, such as I was in 1949, to proclaim that the Communists are our enemies.

I turn now to my own position. I have denied that I am a communist, and I think that in the circumstances I am obliged to state exactly what my political beliefs are.

I have always regarded myself, in the first place, as an African patriot. After all, I was born in Umtata, 46 years ago. My guardian was my cousin, who was the acting paramount chief of Tembuland, and I am related both to the present paramount chief of Tembuland, Sabata Dalindyebo, and to Kaizer Matanzima, the Chief Minister of the Transkei.

Today I am attracted by the idea of a classless society, an attraction which springs in part from Marxist reading and, in part, from my admiration of the structure and organization of early African societies in this country. The land, then the main means of production, belonged to the tribe. There were no rich or poor and there was no exploitation.

It is true, as I have already stated, that I have been influenced by Marxist thought. But this is also true of many of the leaders of the new independent States. Such widely different persons as Gandhi, Nehru, Nkrumah, and Nasser all acknowledge this fact. We all accept the need for some form of socialism to enable our people to catch up with the advanced countries of this world and to overcome their legacy of extreme poverty. But this does not mean we are Marxists.

Indeed, for my own part, I believe that it is open to debate whether the Communist Party has any specific role to play at this particular stage of our political struggle. The basic task at the present moment is the removal of race discrimination and the attainment of democratic rights on the basis of the Freedom Charter. In so far as that Party furthers this task, I welcome its assistance. I realize that it is one of the means by which people of all races can be drawn into our struggle.

From my reading of Marxist literature and from conversations with Marxists, I have gained the impression that communists regard the parliamentary system of the West as undemocratic and reactionary. But, on the contrary, I am an admirer of such a system.

The Magna Carta, the Petition of Rights, and the Bill of Rights are documents which are held in veneration by democrats throughout the world.

I have great respect for British political institutions, and for the country's system of justice. I regard the British Parliament as the most democratic institution in the world, and the independence and impartiality of its judiciary never fail to arouse my admiration.

The American Congress, that country's doctrine of separation of powers, as well as the independence of its judiciary, arouses in me similar sentiments.

I have been influenced in my thinking by both West and East. All this has led me to feel that in my search for a political formula, I should be absolutely impartial and objective. I should tie myself to no particular system of society other than of socialism. I must leave myself free to borrow the best from the West and from the East...

There are certain Exhibits which suggest that we received financial support from abroad, and I wish to deal with this question.

Our political struggle has always been financed from internal sources – from funds raised by our own people and by our own supporters. Whenever we had a special campaign or an important political case – for example, the Treason Trial – we received financial assistance from sympathetic individuals and organizations in the Western countries. We had never felt it necessary to go beyond these sources.

But when in 1961 the Umkhonto was formed, and a new phase of struggle introduced, we realized that these events would make a heavy call on our slender resources, and that the scale of our activities would be hampered by the lack of funds. One of my instructions, as I went abroad in January 1962, was to raise funds from the African states.

I must add that, whilst abroad, I had discussions with leaders of political movements in Africa and discovered that almost every single one of them, in areas which had still not attained independence, had received all forms of assistance from the socialist countries, as well as from the West, including that of financial support. I also discovered that some well-known African states, all of them non-communists, and even anti-communists, had received similar assistance.

On my return to the Republic, I made a strong recommendation to the ANC that we should not confine ourselves to Africa and the Western countries, but that we should also send a mission to the socialist countries to raise the funds which we so urgently needed.

I have been told that after I was convicted such a mission was sent, but I am not prepared to name any countries to which it went, nor am I at liberty to disclose the names of the organizations and countries which gave us support or promised to do so.

As I understand the State case, and in particular the evidence of "Mr X", the suggestion is that Umkhonto was the inspiration of the Communist Party which sought by playing upon imaginary grievances to enrol the African people into an army which ostensibly was to fight for African freedom, but in reality was fighting for a communist state. Nothing could be further from the truth. In fact the suggestion is preposterous. Umkhonto was formed by Africans to further their struggle for freedom in their own land. Communists and others supported the movement, and we only wish that more sections of the community would join us.

Our fight is against real, and not imaginary, hardships or, to use the language of the State Prosecutor, "so-called hardships". Basically, we fight against two features which are the hallmarks of African life in South Africa and which are entrenched by legislation which we seek to have repealed. These features are poverty and lack of human dignity, and we do not need communists or so-called "agitators" to teach us about these things.

South Africa is the richest country in Africa, and could be one of the richest countries in the world. But it is a land of extremes and remarkable contrasts. The whites enjoy what may well be the highest standard of living in the world, whilst Africans live in poverty and misery. Forty per cent of the Africans live in hopelessly overcrowded and, in some cases, drought-stricken Reserves, where soil erosion and the overworking of the soil makes it impossible for them to live properly off the land. Thirty per cent are labourers, labour tenants, and squatters on white farms and work and live under conditions similar to those of the serfs of the Middle Ages. The other 30 per cent live in towns where they have developed economic and social habits which bring them closer in many respects to white standards. Yet most Africans, even in this group, are impoverished by low incomes and high cost of living.

The highest-paid and the most prosperous section of urban African life is in Johannesburg. Yet their actual position is desperate. The latest figures were given on 25 March 1964 by Mr Carr, Manager of the Johannesburg Non-European Affairs Department. The poverty datum line for the average African family in Johannesburg (according to Mr Carr's department) is R42.84 per month. He showed that the average monthly wage is R32.24 and that 46 per cent of all African families in Johannesburg do not earn enough to keep them going.

Poverty goes hand in hand with malnutrition and disease. The incidence of malnutrition and deficiency diseases is very high amongst Africans. Tuberculosis, pellagra, kwashiorkor, gastro-enteritis, and scurvy bring death and destruction of health. The incidence of infant mortality is one of the highest in the world. According to the Medical Officer of Health for Pretoria, tuberculosis kills 40 people a day (almost all Africans), and in 1961 there were 58,491 new cases reported. These diseases not only destroy the vital organs of the body, but they result in retarded mental conditions and lack of initiative, and reduce powers of concentration. The secondary results of such conditions affect the whole community and the standard of work performed by African labourers.

The complaint of Africans, however, is not only that they are poor and the whites are rich, but that the laws which are made by the whites are designed to preserve this situation. There are two ways to break out of poverty. The first is by formal education, and the second is by the worker acquiring a greater skill at his work and thus higher wages. As far as Africans are concerned, both these avenues of advancement are deliberately curtailed by legislation.

The present Government has always sought to hamper Africans in their search for education. One of their early acts, after coming into power, was to stop subsidies for African school feeding. Many African children who attended schools depended on this supplement to their diet. This was a cruel act.

There is compulsory education for all white children at virtually no cost to their parents, be they rich or poor. Similar facilities are not provided for the African children, though there are some who receive such assistance. African children, however, generally have to pay more for their schooling than whites. According to figures quoted by the South African Institute of Race Relations in its 1963 journal, approximately 40 per cent of African children in the age group between seven to fourteen do not attend school. For those who do attend school, the standards are vastly different from those afforded to white children. In 1960-61 the per capita Government spending on African students at State-aided schools was estimated at R12.46. In the same years, the per capita spending on white children in the Cape Province (which are the only figures available to me) was R144.57. Although there are no figures available to me, it can be stated, without doubt, that the white children on whom R144.57 per head was being spent all came from wealthier homes than African children on whom R12.46 per head was being spent.

The quality of education is also different. According to the *Bantu Educational Journal*, only 5,660 African children in the whole of South Africa passed their Junior Certificate in 1962, and in that year only 362 passed matric. This is presumably consistent with the policy of Bantu education about which the present Prime Minister said, during the debate on the Bantu Education Bill in 1953:

'When I have control of Native education I will reform it so that Natives will be taught from childhood to realize that equality with Europeans is not for them... People who believe in equality are not desirable teachers for Natives. When my Department controls Native education it will know for what class of higher education a Native is fitted, and whether he will have a chance in life to use his knowledge.'

The other main obstacle to the economic advancement of the African is the industrial colour-bar under which all the better jobs of industry are reserved for Whites only. Moreover, Africans who do obtain employment in the unskilled and semi-skilled occupations which are open to them are not allowed to form trade unions which have recognition under the Industrial Conciliation Act. This means that strikes of African workers are illegal, and that they are denied the right of collective bargaining which is permitted to the better-paid White workers. The discrimination in the policy of successive South African Governments towards African workers is demonstrated by the so-called "civilized labour policy" under which sheltered, unskilled Government jobs are found for those white workers who cannot make the grade in industry, at wages which far exceed the earnings of the average African employee in industry.

The Government often answers its critics by saying that Africans in South Africa are economically better off than the inhabitants of the other countries in Africa. I do not know whether this statement is true and doubt whether any comparison can be made without having regard to the cost-of-living index in such countries. But even if it is true, as far as the African people are concerned it is irrelevant. Our complaint is not that we are poor by comparison with people in other countries, but that we are poor by comparison with the white people in our own country, and that we are prevented by legislation from altering this imbalance.

The lack of human dignity experienced by Africans is the direct result of the policy of white supremacy. White supremacy implies black inferiority. Legislation designed to preserve white supremacy entrenches this notion. Menial tasks in South Africa are invariably performed by Africans. When anything has to be carried or cleaned the white man will look around for an African to do it for him, whether the African is employed by him or not. Because of this sort of attitude, whites tend to regard Africans as a separate breed. They do not look upon them as people with families of their own; they do not realize that they have emotions – that they fall in love like white people do; that they want to be with their wives and children like white people want to be with theirs; that they want to earn enough money to support their families properly, to feed and clothe them and send them to school. And what "house-boy" or "garden-boy" or labourer can ever hope to do this?

Pass laws, which to the Africans are among the most hated bits of legislation in South Africa, render any African liable to police surveillance at any time. I doubt whether there is a single African male in South Africa who has not at some stage had a brush with the police over his pass. Hundreds and thousands of Africans are thrown into jail each year under pass laws. Even worse than this is the fact that pass laws keep husband and wife apart and lead to the breakdown of family life.

Poverty and the breakdown of family life have secondary effects. Children wander about the streets of the townships because they have no schools to go to, or no money to enable them to go to school, or no parents at home to see that they go to school, because both parents (if there be two) have to work to keep the family alive. This leads to a breakdown in moral standards, to an alarming rise in illegitimacy, and to growing violence which erupts not only politically, but everywhere. Life in the townships is dangerous. There is not a day that goes by without somebody being stabbed or assaulted. And violence is carried out of the townships in the white living areas. People are afraid to walk alone in the streets after dark. Housebreakings and robberies are increasing, despite the fact that the death sentence can now be imposed for such offences. Death sentences cannot cure the festering sore.

Africans want to be paid a living wage. Africans want to perform work which they are capable of doing, and not work which the Government declares them to be capable of. Africans want to be allowed to live where they obtain work, and not be endorsed out of an area because they were not born there. Africans want to be allowed to own land in places where they work, and not to be obliged to live in rented houses which they can never call their own. Africans want to be part of the general population, and not confined to living in their own ghettoes. African men want to have their wives and children to live with them where they work, and not be forced into an unnatural existence in men's hostels. African women want to be with their menfolk and not be left permanently widowed in the Reserves. Africans want to be allowed out after eleven o'clock at night and not to be confined to their rooms like little children. Africans want to be allowed to travel in their own country and to seek work where they want to and not where the Labour Bureau tells them to. Africans want a just share in the whole of South Africa; they want security and a stake in society.

Above all, we want equal political rights, because without them our disabilities will be permanent. I know this sounds revolutionary to the whites in this country, because the majority of voters will be Africans. This makes the white man fear democracy.

But this fear cannot be allowed to stand in the way of the only solution which will guarantee racial harmony and freedom for all. It is not true that the enfranchisement of all will result in racial domination. Political division, based on colour, is entirely artificial and, when it disappears, so will the domination of one colour group by another. The ANC has spent half a century fighting against racialism. When it triumphs it will not change that policy.

This then is what the ANC is fighting. Their struggle is a truly national one. It is a struggle of the African people, inspired by their own suffering and their own experience. It is a struggle for the right to live.

During my lifetime I have dedicated myself to this struggle of the African people. I have fought against white domination, and I have fought against black domination. I have cherished the ideal of a democratic and free society in which all persons live together in harmony and with equal opportunities. It is an ideal which I hope to live for and to achieve. But if needs be, it is an ideal for which I am prepared to die.

On 11 June 1964, at the conclusion of the trial, Mandela and seven others – Walter Sisulu, Govan Mbeki, Raymond Mhlaba, Elias Motsoaledi, Andrew Mlangeni, Ahmed Kathrada and Denis Goldberg – were convicted. Mandela was found guilty on four charges of sabotage and like the others was sentenced to life imprisonment.

quotes

'There can be no keener revelation of a society's soul than the way in which it treats its children.'

'It was religious institutions that gave us strength and hope that we would come back and join our people in the struggle to defeat white supremacy.'

'If I were to be granted one wish it would be that all South Africans should rededicate ourselves to turning this into the land of our dreams: a place that is free of hatred and discrimination; a place from which hunger and homelessness have been banished; a safe place for our children to grow into our future leaders.'

'One of the striking features of modern times is the number of men and women all over the globe, in all continents, who fight oppression of human rights. Many communities in the world now have been able to solve their problems because of the efforts of those men and women who have vision, who have courage to stand for the truth and who are prepared to suffer for it.'

'I am an ordinary human being, with frailties, with weaknesses. Especially because of the way I have been treated by the mass media, being elevated to the position of a messiah, it was necessary to tell the public who I am, that I'm an ordinary person, I have made serious mistakes, I have serious weaknesses.'

'Whenever the noble ideas and values of religion have been joined with practical action to realize them, it has strengthened us and at the same time nurtured those ideals.'

'Future generations will ask themselves what errors were made that allowed the apartheid to be established in the wake of the adoption of the Universal Declaration of Human Rights and in the aftermath of the trials at Nuremberg.'

'It was encouraging to hear of the God who did not tolerate oppression, but who stood with the oppressed.'

'Real leaders' messages are based on hope rather than fear, on the optimism of hard work rather than the pessimism of armchair whining.'

'It will forever remain an accusation and a challenge to all men and women of conscience that it took as long as it has before all of us stood up to say enough is enough. The United Nations was established primarily because of the determination of all humanity not to allow racism to again dragoon the world into the clutches of war. And yet, for all that, a racist tyranny established itself in our country.'

'I thank my mother and uncles who sent me to Sunday school and to the mission schools where I was nurtured. Although youth is supposed to rebel against a strict church, I look back fondly on the instruction I received.'

'We went to jail because it was impossible to sit still while the obscenity of the apartheid system was being imposed on our people. It would have been immoral to keep quiet while the racist tyranny sought to reduce an entire people into a status worse than the beasts of the forest.'

'Never, never and never again shall it be that this beautiful land will again experience the oppression of one by another and suffer the indignity of being the skunk of the world. The sun shall never set on so glorious a human achievement. Let freedom reign. God bless Africa.'

'During the proceedings, the magistrate was diffident and uneasy, and would not look at me directly. The other attorneys also seemed embarrassed, and at that moment I had something of a revelation. These men were not only uncomfortable because I was a colleague brought low, but because I was an ordinary man being punished for his beliefs. In a way I had never quite comprehended before, I realized the role I could play in court and the possibilities before me as a defendant. I was the symbol of justice in the court of the oppressor, the representative of the great ideas of freedom, fairness and democracy in a society that dishonored those virtues. I realized then and there that I could carry on the fight even within the fortress of the enemy.'

'It confirmed to me how apartheid was a poison that bred moral decay in all areas.'

'I was prepared to die secure in the knowledge that my death would be an inspiration to the cause for which I was giving my life.'

'I thought of the line from Shakespeare: 'Be absolute for death; for either death or life shall be the sweeter.'

Mohandas Gandhi

LAWYER, HUMANITARIAN AND CIVIL RIGHTS LEADER

'Be the change you wish to see in the world.'

The Life of Mohandas Karamchand Gandhi

1869	2 October: Born in Porbandar, India.
1883	Marries at age 13.
1885	Father dies.
1888	September, leaves family to study Law in London.
1891	Returns to India.
1892	Fails as lawyer in India.
1893	Goes to South Africa.
1906	Announces Celibacy (Brahmacharya) at age 37.
1908	Arrested and imprisoned.
1915	Returns to India.
1930	Salt March.
1944	Wife, Kasturba, dies.
1947	Negotiates end to 190 years of British rule.
1947	14 August: India celebrates independence.
1948	30 January: Killed by Hindu fanatic.

biography

The Story of My Experiments With Truth is the title of Gandhi's auto-biography. It is also a fitting title to describe his extraordinary life – from being married at the age of thirteen, leaving his wife to go and study Law in London, failing as a lawyer in India, then working as a lawyer and social activist in South Africa for 21 years, until at the age of 45 returning to India to create the legend of the Mahatma – the great soul!

It was indeed an ongoing search for truth, a search for an ultimate wisdom that would be both an explanation and a guide for how to make one's way in the world. It was a search along many paths.

No single short quotation can do that journey justice. Nehru's daughter Indira Gandhi said of him: 'More than his words, his life was his message.' And that life was certainly varied and eventful… He was a man of many faces…

Despite all his flaws, mistakes, obsessions and seeming contradictions, this leader of one-fifth of the world's population was able to live an iconic life that symbolised love and non-violence for millions around the world, in his own times, and for as long as the memory of him remains…

In the end, the grand experiment did appear to produce a major result… Love was the greatest truth.

'In the midst of death, life persists. In the midst of untruth, truth persists. In the midst of darkness, light persists. Hence I gather that God is life, truth, light. He is love. He is the supreme good.'

Mohandas Karamchand Gandhi was born in the port city of Porbandar on 2 October 1869, the youngest of four children. His father was a local politician, who had no aspirations to accumulate great wealth. His mother was a highly religious woman whom he revered greatly.

In 1883 at the age of 13, Gandhi was married to Kasturba, aged 12, in a marriage arranged by their parents, as was the Hindu custom. They were to produce a family of four sons, two born in India, and two in South Africa. He was a possessive husband and a strict father, a demanding and severe head of the household.

Gandhi had many faces, and had a quirky personality. He was afraid of the dark, and slept with a candle burning. Yet throughout most of his life he was cheeky and playful, with a ready sense of humour. When visiting the King of Britain in Buckingham Palace, he wore his trademark robes and was criticized for not showing due respect. His response was that the king 'was wearing enough for both of us.' When asked what he thought about western civilisation he replied: 'I think it would be a great idea.'

As a boy, he had stolen some loose change from around the house to buy some cigarettes. This so filled him with guilt that he had to confess to his father. Fearing physical punishment, he wrote him a note. His father was so taken by the honesty of this confession, that he burst into tears, whereupon the young Gandhi entered and they were both in tears. It was an incident he never forgot, it was like a "cleansing" of guilt.

But he was to be forever guilt-stricken when at the age of just 16, he left his ailing father's bedside, to run upstairs to his wife's bed. Less than 10 minutes later, the servant ran upstairs to announce that his father had just died. It was an incident that haunted him to the end of his days.

In September 1888, he left his family behind to study Law in London for three years, passing his Bar exams in June 1891. He was shy and naïve and intimidated by the big city; he himself said: 'There was no end to my helplessness and fear.'

However, he was still seduced by all things British, and at the time his ambition was to be an English gentleman, so he sported a top hat and a silver-tipped cane and wore tails. He also took dancing, violin, elocution and French lessons.

He returned to India in 1891 to practice law. His very first case was a very minor matter, which he had to argue in court. He went to the court and was totally tongue-tied – he could not speak – it was an absolute disaster. Thus humiliated, he had difficulty gaining work and in 1893 was fortunate to secure a short-term contract to do some legal work in South Africa. However, his family was left behind again.

He had to make a train trip to Pretoria, and having paid for a first class ticket, set off on the journey. However another passenger complained that Gandhi, as a "colored person" was not in third class where he should have been, and he was forcibly ejected from the train when he refused to move. He spent the whole night freezing at Maritzburg station. He referred to this night as 'the most creative experience of my life,' and later proclaimed that it was 'in this godless country that I found my God.'

When he attempted to claim his rights as a British subject he found himself abused and discriminated against, and saw that all Indians as well as other colored people suffered similar treatment. At the age of 24 he began organising Indian immigrants to try and better their situation, and in the spring of 1894, Gandhi founded the Natal Indian Congress. The first steps had been taken along the path to becoming the Mahatma.

At first he was very naïve, expecting that by challenging and changing the law, social behaviours would thus comply, but the British were always a step ahead. Still he persevered.

In the spring of 1896 he returned to India to collect his family, returning with them in December.

Gandhi worked as a lawyer and social activist in South Africa for some 21 years, helping to secure rights for people of Indian background.

He also maintained regular contact with India and the Indian nationalists, becoming increasingly interested and involved in developments in India itself. In 1901 he went to India to attend the Indian National Congress, where he was introduced to nationalist leaders.

However, even in 1906 he was still a loyal British subject, singing God Save The King and becoming a stretcher bearer for the English forces in the Boer War.

He was a complex character; and despite fighting for the rights of others, he was still stern with, and some said, inconsiderate to his family. With his Hindu background, he had been concerned for some time with matters such as personal purity, and attaining "Brahmacharya" or celibacy. In 1906, at the age of 37, he declared to his wife the end of his sexual activity. He had not discussed the matter with her beforehand, and simply announced his decision to her.

In 1906 new laws were announced to allow the fingerprinting and classification of all Indians. Three thousand Indians met in Johannesburg on 11 September to plan a response. Gandhi became convinced that justice would be best served by going to prison rather than obeying unjust laws.

He had been contemplating the best way forward in the circumstances, and realised that a violent response would result in a bloodbath. He addressed the crowd and a campaign of non-violent resistance was launched to protest discrimination against Indians.

He called this approach "Satyagraha", made up from two Sanskrit words for "truth and committed pursuit of". Satyagraha came to mean "soul force".

Together with "Ahimsa", meaning non-violence and a respect for life, these two words were a simple, symbolic summary of the Gandhi approach.

Gandhi was greatly influenced in his approach by both Indian and Christian religious teachings, as well as Leo Tolstoy and the 19th-century American writer Henry David Thoreau (especially his essay "Civil Disobedience").

Gandhi translated Tolstoy's *Letter to a Hindu* and endorsed it with: 'One need not accept all that Tolstoy says – some of his facts are not accurately stated – to realise the central truth of his indictment of the present system, which is to understand and act upon the irresistible power of the soul over the body, of love, which is an attribute of the soul, over the brute or body force generated by the stirring in us of evil passions.

'There is no doubt that there is nothing new in what Tolstoy preaches. But his presentation of the old truth is refreshingly forceful. His logic is unassailable. And above all he endeavours to practise what he preaches. He preaches to convince. He is sincere and in earnest. He commands attention.'

Tolstoy had written to an Indian publication:

'A commercial company enslaved a nation comprising two hundred millions. Tell this to a man free from superstition and he will fail to grasp what these words mean. What does it mean that thirty thousand people, not athletes, but rather weak and ordinary people, have enslaved two hundred millions of vigorous, clever, capable, freedom-loving people? Do not the figures make it clear that not the English, but the Indians, have enslaved themselves?'.

And further: 'You say that the English have enslaved your people and hold them in subjection because the latter have not resisted resolutely enough and have not met force by force.

'But the case is just the opposite. If the English have enslaved the people of India it is just because the latter recognized, and still recognize, force as the fundamental principle of the social order. In accord with that principle they submitted to their little rajahs, and on their behalf struggled against one another, fought the Europeans, the English, and are now trying to fight with them again.'

The makings of major change were developing.

Major civil disturbances followed as the fight for greater civil rights for Indians continued across South Africa and the movement gained strength, with Gandhi increasingly the prime mover.

In January 1908 he was arrested and sentenced to two months in prison, and in October he was arrested again, this time spending a month in jail.

He was no longer the naïve little learner lawyer. By this time his network was extensive, not only in South Africa, but in India and Britain as well. His methods were attracting attention and he was creating a very distinct profile for himself and his approach. His idiosyncratic "search for truth" was taking him some way along extraordinary paths.

In 1909 he travelled to London, campaigning for the rights of South African Indians, and in November 1913, under Gandhi's leadership, Indians in Natal and the Transvaal marched peacefully to protest against racist poll tax and marriage laws. The marches continued through the winter.

When in 1913, he led 2,500 Indians in another protest, violent arrests occurred. When Gandhi refused to pay a fine, he was jailed again, his supporters responding with further demonstrations, at which Natal police fired into the crowd, killing two and injuring many. In June 1914 Gandhi and the Prime Minister of the Transvaal, Smuts, finally reached an agreement, ending the protests.

He had by then decided that his destiny lay in the greater fight of achieving independence for India herself. In July 1914 Gandhi sailed to England again, arriving just at the outbreak of World War I.

On 9 January 1915, at the age of 45, he returned to India to a hero's welcome. He had gained valuable experience in South Africa, which would be very useful in his next challenge.

In May of that year Gandhi and his followers founded Satyagraha Ashram, the religiously oriented communal farm where Gandhi, his family, and his followers would live.

India was the jewel in the British Empire crown. It was a large and rich domain, which had been successfully subjugated for some 200 years. The economy was totally controlled by the British and they were able to use the wealth of the nation to maintain their rule. Three hundred million Indians were controlled by a contingent of a mere 100,000 or so English.

During World War I the resources of India were very useful to the British in their war effort, and at the conclusion of the war, many expected that it would be "business as usual". But times had changed. An experienced and determined Gandhi was back – and he was nothing like anything the British rulers had ever experienced before.

On 6 April 1919 the Indian Nationalists held a hartal, or day of fasting and prayer, in protest against the Rowlatt Act, which harshly sought to curtail civil liberties in India.

On 13 April 1919, in the village of Amritsar, some 2,000 Indians had gathered, unaware that General Reginald Dyer had very recently banned public assemblies. Without warning he mobilised 50 Indian troops equipped with rifles and the rapid firing Gatling Guns, and ordered them to open fire. In the slaughter, they killed 379 people and wounded over a thousand. They only stopped firing because they ran out of ammunition.

Dyer was determined to put the local population back in its place. The massacre was followed up by the infamous "crawling decree" whereby the local population could be forced to wriggle on their bellies like worms, or be flogged – to death!

Such a violent and powerful authority had to be carefully countered… and Gandhi was at the forefront. His values and those of his people, would be put to the most demanding test.

Gandhi was a shrewd political operator and now well-connected around the world. He was no simple villager that could be easily intimidated by men with guns.

Gandhi's heart could inspire, but he also had an ear to international opinion, especially in Britain, Europe and the USA. And he had a mind that was shrewd, capable, well-versed in matters of large scale social protest, and full of surprises.

While the British were readying their guns and laws, Gandhi was working on hearts and minds.

He exhorted his people not to hate the English, saying that 'they are not our enemies, they are our friends. They need to be liberated as much as we do.'

He was developing a method of direct social action based on Satyagraha and Ahimsa principles, promoting non-violence and civil disobedience as the most appropriate methods for obtaining political and social goals.

As much as it may have been guided by Gandhi's moral perspective, it was a shrewd political strategy that was brilliant in the circumstances. Not that it was easy, comfortable or safe – far from it. But it was an approach that took on an opponent who was much better armed, and then engaged that opponent using that opponent's own professed principles. It was a strategy of fighting from the higher moral ground.

Gandhi also attracted wide attention across the world by fasting in support of his protests, and to impress upon others the need to be non-violent. It was a tactic that he used many times.

He was also not afraid to go to jail in support of his position. He was arrested many times by the British for his activities in both South Africa and India, and believed it was honourable to go to jail for a just cause. He spent a total of some seven years in prison for his political activities.

In August 1920, Gandhi called for a widespread campaign of non-cooperation and civil disobedience across the nation. Then on 10 March 1922 he was arrested for sedition, and remained in prison until January 1924.

The period from 1924 to 1928 saw Gandhi diminish his direct involvement in politics, focusing his writings on the improvement of India and exploring other paths in his ongoing "experiment with truth". Even so, he was elected President of the Indian National Congress in 1925. By this time he was being increasingly referred to as Mahatma – the great soul.

He was also gaining greater visibility and developing an iconic status with his idiosyncratic habits and clothing.

Meanwhile, his methods were increasingly gaining adherents... from February to August 1928 residents in the Bardoli district protested against high rents, using Gandhi-inspired non-cooperation tactics.

He was also encouraging a kind of cultural nationalism. Foreign clothing was burned in huge bonfires, and the local population was encouraged to spin their own cloth and wear traditional clothing made from it. By way of example, he would very visibly spend an hour a day spinning thread on a rudimentary spinning wheel. Even many of his supporters considered he was overdoing the symbolism, and that surely a man in his position of national importance had better things to do with his time. But the Mahatma was doing it his way – sticking to his principles, while being very much aware of the political and social impacts – in India and around the world.

Getting out from under the British yoke was proving to be a long haul, and it was not until 26 January 1930 that Gandhi published the *Declaration of Independence of India*. And then a civil disobedience campaign with a difference began.

On 2 March 1930, Gandhi warned the Viceroy of India, Lord Irwin (who later took the title Lord Halifax) of his intention to disobey the Salt Laws as a gesture of defiance against the British monopoly on salt production in particular and the economy generally. Only the British could harvest salt. The economy was strictly regulated and the means of production and commerce were severely restricted to ensure British control and profits. After all, one needs a lot of money to run an empire, and who better to pay for it than the subjects themselves.

The Viceroy had a considerable respect for Gandhi, referring to him as 'the little man', and was loath to move against him. So he allowed the march to proceed.

On 12 March 1930, Gandhi and some 80 companions started his march of approximately 240 miles to the Gujarat Coast of the Arabian Sea, where he would take some salt from the sea in contravention of the law.

They marched some 10 miles a day, so the journey would take 24 days. Of course this provided a lot of time for the news to spread all over the world as well as India, with reporters arriving from around the globe. As they proceeded, the crowd swelled, the photo opportunities became endless, and by the time they reached the coast, the world was watching Bapu, the 'little father' and his flock.

At the ocean's edge on 6 April, Gandhi raised a pinch of salt in his fingers and announced 'with this salt I resist the might of the British Empire. Join me in this struggle of right against might.' And then waited for the full response of the Empire.

The country erupted as the citizens followed his example – everyone was making their own salt. Mass meetings materialised across the country and the Indian National Congress even orchestrated the sale of illegal salt in huge quantities.

Of course the march was of little immediate practical economic conse-quence, but the political impact was seismic. Despite the western world's stock market crashes and looming depression, the 'little man' now held the world's attention. Indian independence was on the international radar.

Satyagraha and Ahimsa had been let loose on an enormous scale. The British Government responded robustly, censoring the press and filling the prisons with non-violent and non-complying Indians, but it was crisis time. Indian leaders were arrested, including Jawaharlal Nehru (who was to become the first Prime Minister of India) and Gandhi who was arrested on 5 May. But the demonstrations went on until January 1931, when the prisoners were finally released.

The Empire was in trouble… so a meeting was arranged between Gandhi and the Viceroy Lord Irwin. Gandhi went from prison to palace, and sitting with the Viceroy, was offered the glass of warm water that he had requested. From his clothing he apparently produced a substance which he sprinkled into the water. When asked what it was, he replied: 'don't tell anybody, but it is the salt I have illegally manufactured'.

Gandhi could certainly be exasperating. He allegedly observed one day of silence per week as one of his disciplines. Occasionally the Viceroy would need to confer with him and get him to the palace, where, upon asking him a question, Gandhi would respond with a finger to his lips – it was his day of silence!

During the course of this meeting however, Gandhi was speaking, and it was agreed that the Indian National Congress could send a representative to the Round Table Conference in London that year.

It was no surprise who that representative would be, and it would be a public relations triumph for the cause of Indian independence.

Gandhi was awarded a generally rapturous welcome in Britain – he was a major curiosity. Prominent people from all over Britain, including the King and George Bernard Shaw, asked for interviews, and large crowds followed him everywhere. This was one of the international peaks of his career. Of course there were dissenting voices – losing India was not a pleasant prospect to some, including Winston Churchill, later to be Britain's legendary wartime Prime Minister, who rumbled about the collapse of the British Empire and referred to Gandhi as a "half-naked fakir".

Gandhi made a point of visiting the poor in London and the industrial cities, and stayed among them in the East End. The crowds turned out in huge numbers. He travelled by third class train and duly observed his daily disciplines, appearing in his traditional robes. There was certainly no longer any hint of a top hat, silver-tipped cane or violin.

It was these public relations initiatives that were the most successful part of the conference for India. Gandhi was masterful at building maximum support among the British public for Indian independence.

But no actual plan for independence or home rule could be agreed upon at the Conference itself. In that respect, it was a non-event; among other matters, the British were worried about the future of minorities (especially Muslims). This was a real and recurring issue, as Muhammed Ali Jinnah's Muslim League was now a significant player. The road to independence was to be a rough and tortuous one.

Nevertheless, Gandhi left no one in any doubt: 'it is complete independence that we want'.

On 28 December 1931, Gandhi returned to India. It was only 4 January 1932 when he was arrested for sedition, and held without a trial without any charges being brought. He was simply held at the discretion of the British Government to keep him out of play in what was a complex and high stakes game.

Taking advantage of his isolation, the British endeavoured to create separate electoral systems for Hindus, Muslims and untouchables, which were supposed to ensure representation in provincial legislatures for each. Gandhi found the notion of dividing Indians by religion reprehensible enough, but dividing them by caste was just untenable. The untouchables, who Gandhi referred to as the Harijans or "God's Children" were one of his special causes.

Gandhi called for social reforms and a boycott on British goods, and from 20 September 1932, committed himself to a "fast unto the death". Six days later a settlement was negotiated. But this fast did have significant re-percussions on his health. His own personal survival had become an issue.

And the political situation was not getting any simpler or clearer. Gandhi made plans to move more into the background, and resolved to concentrate on the "constructive work", of improving the daily lives of his fellow Indians. When, in 1934 he announced another fast for self-purification in preparation for his constructive work, he was released from prison as the authorities could no longer afford to make a martyr of him.

The years from 1934 to 1938 were years of avoiding politics – there were plenty of other players, including the charismatic Nehru. Gandhi spent his time travelling through the country. His search for truth involved more than just politics. He was still promoting his spinning wheel, travelling barefoot from village to village, and teaching the population about his views on hygiene, harmony, love, etc, and promoting traditional village lifestyles. He even promoted the Italian Montessori education system because it combined practical instruction with book-based learning.

However his life was not without tragedy – his older son became a Muslim, alcoholic and a prostitute and in 1938 Gandhi was to have said "He is no longer my son."

In 1935 the Government of India Act was passed in the British Parliament and implemented in India; it was the first significant move towards independence (Winston Churchill resigned from the cabinet in protest).

The objective of the Act was to engender a move towards an Indian federation under which all the provinces and princely states would be united. However, local politicians had their own ideas, and the Act was rejected both by the Congress and their increasingly difficult major opponent, Jinnah's Muslim League, although the ancillary provisions of the Act did go into effect. So by 1937 local legislatures, made up of elected Indians, held effective control on the provincial level, while the British still ruled India on the national level.

When World War II started in September 1939, India was brought into the conflict without consulting the nationalist leadership. The Congress and the Muslim League were outraged, but Gandhi was invited to see Viceroy Lord Linlithgow.

Gandhi had no time for Nazism, he still had his passion for things British, and pledged his personal support to Britain and the allies. Nehru was not nearly as keen. Instead, the Congress leaders essentially asked for complete independence in return for Indian support in the war. Gandhi reluctantly complied.

But Prime Minister Churchill had no interest in Indian independence, especially now. A small scale civil disobedience campaign resulted in the Congress leaders spending time in jail. In 1942 Sir Stafford Cripps arrived to offer India Dominion status in the British Commonwealth after the war (de facto independence).

The Cripps mission failed when the parties could not agree. All the Congress leaders, including Gandhi, were arrested in August 1942 and imprisoned in a palace. When India exploded into violence, the Viceroy demanded Gandhi speak out. He refused, preferring to begin another fast in February 1943 that lasted for three weeks. While concerned that he might die, the authorities still kept him, his friends and his family in the palace, where they could at least keep an eye on them. For the next two years, Gandhi would lead the ever-growing (and ever more complex) rebellion from the palace.

A month before D-Day, in May of 1944, Gandhi was released. His wife of 62 years had died in his arms on 22 February.

He now faced a prospect he dreaded – the partition of India. In 1942 he met with Jinnah who wanted an independent Muslim state, a "Pakistan". Gandhi argued that partition would lead to violence and forced migration. 'You can cut me in two if you wish,' said Gandhi, 'but don't cut India in two.' Jinnah remained obdurate.

When Churchill lost the British elections, the winning Labour Party hurried to rid themselves of an ungovernable subcontinent. New elections in India elected Muslim League representatives from Muslim districts, and Congress Party representatives everywhere else. The divisions were now between Indians, no longer the British and the Indians.

In May 1946 the British Cabinet Mission published a proposal for an

Indian state without partition, but Jinnah and the Muslim League rejected it.

Nehru became the provisional government leader and religious riots erupted in Calcutta. From Calcutta, Gandhi walked through rural villages, preaching love and understanding to thousands, including large Muslim populations, trying to keep the country together.

The British were now determined to achieve a resolution as soon as possible, and sent the skilled diplomat Lord Mountbatten as last Viceroy of India. Charged with achieving independence within a year, he arrived in March 1947 and summoned Gandhi to meet with Jinnah in Delhi.

Jinnah remained unyielding, but Mountbatten refused his more extreme demands. The Congress leaders, led by Nehru, accepted partition as the price of independence. A border was established and independence was celebrated on 14 August 1947. Gandhi was heartbroken, and asked 'Why do they rejoice? I see only rivers of blood.'

Violence swept the country with some 500,000 dying in the conflict and nearly fifteen million being forced from their homes.

Gandhi was devastated. 'There is darkness everywhere' he despaired, 'men are behaving worse than beasts.' His own people had let him – and themselves, down.

The presence of the Mahatma was still of some consequence. His Independence Day pledge to fast until violence in Calcutta ceased, brought an end to the riots in three days. But there was violence everywhere, so he threw himself into a campaign to spread the message of peace, travelling through the villages and towns. In the first days, some of the responses were very disappointing; 'let Gandhi die' some called, but gradually he started to achieve his desired effect.

From Delhi, he went to the Punjab and back to Delhi, where on 13 January, he began another fast 'unto death'. It took five days for Muslim and Hindu leaders to make peace. The 78-year-old Gandhi then concentrated on recuperating, hoping to return to the Punjab.

He was well aware that he was an assassination target, and spoke of dying well if the time came, saying: 'My death must achieve what my life has not.'

Gandhi had made India ungovernable for the British, but in 1947 the country as a whole entity had become ungovernable by anyone.

On the evening of Friday, 30 January 1948, he was in his garden when a Hindu nationalist came up to him, and, after receiving a blessing from the Mahatma, shot him three times. The last word uttered by Gandhi was "Rama" – God.

The assassin had hoped Gandhi's death would lead to war between India and Pakistan and the elimination of the Muslim state. But violence across the country ceased overnight.

Over one million people turned up at his funeral. When his body was cremated, his ashes were spread upon the waters.

The world mourned; flags flew at half-mast, leaders and dignitaries sent their condolences. Nehru, his voice choking with emotion, declared, 'the light has gone out of our lives and there is darkness everywhere.'

One man's experiment with truth was done.

But there were now two nations with their own destinies, not exactly what the Mahatma had desired, but two nations ruled by their own people.

Not all his dreams came to pass as he would have desired. Yet he left an indelible mark on the history of the world, and provided inspiration for other great leaders as well as millions of ordinary folk around the world. Martin Luther King, Nelson Mandela, the Dalai Lama and many of the peace movements of the world have lionised him. He has now become a citizen of the world and an iconic symbol for ethical and non-violent rebellion.

India is now not as he may have imagined – an industrial and atomic power, rather than villagers spinning their own thread. There is some argument that the collapse of the British Raj from the mid 1930s was due to a variety of historical, cultural, technical, economic and political factors around the world, as well as Gandhi and events in India. But Gandhi certainly gave it a symbolic public face.

Although an iconic creator of a philosophy of passive resistance and non-violence, he had an idiosyncratic personal life. Apart from politics and the law, he spent much time on eccentric theories of diet, bowel movements and human excrement. His later experiments included sleeping with naked young women by his side so he could prove he had mastered his physical urges. He also believed that control over his vital fluids would enhance his spiritual powers.

And as for his ascetic lifestyle, some saw it as a highly-stylised public relations exercise. As the poet Sarojini Naidu joked, it cost the nation a fortune to keep Gandhi living in poverty.

Like many great people who may appear superhuman in their particular ways, the deeper you dig, the more human they become.

And in that mixture of greatness and common humanity, there may lie the wisdom we all need.

I have nothing new to teach the world. Truth and non violence are as old as the hills.

Keep my word positive. Words become my behaviors. Keep my behaviors positive. Behaviors become my habits. Keep my habits positive. Habits become my values. Keep my values positive. Values become my destiny.

– MOHANDAS GANDHI, from the introduction to his autobiography, *The Story of My Experiments With Truth*

wisdom

How do you just decide to get up and write a book after being sacked?

There was never a time when I presented *Collective Wisdom* where I was not asked this question or a variant on this theme! And it is amazing that if you are forced time and again in so many varied circumstances to answer essentially the same question how much more insight one gains on the matter being considered.

Essentially when I lost my job I decided to reconsider everything about me as a person; who I was, what I stood for and believed in every respect and as a result what I would do going forward.

When I read Gandhi saying, *'I have found by experience that man makes his plans to be often upset by God, but, at the same time, where the ultimate goal is the search of truth, no matter how a man's plans are frustrated the issue is never injurious and often better than anticipated,'* I could not have agreed more, and life, to date, has proved as much.

So when a Gandhi quote said to me 'You must be the change you wish to see in the world' I agreed with him. I read him also to say, 'Non-cooperation with evil is a sacred duty. You assist an evil system most effectively by obeying its orders and decrees. An evil system never deserves such allegiance. Allegiance to it means partaking of the evil. A good person will resist an evil system with his or her whole soul', and knew I had found an answer.

Now, as with Gandhi, coming to understand and find one's place in life can be a very long and winding road. A journey of despair, joy, anger, fun, utter desperation, failure and triumph but one sustained by hope.

Gandhi was married at 13. Soon after, he left his ailing father's side to make love to his wife. His father died during that short time – the guilt was with him forever.

As a teenager, he left his wife and family in India to go and study Law in England, his ambition at the time was to be an English Gentleman, and he sported a silver-tipped cane and a top hat! Failing as a lawyer in India, he then spent over 20 years in South Africa before returning to India in his mid-forties to begin the work for which he was to become one of the most famous people on earth.

It is interesting to remember that Mother Teresa taught in a school in Calcutta for many years before setting up her order of the Sisters of Charity when she was nearly 40 years old. Nelson Mandela was more than 70 years of age when released from prison to be President of South Africa and John Paul II was close to 60 years of age when he became Pope.

Driven by a deep sense of the need for justice, Gandhi was courageous and determined. He preached the way of non-violence, and promoted the all encompassing message of love for all, even his enemies. It took extra-ordinary courage to take on one of the most powerful regimes on the planet, the English establishment.

He had a great and abiding faith and a hope which he was able to communicate to millions.

He sought dignity for his people and oppressed people everywhere, and stood as an icon for what could be achieved by them through non-violent struggle.

What has all this got to do with me? Essentially Gandhi, and others like him, showed me a way to look at myself as the root of the problem to be conquered. Rather than succumbing to the desire to blame others and endlessly point out their faults, Gandhi showed me that I have the power to cooperate or not.

It is a common association to think of Gandhi being about non-violent resistance to bring down systems of oppression. He certainly did this. However for me, the great insight I learned from him, is that we are all free to choose to what level we will cooperate with desires that we may have that are "second-rate-version-of-ourselves stuff". Gandhi even codified seven observations, in short, that he considered represented the struggle between the higher v lower way for a person, as follows:

1. *Wealth without Work*
2. *Pleasure without Conscience*
3. *Science without Humanity*
4. *Knowledge without Character*
5. *Politics without Principle*
6. *Commerce without Morality*
7. *Worship without Sacrifice*

His whole ethos was one of a mastery of self that would create the space to act in freedom. He famously decided, at age 37 to become celibate, slept in a bed full of young virgins, fasted for days on end and the like – these were exercises for him in building self-discipline, something he considered indispensable.

Knowing that he could control himself, Gandhi could resist anyone or anything's attempt to control him; he had mastered himself in every sphere.

So when I lost my job I realised I had to choose to become a loser by blaming others or master myself. Looking deeply into my own brokenness

I decided to choose – and it is in the active choosing, and following through on these choices, that I found the strength to pick myself up and make a contribution. Gandhi showed me that you are never too young nor too old to, 'be the change you wish to see in the world'.

wisdom

words

The Quit India Speeches

Gandhi address (in Hindustani) to the AICC, outlining his plan of action, in Bombay – 8 August 1942.

I

Before you discuss the resolution, let me place before you one or two things, I want you to understand two things very clearly and to consider them from the same point of view from which I am placing them before you. I ask you to consider it from my point of view, because if you approve of it, you will be enjoined to carry out all I say. It will be a great responsibility. There are people who ask me whether I am the same man that I was in 1920, or whether there has been any change in me. You are right in asking that question.

Let me, however, hasten to assure that I am the same Gandhi as I was in 1920. I have not changed in any fundamental respect. I attach the same importance to non-violence that I did then. If at all, my emphasis on it has grown stronger. There is no real contradiction between the present resolution and my previous writings and utterances.

Occasions like the present do not occur in everybody's and but rarely in anybody's life. I want you to know and feel that there is nothing but purest Ahimsa in all that I am saying and doing today. The draft resolution of the Working Committee is based on Ahimsa, the contemplated struggle similarly has its roots in Ahimsa. If, therefore, there is any among you who has lost faith in Ahimsa or is wearied of it, let him not vote for this resolution.

Let me explain my position clearly. God has vouchsafed to me a priceless gift in the weapon of Ahimsa. I and my Ahimsa are on our trail today. If in the present crisis, when the earth is being scorched by the flames of Himsa and crying for deliverance, I failed to make use of the God given talent, God will not forgive me and I shall be judged unwrongly of the great gift. I must act now. I may not hesitate and merely look on, when Russia and China are threatened.

Ours is not a drive for power, but purely a non-violent fight for India's independence. In a violent struggle, a successful general has been often known to effect a military coup and to set up a dictatorship. But under the Congress scheme of things, essentially non-violent as it is, there can be no room for dictatorship. A non-violent soldier of freedom will covet nothing for himself, he fights only for the freedom of his country. The Congress is unconcerned as to who will rule, when freedom is attained. The power, when it comes, will belong to the people of India, and it will be for them to decide to whose hands that power is entrusted. May be that the reins will be placed in the hands of the Parsis, for instance – as I would love to see happen – or they may be handed to some others whose names are not heard in Congress today. It will not be for you then to object saying, 'This community is microscopic. That party did not play its due part in the freedom's struggle; why should it have all the power?' Ever since its inception the Congress has kept itself meticulously free of the communal taint. It has thought always in terms of the whole nation and has acted accordingly.

I know how imperfect our Ahimsa is and how far away we are still from the ideal, but in Ahimsa there is no final failure or defeat. I have faith, therefore, that if, in spite of our shortcomings, the big thing does happen, it will be because God wanted to help us by crowning with success our silent, unremitting Sadhana for the last twenty-two years.

I believe that in the history of the world, there has not been a more genuinely democratic struggle for freedom than ours. I read Carlyle's French Revolution while I was in prison, and Pandit Jawaharlal has told me something about the Russian Revolution. But it is my conviction that inasmuch as these struggles were fought with the weapon of violence they failed to realize the democratic ideal. In the democracy which I have envisaged, a democracy established by non-violence, there will be equal freedom for all. Everybody will be his own master. It is to join a struggle for such democracy that I invite you today. Once you realize this you will forget the differences between the Hindus and Muslims, and think of yourselves as Indians only, engaged in the common struggle for independence.

Then, there is the question of your attitude towards the British. I have noticed that there is hatred towards the British among the people. The people say they are disgusted with their behaviour. The people make no distinction between British imperialism and the British people. To them, the two are one. This hatred would even make them welcome the Japanese. It is most dangerous. It means that they will exchange one slavery for another. We must get rid of this feeling. Our quarrel is not with the British people, we fight their imperialism. The proposal for the withdrawal of British power did not come out of anger. It came to enable India to play its due part at the present critical juncture. It is not a happy position for a big country like India to be merely helping with money and material obtained willy-nilly from her while the United Nations are conducting the war. We cannot evoke the true spirit of sacrifice and valour, so long as we are not free. I know the British Government will not be able to withhold freedom from us, when we have made enough self-sacrifice. We must, therefore, purge ourselves of hatred. Speaking for myself, I can say that I have never felt any hatred. As a matter of fact, I feel myself to be a greater friend of the British now than ever before. One reason is that they are today in distress. My very friendship, therefore, demands that I should try to save them from their mistakes. As I view the situation, they are on the brink of an abyss. It, therefore, becomes my duty to warn them of their danger even though it may, for the time being, anger them to the point of cutting off the friendly hand that is stretched out to help them. People may laugh, nevertheless that is my claim. At a time when I may have to launch the biggest struggle of my life, I may not harbour hatred against anybody.

II

I congratulate you on the resolution that you have just passed. I also congratulate the three comrades on the courage they have shown in pressing their amendments to a division, even though they knew that there was an overwhelming majority in favour of the resolution, and I con-gratulate the thirteen friends who voted against the resolution. In doing so, they had nothing to be ashamed of. For the last twenty years we have tried to learn not to lose courage even when we are in a hopeless minority and are laughed at. We have learned to hold on to our beliefs in the confidence that we are in the right. It behoves us to cultivate this courage of con-viction, for it ennobles man and raises his moral stature. I was, therefore, glad to see that these friends had imbibed the principle which I have tried to follow for the last fifty years and more.

Having congratulated them on their courage, let me say that what they asked this Committee to accept through their amendments was not the correct representation of the situation. These friends ought to have pondered over the appeal made to them by the Maulana to withdraw their amendments; they should have carefully followed the explanations given by Jawaharlal. Had they done so, it would have been clear to them that the right which they now want the Congress to concede has already been conceded by the Congress.

Time was when every Mussulman claimed the whole of India as his motherland. During the years that the Ali brothers were with me, the assumption underlying all their talks and discussions was that India belonged as much to the Mussulmans as to the Hindus. I can testify to the fact that this was their innermost conviction and not a mask; I lived with them for years. I spent days and nights in their company. And I make bold to say that their utterances were the honest expression of their beliefs. I know there are some who say that I take things too readily at their face value, that I am gullible. I do not think I am such a simpleton, nor am I so gullible as these friends take me to be. But their criticism does not hurt me. I should prefer to be considered gullible rather than deceitful.

What these Communist friends proposed through their amendments is nothing new. It has been repeated from thousands of platforms. Thousands of Mussulmans have told me, that if the Hindu-Muslim question was to be solved satisfactorily, it must be done in my lifetime. I should feel flattered at this; but how can I agree to a proposal which does not appeal to my reason? Hindu-Muslim unity is not a new thing. Millions of Hindus and Mussulmans have sought after it. I consciously strove for its achie-vement from my boyhood. While at school, I made it a point to cultivate the friendship of Muslims and Parsi co-students. I believed even at that tender age that the Hindus in India, if they wished to live in peace and amity with the other communities, should assiduously cultivate the virtue of neighbourliness. It did not matter, I felt, if I made no special effort to cultivate the friendship with Hindus, but I must make friends with at least a few Mussulmans. It was as counsel for a Mussulmans' merchant that I went to South Africa. I made friends with other Mussulmans there, even with the opponents of my client, and gained a reputation for integrity and good faith. I had among my friends and co-workers Muslims as well as Parsis. I captured their hearts and when I left finally for India, I left them sad and shedding tears of grief at the separation.

In India too I continued my efforts and left no stone unturned to achieve that unity. It was my life-long aspiration for it that made me offer my fullest co-operation to the Mussulmans in the Khilafat movement. Muslims throughout the country accepted me as their true friend.

How then is it that I have now come to be regarded as so evil and detestable? Had I any axe to grind in supporting the Khilafat movement? True, I did in my heart of hearts cherish a hope that it might enable me to save the cow. I am a worshipper of the cow. I believe the cow and myself to be the creation of the same God, and I am prepared to sacrifice my life in order to save the cow. But, whatever my philosophy of life and my ultimate hopes, I joined the movement in no spirit of bargain. I co-operated in the struggle for the Khilafat solely in order to discharge my obligation to my neighbour who, I saw, was in distress. The Ali brothers, had they been alive today, would have testified to the truth of this assertion. And so would many others bear me out in that it was not a bargain on my part for saving the cow. The cow like the Khilafat stood on her own merits. As an honest man, a true neighbour and a faithful friend, it was incumbent on me to stand by the Mussulmans in the hour of their trial.

In those days, I shocked the Hindus by dining time they have now got used to it. Maulana Bari told me, however, that though he would not allow me to dine with him, lest some day he should be accused of a sinister motive. And so, whenever I had occasion to stay with him, he called a Brahmana cook and made social arrangements for separate cooking. Firangi, Mahal, his residence, was an old-styled structure with limited accommodation; yet he cheerfully bore all hardships and carried out his resolve from which I could not dislodge him. It was the spirit of courtesy, dignity and nobility that inspired us in those days. They respected one another's religious feelings, and considered it a privilege to do so. Not a trace of suspicion lurked in anybody's heart. Where has all that dignity, that nobility of spirit, disappeared now? I should ask all Mussulmans, including Quaid-i-Azam Jinnah, to recall those glorious days and to find out what has brought us to the present impasse. Quaid-i-Azam Jinnah himself was at one time a Congressman. If today the Congress has incurred his wrath, it is because the canker of suspicion has entered his heart. May God bless him with long life, but when I am gone, he will realize and admit that I had no designs on Mussulmans and that I had never betrayed their interests. Where is the escape for me, if I injure their cause or betray their interests? My life is entirely at their disposal. They are free to put an end to it, whenever they wish to do so. Assaults have been made on my life in the past, but God has spared me till now, and the assailants have repented for their action. But if someone were to shoot me in the belief that he was getting rid of a rascal, he would kill not the real Gandhi, but the one that appeared to him a rascal.

To those who have been indulging in a campaign of abuse and vilification I would say, 'Islam enjoins you not to revile even an enemy. The Prophet treated even enemies with kindness and tried to win them over by his fairness and generosity. Are you followers of that Islam or of any other? If you are followers of the true Islam, does it behove you to distrust the words of one who makes a public declaration of his faith? You may take it from me that one day you will regret the fact that you distrusted and killed one who was a true and devoted friend of yours'. It cuts me to the quick to see that the more I appeal and the more the Maulana importunes, the more intense does the campaign of vilification grow. To me, these abuses are like bullets. They can kill me, even as a bullet can put an end to my life. You may kill me. That will not hurt me. But what of those who indulge in abusing? They bring discredit to Islam. For the fair name of Islam, I appeal to you to resist this unceasing campaign of abuse and vilification.

Maulana Saheb is being made a target for the filthiest abuse. Why? Because he refuses to exert on me the pressure of his friendship. He realizes that it is a misuse of friendship to seek up to compel a friend to accept as truth what he knows is an untruth.

To the Quaid-i-Azam I would say: Whatever is true and valid in the claim for Pakistan is already in your hands. What is wrong and untenable is in nobody's gift, so that it can be made over to you. Even if someone were to succeed in imposing an untruth on others, he would not be able to enjoy for long the fruits of such a coercion. God dislikes pride and keeps away from it. God would not tolerate a forcible imposition of an untruth.

The Quaid-i-Azam says that he is compelled to say bitter things but that he cannot help giving expression to his thoughts and his feelings. Similarly I would say: 'I consider myself a friend of Mussulmans. Why should I then not give expression to the things nearest to my heart, even at the cost of displeasing them? How can I conceal my innermost thoughts from them? I should congratulate the Quaid-i-Azam on his frankness in giving expression to his thoughts and feelings, even if they sound bitter to his hearers. But even so why should the Mussulmans sitting here be reviled, if they do not see eye to eye with him? If millions of Mussulmans are with you can you not afford to ignore the handful of Mussulmans who may appear to you to be misguided? Why should one with the following of several millions be afraid of a majority community, or of the minority being swamped by the majority? How did the Prophet work among the Arabs and the Mussulmans? How did he propagate Islam? Did he say he would propagate Islam only when he commanded a majority? I appeal to you for the sake of Islam to ponder over what I say. There is neither fair play nor justice in saying that the Congress must accept a thing, even if it does not believe in it and even if it goes counter to principles it holds dear.'

Rajaji said: 'I do not believe in Pakistan. But Mussulmans ask for it, Mr Jinnah asks for it, and it has become an obsession with them. Why not then say, "yes" to them just now? The same Mr Jinnah will later on realize the disadvantages of Pakistan and will forgo the demand.' I said: 'It is not fair to accept as true a thing which I hold to be untrue, and ask others to do or say in the belief that the demand will not be pressed when the time comes for settling in finally. If I hold the demand to be just, I should concede it this very day. I should not agree to it merely in order to placate Jinnah Saheb. Many friends have come and asked me to agree to it for the time being to placate Mr Jinnah, disarm his suspicions and to see how he reacts to it. But I cannot be party to a course of action with a false promise. At any rate, it is not my method.'

The Congress has no sanction but the moral one for enforcing its decisions. It believes that true democracy can only be the outcome of non-violence. The structure of a world federation can be raised only on a foundation of non-violence, and violence will have to be totally abjured from world affairs. If this is true, the solution of the Hindu-Muslim question, too, cannot be achieved by a resort to violence. If the Hindus tyrannize the Mussulmans, with what face will they talk of a world federation? It is for the same reason that I do not believe in the possibility of establishing world peace through violence as the English and American statesmen propose to do. The Congress has agreed to submitting all the differences to an impartial international tribunal and to abide by its decisions. If even this fairest of proposals is unacceptable, the only course that remains open is that of the sword, of violence. How can I persuade myself to agree to an impossibility? To demand the vivisection of a living organism is to ask for its very life. It is a call to war. The Congress cannot be party to such a fratricidal war. Those Hindus who, like Dr Moonje and Shri Savarkar, believe in the doctrine of the sword may seek to keep the Mussulmans under Hindus domination. I do not represent that section. I represent the Congress. You want to kill the Congress which is the goose that lays golden eggs. If you distrust the Congress, you may rest assured that there is to be perpetual war between the Hindus and the Mussulmans, and the country will be doomed to continue warfare and bloodshed. If such warfare is to be our lot, I shall not live to witness it.

It is for that reason that I say to Jinnah Saheb, "You may take it from me that whatever in your demand for Pakistan accords with considerations of justice and equity is lying in your pocket; whatever in the demand is contrary to justice and equity you can take only by the sword and in no other manner."

There is much in my heart that I would like to pour out before this assembly. One thing which was uppermost in my heart I have already dealt with. You may take it from me that it is with me a matter of life and death. If we Hindus and Mussulmans mean to achieve a heart unity, without the slightest mental reservation on the part of either, we must first unite in the effort to be free from the shackles of this empire. If Pakistan after all is to be a portion of India, what objection can there be for Mussulmans against joining this struggle for India's freedom? The Hindus and Mussulmans must, therefore, unite in the first instance on the issue of fighting for freedom. Jinnah Saheb thinks the war will last long. I do not agree with him. If the war goes on for six months more, how shall we be able to save China?

I, therefore, want freedom immediately, this very night, before dawn, if it can be had. Freedom cannot now wait for the realization of communal unity. If that unity is not achieved, sacrifices necessary for it will have to be much greater than would have otherwise sufficed. But the Congress must win freedom or be wiped out in the effort. And forget not that the freedom which the Congress is struggling to achieve will not be for the Congressmen alone but for all the forty cores of the Indian people. Congressmen must forever remain humble servants of the people.

The Quaid-i-Azam has said that the Muslim League is prepared to take over the rule from the Britishers if they are prepared to hand it over to the Muslim League, for the British took over the empire from the hands of the Muslims. This, however, will be Muslim Raj. The offer made by Maulana Saheb and by me does not imply establishment of Muslim Raj or Muslim domination. The Congress does not believe in the domination of any group or any community. It believes in democracy which includes in its orbit Muslims, Hindus, Christians, Parsis, Jews – every one of the communities inhabiting this vast country. If Muslim Raj is inevitable, then let it be; but how can we give it the stamp of our assent? How can we agree to the domination of one community over the others?

Millions of Mussulmans in this country come from Hindu stock. How can their homeland be any other than India? My eldest son embraced Islam some years back. What would his homeland be – Porbandar or the Punjab? I ask the Mussulmans: 'If India is not your homeland, what other country do you belong to? In what separate homeland would you put my son who embraced Islam?' His mother wrote him a letter after his conversion, asking him if he had on embracing Islam given up drinking which Islam forbids to its follower. To those who gloated over the conversion, she wrote to say: 'I do not mind his becoming a Mussulman, so much as his drinking. Will you, as pious Mussulmans, tolerate his drinking even after his conversion? He has reduced himself to the state of a rake by drinking. If you are going to make a man of him again, his conversion will have been turned to good account. You will, therefore, please see that he as a Mussulman abjures wine and women. If that change does not come about, his conversion goes in vain and our non-cooperation with him will have to continue.'

India is without doubt the homeland of all the Mussulmans inhabiting this country. Every Mussulman should therefore co-operate in the fight for India's freedom. The Congress does not belong to any one class or community; it belongs to the whole nation. It is open to Mussulmans to take possession of the Congress. They can, if they like, swamp the Congress by their numbers, and can steer it along the course which appeals to them. The Congress is fighting not on behalf of the Hindu but on behalf of the whole nation, including the minorities. It would hurt me to hear of a single instance of a Mussulman being killed by a Congressman. In the coming revolution, Congressmen will sacrifice their lives in order to protect the Mussulman against a Hindu's attack and vice versa. It is a part of their creed, and is one of the essentials of non-violence. You will be expected on occasions like these not to lose your heads. Every Congressman, whether a Hindu or a Mussulman, owes this duty to the organization which will render a service to Islam. Mutual trust is essential for success in the final nation-wide struggle that is to come.

I have said that much greater sacrifice will have to be made this time in the wake of our struggle because of the opposition from the Muslim League and from Englishmen. You have seen the secret circular issued by Sir Frederick Puckle. It is a suicidal course that he has taken. It contains an open incitement to organizations which crop up like mushrooms to combine to fight the Congress. We have thus to deal with an Empire whose ways are crooked. Ours is a straight path which we can tread even with our eyes closed. That is the beauty of Satyagraha.

In Satyagraha, there is no place for fraud or falsehood, or any kind of untruth. Fraud and untruth today are stalking the world. I cannot be a helpless witness to such a situation. I have traveled all over India as perhaps nobody in the present age has. The voiceless millions of the land saw in me their friend and representative, and I identified myself with them to an extent it was possible for a human being to do. I saw trust in their eyes, which I now want to turn to good account in fighting this Empire upheld on untruth and violence. However gigantic the preparations that the Empire has made, we must get out of its clutches. How can I remain silent at this supreme hour and hide my light under the bushel? Shall I ask the Japanese to tarry awhile? If today I sit quiet and inactive, God will take me to task for not using up the treasure He had given me, in the midst of the conflagration that is enveloping the whole world. Had the condition been different, I should have asked you to wait yet awhile. But the situation now has become intolerable, and the Congress has no other course left for it.

Nevertheless, the actual struggle does not commence this moment. You have only placed all your powers in my hands. I will now wait upon the Viceroy and plead with him for the acceptance of the Congress demand. That process is likely to take two or three weeks. What would you do in the meanwhile? What is the programme, for the interval, in which all can participate? As you know, the spinning wheel is the first thing that occurs to me. I made the same answer to the Maulana. He would have none of it, though he understood its import later. The fourteen fold constructive programme is, of course, there for you to carry out. What more should you do? I will tell you. Every one of you should, from this moment onwards, consider yourself a free man or woman, and act as if you are free and are no longer under the heel of this imperialism.

It is not a make-believe that I am suggesting to you. It is the very essence of freedom. The bond of the slave is snapped the moment he considers himself to be a free being. He will plainly tell the master: 'I was your bond slave till this moment, but I am a slave no longer. You may kill me if you like, but if you keep me alive, I wish to tell you that if you release me from the bondage, of your own accord, I will ask for nothing more from you. You used to feed and clothe me, though I could have provided food and clothing for myself by my labour. I hitherto depended on you instead of on God, for food and raiment. But God has now inspired me with an urge for freedom and I am today a free man, and will no longer depend on you.'

You may take it from me that I am not going to strike a bargain with the Viceroy for ministries and the like. I am not going to be satisfied with anything short of complete freedom. Maybe, he will propose the abolition of salt tax, the drink evil, etc. But I will say, 'Nothing less than freedom.'

Here is a mantra, a short one, that I give you. You may imprint it on your hearts and let every breath of yours give expression to it. The mantra is: "Do or Die". We shall either free India or die in the attempt; we shall not live to see the perpetuation of our slavery. Every true Congressman or woman will join the struggle with an inflexible determination not to remain alive to see the country in bondage and slavery. Let that be your pledge. Keep jails out of your consideration. If the Government keep me free, I will not put on the Government the strain of maintaining a large number of prisoners at a time, when it is in trouble. Let every man and woman live every moment of his or her life hereafter in the consciousness that he or she eats or lives for achieving freedom and will die, if need be, to attain that goal. Take a pledge, with God and your own conscience as witness, that you will no longer rest till freedom is achieved and will be prepared to lay down your lives in the attempt to achieve it. He who loses his life will gain it; he who will seek to save it shall lose it. Freedom is not for the coward or the faint-hearted.

A word to the journalists. I congratulate you on the support you have hitherto given to the national demand. I know the restrictions and handicaps under which you have to labour. But I would now ask you to snap the chains that bind you. It should be the proud privilege of the newspapers to lead and set an example in laying down one's life for freedom.

You have the pen which the Government can't suppress. I know you have large properties in the form of printing presses, etc., and you would be afraid lest the Government should attack them. I do not ask you to invite an attack of the printing-press voluntarily. For myself, I would not suppress my pen, even if the press was to be attacked. As you know my press was attacked in the past and returned later on. But I do not ask from you that final sacrifice. I suggest a middle way. You should now wind up your standing committee, and you may declare that you will give up the pen only when India has won her freedom. You may tell Sir Frederick Puckle that he can't expect from you a command performance, that his press notes are full of untruth, and that you will refuse to publish them. You will openly declare that you are wholeheartedly with the Congress. If you do this, you will have changed the atmosphere before the fight actually begins.

From the Princes I ask with all respect due to them a very small thing. I am a well-wisher of the Princes. I was born in a State. My grandfather refused to salute with his right hand any Prince other than his own. But he did not say to the Prince, as I felt he ought to have said, that even his own master could not compel him, his minister, to act against his conscience. I have eaten the Prince's salt and I would not be false to it. As a faithful servant, it is my duty to warn the Princes that if they will act while I am still alive, the Princes may come to occupy an honourable place in free India. In Jawaharlal's scheme of free India, no privileges or the privileged classes have a place. Jawaharlal considers all property to be State-owned. He wants planned economy. He wants to reconstruct India according to plan. He likes to fly; I do not. I have kept a place for the Princes and the Zamindars in India that I envisage. I would ask the Princes in all humility to enjoy through renunciation. The Princes may renounce ownership over their properties and become their trustees in the true sense of the term. I visualize God in the assemblage of people. The Princes may say to their people: 'You are the owners and masters of the State and we are your servants.' I would ask the Princes to become servants of the people and render to them an account of their own services. The Empire too bestows power on the Princes, but they should prefer to derive power from their own people; and if they want to indulge in some innocent pleasures, they may seek to do so as servants of the people. I do not want the Princes to live as paupers. But I would ask them: 'Do you want to remain slaves for all time? Why should you, instead of paying homage to a foreign power, not accept the sovereignty of your own people?' You may write to the Political Department: 'The people are now awake. How are we to withstand an avalanche before which even the large Empire is crumbling? We, therefore, shall belong to the people from today onwards. We shall sink or swim with them.' Believe me, there is nothing unconstitutional in the course I am suggesting. There are, so far as I know, no treaties enabling the Empire to coerce the Princes. The people of the States will also declare that though they are the Princes' subjects, they are part of the Indian nation and that they will accept the leadership of the Princes, if the latter cast their lot with the people, the latter will meet death bravely and unflinchingly, but will not go back on their word.

Nothing, however, should be done secretly. This is an open rebellion. In this struggle secrecy is a sin. A free man would not engage in a secret movement. It is likely that when you gain freedom you will have a C.I.D.

of your own, in spite of my advice to the contrary. But in the present struggle, we have to work openly and to receive bullets on our chest, without taking to heels.

I have a word to say to Government servants also. They may not, if they like, resign their posts yet. The late Justice Ranade did not resign his post, but he openly declared that he belonged to the Congress. He said to the Government that though he was a judge, he was a Congressman and would openly attend the sessions of the Congress, but that at the same time he would not let his political views warp his impartiality on the bench. He held a Social Reform Conference in the very Pandal of the Congress. I would ask all the Government servants to follow in the footsteps of Ranade and to declare their allegiance to the Congress as an answer to the secret circular issued by Sir Frederick Puckle.

This is all that I ask of you just now. I will now write to the Viceroy. You will be able to read the correspondence not just now but when I publish it with the Viceroy's consent. But you are free to aver that you support the demand to be put forth in my letter. A judge came to me and said: 'We get secret circulars from high quarters. What are we to do?' I replied, 'If I were in your place, I would ignore the circulars. You may openly say to the Government: "I have received your secret circular. I am, however, with the Congress. Though I serve the Government for my livelihood, I am not going to obey these secret circulars or to employ underhand methods." '

Soldiers too are covered by the present programme. I do not ask them just now to resign their posts and to leave the army. The soldiers come to me, Jawaharlal and the Maulana and say: 'We are wholly with you. We are tired of the Governmental tyranny.' To these soldiers I would say: You may say to the Government, 'Our hearts are with the Congress. We are not going to leave our posts. We will serve you so long as we receive our salaries. We will obey your just orders, but will refuse to fire on our own people.'

To those who lack the courage to do this much I have nothing to say. They will go their own way. But if you can do this much, you may take it from me that the whole atmosphere will be electrified. Let the Government then shower bombs, if they like. But no power on earth will then be able to keep you in bondage any longer.

If the students want to join the struggle only to go back to their studies after a while, I would not invite them to it. For the present, however, till the time that I frame a programme for the struggle, I would ask the students to say to their professors: 'We belong to the Congress. Do you belong to the Congress, or to the Government? If you belong to the Congress, you need not vacate your posts. You will remain at your posts but teach us and lead us unto freedom.' In all fights for freedom, the world over, the students have made very large contributions.

If in the interval that is left to us before the actual fight begins, you do even the little I have suggested to you, you will have changed the atmosphere and will have prepared the ground for the next step.

There is much I should yet like to say. But my heart is heavy. I have already taken up much of your time. I have yet to say a few words in English also. I thank you for the patience and attention with which you have listened to me even at this late hour. It is just what true soldiers would do. For the last 22 years, I have controlled my speech and pen and have stored up my energy. He is a true Brahmacharri who does not fritter away his energy. He will, therefore, always control his speech. That has been my conscious effort all these years. But today the occasion has come when I had to unburden my heart before you. I have done so, even though it meant putting a strain on your patience; and I do not regret having done it. I have given you my message and through you I have delivered it to the whole of India.

III

I have taken such an inordinately long time over pouring out, what was agitating my soul, to those whom I had just now the privilege of serving. I have been called their leader or, in the military language, their commander. But I do not look at my position in that light. I have no weapon but love to wield my authority over anyone. I do sport a stick which you can break into bits without the slightest exertion. It is simply my staff with the help of which I walk. Such a cripple is not elated, when he has been called upon to bear the greatest burden. You can share that burden only when I appear before you not as your commander but as a humble servant. And he who serves best is the chief among equals.

Therefore, I was bound to share with you such thoughts as were welling up in my breast and tell you, in as summary a manner as I can, what I expect you to do as the first step.

Let me tell you at the outset that the real struggle does not commence today. I have yet to go through much ceremonial as I always do. The burden, I confess, would be almost unbearable. I have to continue to reason in those circles with whom I have lost my credit and who have no trust left in me. I know that in the course of the last few weeks I have forfeited my credit with a large number of friends, so much so, that they have begun to doubt not only my wisdom but even my honesty. Now I hold my wisdom is not such a treasure which I cannot afford to lose; but my honesty is a precious treasure to me and I can ill-afford to lose it. I seem however to have lost it for the time being.

FRIEND OF THE EMPIRE

Such occasions arise in the life of the man who is a pure seeker after truth and who would seek to serve the humanity and his country to the best of his lights without fear or hypocrisy. For the last 50 years I have known no other way. I have been a humble servant of humanity and have rendered on more than one occasion such services as I could to the Empire, and here let me say without fear of challenge that throughout my career never have I asked for any personal favour. I have enjoyed the privilege of friendship as I enjoy it today with Lord Linlithgow. It is a friendship which has outgrown official relationship. Whether Lord Linlithgow will bear me out, I do not know, but there is a personal bond between him and myself. He once introduced me to his daughter. His son-in law, the A.D.C. was drawn towards me. He fell in love with Mahadev more than with me and Lady Anna and he came to me. She is an obedient and favourite daughter. I take interest in their welfare. I take the liberty to give out these personal and sacred tit-bits only to give you an example of the personal bond that will never interfere with the stubborn struggle on which, if it falls to my lot, I may have to launch against Lord Linlithgow, as the representative of the Empire. I will have to resist the might of that Empire with the might of the dumb millions with no limit but of non-violence as policy confined to this struggle. It is a terrible job to have to offer resistance to a Viceroy with whom I enjoy such relations. He has more than once trusted my word, often about my people. I would love to repeat that experiment, as it stands to his credit. I mention this with great pride and pleasure. I mention it as an example of my desire to be true to the Empire when that Empire for-feited my trust and the Englishman who was its Viceroy came to know it.

CHARLIE ANDREWS

Then there is the sacred memory of Charlie Andrews which wells up within me. At this moment the spirit of Andrews hovers about me. For me he sums up the brightest traditions of English culture. I enjoyed closer relations with him than with most Indians. I enjoyed his confidence. There were no secrets between us. We exchanged our hearts every day. Whatever was in his heart, he would blurt out without the slightest hesitation or reservation. It is true he was a friend of Gurudev but he looked upon Gurudev with awe. He had that peculiar humility. But with me he became the closest friend. Years ago he came to me with a note of introduction from Gokhale. Pearson and he were the first-rank specimens of Englishmen. I know that his spirit is listening to me.

Then I have got a warm letter of congratulations from the Metropolitan of Calcutta. I hold him to be a man of God. Today he is opposed to me.

VOICE OF CONSCIENCE

With all this background, I want to declare to the world, although I may have forfeited the regard of many friends in the West and I must bow my head low; but even for their friendship or love I must not suppress the voice of conscience – the promptings of my inner basic nature today. There is something within me impelling me to cry out my agony. I have known humanity. I have studied something of psychology. Such a man knows exactly what it is. I do not mind how you describe it. That voice within tells me, 'You have to stand against the whole world although you may have to stand alone. You have to stare in the face the whole world although the world may look at you with bloodshot eyes. Do not fear. Trust the little voice residing within your heart.' It says: 'Forsake friends, wife and all; but testify to that for which you have lived and for which you have to die. I want to live my full span of life. And for me I put my span of life at 120 years. By that time India will be free, the world will be free.'

REAL FREEDOM

Let me tell you that I do not regard England or for that matter America as free countries. They are free after their own fashion, free to hold in bondage coloured races of the earth. Are England and America fighting for the liberty of these races today? If not, do not ask me to wait until after the war. You shall not limit my concept of freedom. The English and American teachers, their history, their magnificent poetry have not said that you shall not broaden the interpretation of freedom. And according to my interpretation of that freedom I am constrained to say they are strangers to that freedom which their teachers and poets have described. If they will know the real freedom they should come to India. They have to come not with pride or arrogance but in the spirit of real earnest seekers of truth. It is a fundamental truth which India has been experimenting with for 22 years.

CONGRESS AND NON-VIOLENCE

Unconsciously from its very foundations long ago the Congress has been building on non-violence known as constitutional methods. Dadabhai and Pherozeshah who had held the Congress India in the palm of their hands became rebels. They were lovers of the Congress. They were its masters. But above all they were real servants. They never countenanced murder, secrecy and the like. I confess there are many black sheep amongst us Congressmen. But I trust the whole of India today to launch upon a non-violent struggle. I trust because of my nature to rely upon the innate goodness of human nature which perceives the truth and prevails during the crisis as if by instinct. But even if I am deceived in this I shall not swerve. I shall not flinch. From its very inception the Congress based its policy on peaceful methods, included Swaraj and the subsequent generations added non-violence. When Dadabhai entered the British Parliament, Salisbury dubbed him as a black man; but the English people defeated Salisbury and Dadabhai went to the Parliament by their vote. India was delirious with joy. These things however India has outgrown.

I WILL GO AHEAD

It is, however, with all these things as the background that I want Englishmen, Europeans and all the United Nations to examine in their hearts what crime had India committed in demanding Independence. I ask, is it right for you to distrust such an organization with all its background, tradition and record of over half a century and misrepresent its endeavours before all the world by every means at your command? Is it right that by hook or by crook, aided by the foreign press, aided by the President of the USA, or even by the Generalissimo of China who has yet to win his laurels, you should present India's struggle in shocking caricature? I have met the Generalissimo. I have known him through Madame Shek who was my interpreter; and though he seemed inscrutable to me, not so Madame Shek; and he allowed me to read his mind through her. There is a chorus of disapproval and righteous protest all over the world against us. They say we are erring, the move is inopportune. I had great regard for British diplomacy which has enabled them to hold the Empire so long. Now it stinks in my nostrils, and others have studied that diplomacy and are putting it into practice. They may succeed in getting, through these methods, world opinion on their side for a time; but India will speak against that world opinion. She will raise her voice against all the organized propaganda. I will speak against it. Even if all the United Nations opposed me, even if the whole of India forsakes me, I will say, "You are wrong. India will wrench with non-violence her liberty from unwilling hands." I will go ahead not for India's sake alone, but for the sake of the world. Even if my eyes close before there is freedom, non-violence will not end. They will be dealing a mortal blow to China and to Russia if they oppose the freedom of non-violent India which is pleading with bended knees for the fulfillment of debt long overdue. Does a creditor ever go to a debtor like that? And even when, India is met with such angry opposition, she says, 'We won't hit below the belt, we have learnt sufficient gentlemanliness. We are pledged to non-violence.' I have been the author of non-embarrassment policy of the Congress and yet today you find me talking this strong language. I say it is consistent with our honour. If a man holds me by the neck and wants to drown me, may I not struggle to free myself directly? There is no inconsistency in our position today.

APPEAL TO UNITED NATIONS

There are representatives of the foreign press assembled here today. Through them I wish to say to the world that the United Powers who somehow or other say that they have need for India, have the opportunity now to declare India free and prove their bona fides. If they miss it, they will be missing the opportunity of their lifetime, and history will record that they did not discharge their obligations to India in time, and lost the battle. I want the blessings of the whole world so that I may succeed with them. I do not want the United Powers to go beyond their obvious limitations. I do not want them to accept non-violence and disarm today. There is a fundamental difference between fascism and this imperialism which I am fighting. Do the British get from India which they hold in bondage. Think what difference it would make if India was to participate as a free ally. That freedom, if it is to come, must come today. It will have no taste left in it today. You who have the power to help cannot exercise it. If you can exercise it, under the glow of freedom what seems impossible, today, will become possible tomorrow. If India feels that freedom, she will command that freedom for China. The road for running to Russia's help will be open. The Englishmen did not die in Malaya or on Burma soil. What shall enable us to retrieve the situation? Where shall I go, and where shall I take the 4 crores of India? How is this vast mass of humanity to be aglow in the cause of world deliverance, unless and until it has touched and felt freedom. Today they have no touch of life left. It has been crushed out of them. If lustre is to be put into their eyes, freedom has to come not tomorrow, but today.

Do or Die.

I have pledged the Congress and the Congress will do or die.

quotes

'A coward is incapable of exhibiting love; it is the prerogative of the brave.'

'Non-cooperation with evil is a sacred duty.'

'You assist an evil system most effectively by obeying its orders and decrees. An evil system never deserves such allegiance. Allegiance to it means partaking of the evil.'

'A good person will resist an evil system with his or her whole soul.'

'Non-violence is the greatest force at the disposal of mankind. It is mightier than the mightiest weapon of destruction devised by the ingenuity of man.'

'It may be long before the law of love will be recognized in international affairs. The machineries of government stand between and hide the hearts of one people from those of another.'

'To forgive is not to forget. The merit lies in loving in spite of the vivid knowledge that the one that must be loved is not a friend.'

'You must be the change you wish to see in the world.'

'Whether humanity will consciously follow the law of love, I do not know. But that need not disturb me. The law will work just as the law of gravitation works, whether we accept it or not. The person who discovered the law of love was a far greater scientist than any of our modern scientists. Only our explorations have not gone far enough and so it is not possible for everyone to see all its workings.'

'Power is of two kinds. One is obtained by the fear of punishment and the other by acts of love. Power based on love is a thousand times more effective and permanent than the one derived from fear of punishment.'

'As soon as we lose the moral basis, we cease to be religious. There is no such thing as religion over-riding morality. Man, for instance, cannot be untruthful, cruel or incontinent and claim to have God on his side.'

'Non-violence and cowardice are contradictory terms. Non-violence is the greatest virtue, cowardice the greatest vice. Non-violence springs from love, cowardice from hate. Non-violence always suffers, cowardice would always inflict suffering. Perfect non-violence is the highest bravery. Non-violent conduct is never demoralizing, cowardice always is.'

'Non-violence is not a garment to be put on and off at will. Its seat is in the heart, and it must be an inseparable part of our being.'

'Fear of death makes us devoid both of valour and religion. For want of valour is want of religious faith.'

'There are times when you have to obey a call which is the highest of all, i.e. the voice of conscience even though such obedience may cost many a bitter tear, and even more, separation from friends, from family, from the state to which you may belong, from all that you have held as dear as life itself. For this obedience is the law of our being.'

'Whenever I see an erring man, I say to myself I have also erred; when I see a lustful man I say to myself, so was I once; and in this way I feel kinship with everyone in the world and feel that I cannot be happy without the humblest of us being happy.'

'An error does not become truth by reason of multiplied propagation, nor does truth become error because nobody will see it.'

'Suffering cheerfully endured, ceases to be suffering and is transmuted into an ineffable joy.'

'Non-violence requires a double faith, faith in God and also faith in man.'

'Non-cooperation is directed not against men but against measures. It is not directed against the Governors, but against the system they administer. The roots of non-cooperation lie not in hatred but in justice, if not in love.'

'I will far rather see the race of man extinct than that we should become less than beasts by making the noblest of God's creation, woman, the object of our lust.'

'The spirit of non-violence necessarily leads to humility. Non-violence means reliance on God, the rock of ages. If we would seek His aid, we must approach Him with a humble and contrite heart.'

'Abstract truth has no value unless it incarnates in human beings who represent it, by proving their readiness to die for it.'

'There is a higher court than courts of justice and that is the court of conscience. It supersedes all other courts.'

'God is, even though the whole world deny Him. Truth stands, even if there be no public support. It is self-sustained.'

'It is my own firm belief that the strength of the soul grows in proportion as you subdue the flesh.'

'My trust is solely in God. And I trust men only because I trust God. If I had no God to rely upon, I should be like Timon, a hater of my species.'

'It is any day better to stand erect with a broken and bandaged head then to crawl on one's belly, in order to be able to save one's head.'

'I am but a poor struggling soul yearning to be wholly good, wholly truthful and wholly non-violent in thought, word and deed, but ever failing to reach the ideal which I know to be true. It is a painful climb, but the pain of it is a positive pleasure to me. Each step upwards makes me feel stronger and fit for the next.'

'Moral authority is never retained by any attempt to hold on to it. It comes without seeking and is retained without effort.'

'Love never claims, it ever gives. Love ever suffers, never resents, never revenges itself.'

'Man has reason, discrimination and free-will such as it is. The brute has no such thing. It is not a free agent, and knows no distinction between virtue and vice, good and evil. Man, being a free agent, knows these distinctions, and when he follows his higher nature, shows himself far superior to the brute, but when he follows his baser nature can show himself lower then the brute.'

'A principle is the expression of perfection, and as imperfect beings like us cannot practise perfection, we devise every moment limits of its compromise in practice.'

'There is no principle worth the name if it is not wholly good.'

'It is easy enough to say, "I do not believe in God." For God permits all things to be said of Him with impunity. He looks at our acts. And any breach of His Law carries with it not its vindictive, but its purifying, compelling punishment.'

'Truth is by nature self-evident, as soon as you remove the cobwebs of ignorance that surround it, it shines clear.'

'I have found by experience that man makes his plans to be often upset by God, but, at the same time, where the ultimate goal is the search of truth, no matter how a man's plans are frustrated the issue is never injurious and often better then anticipated.'

'A "no" uttered from deepest conviction is better and greater than a "yes" merely uttered to please, or what is worse, to avoid trouble.'

'A clean confession, combined with a promise never to commit the sin again, when offered before one who has the right to receive it, is the purest type of repentance.'

'Purity of personal life is the one indispensable condition for building up a sound education.'

'Service which is rendered without joy helps neither the servant nor the served. But all other pleasures and possessions pale into nothingness before service which is rendered in a spirit of joy.'

'A true soldier does not argue as he marches, how success is going to be ultimately achieved. But he is confident that if he only plays his humble part well, somehow or other the battle will be won. It is in that spirit that every one of us should act. It is not given to us to know the future. But it is given to everyone of us to know how to do our own part well.'

'I do not want any patronage, as I do not give any. I am a lover of my own liberty, and so I would do nothing to restrict yours. I simply want to please my own conscience, which is God.'

'Of all the animal creation of God, man is the only animal who has been created in order that he may know his Maker. Man's aim in life is not therefore to add from day to day to his material prospects and to his material possessions, but his predominant calling is, from day to day to come nearer to his own Maker.'

'It has always been a mystery to me how men can feel themselves honoured by the humiliation of their fellow beings.'

'Spiritual relationship is far more precious than physical. Physical relationship divorced from spiritual is body without soul.'

'All the religions of the world, while they may differ in other respects, unitedly proclaim that nothing lives in this world but Truth.'

'Morality is the basis of things and truth is the substance of all morality.'

'Real suffering, bravely borne, melts even a heart of stone. Such is the potency of suffering. And there lies the key to Satyagraha.'

'There is an orderliness in the universe, there is an unalterable law governing everything and every being that exists or lives. It is no blind law; for no blind law can govern the conduct of living beings.'

'Where love is, there God is also.'

'There will have to be rigid and iron discipline before we achieve anything great and enduring, and that discipline will not come by mere academic argument and appeal to reason and logic. Discipline is learnt in the school of adversity.'

'Non-violence is not a quality to be evolved or expressed to order. It is an inward growth depending for sustenance upon intense individual effort.'

'I do dimly perceive that whilst everything around me is ever-changing, ever-dying, there is underlying all that change a living Power that is changeless, that holds all together, that creates, dissolves and recreates. That informing power or spirit is God. And since nothing else I see merely through the senses can or will persist, He alone is.'

'It is man's social nature which distinguishes him from the brute creation. If it is his privilege to be independent, it is equally his duty to be inter-dependent. Only an arrogant man will claim to be independent of everybody else and be self-contained.'

'Manliness consists not in bluff, bravado or lordliness. It consists in daring to do what is right and facing consequences whether it is in matters social, political or other. It consists in deeds, not in words.'

'Healthy discontent is the prelude to progress.'

'I reject any religious doctrine that does not appeal to reason and is in conflict with morality.'

'Breach of promise is a base surrender of truth.'

'Intellect takes us along in the battle of life to a certain limit, but at the crucial moment it fails us. Faith transcends reason. It is when the horizon is the darkest and human reason is beaten down to the ground that faith shines brightest and comes to our rescue.'

'Breach of promise is no less an act of insolvency than a refusal to pay one's debt.'

'Prayer is not asking. It is a longing of the soul. It is daily admission of one's weakness. It is better in prayer to have a heart without words than words without a heart.'

'The law of sacrifice is uniform throughout the world. To be effective it demands the sacrifice of the bravest and the most spotless.'

'Man becomes great exactly in the degree in which he works for the welfare of his fellow-men.'

'There should be truth in thought, truth in speech, and truth in action. To the man who has realised this truth in perfection, nothing else remains to be known because all knowledge is necessarily included in it.'

'I saw that nations like individuals could only be made through the agony of the Cross and in no other way. Joy comes not out of infliction of pain on others but out of pain voluntarily borne by oneself.'

'Courage has never been known to be a matter of muscle; it is a matter of the heart. The toughest muscle has been known to tremble before an imaginary fear. It was the heart that set the muscle atrembling.'

'When restraint and courtesy are added to strength, the latter becomes irresistible.'

'Have I not gazed at the marvellous mystery of the starry vault, hardly ever tiring of the great panorama?'

'An ounce of practice is worth more than tons of preaching.'

'To me art in order to be truly great must, like the beauty of Nature, be universal in its appeal. It must be simple in its presentation and direct in its expression, like the language of Nature.'

'God sometimes does try to the uttermost those whom He wishes to bless.'

'Suffering has its well-defined limits. Suffering can be both wise and unwise, and when the limit is reached, to prolong it would be not unwise but the height of folly.'

'I have worshipped woman as the living embodiment of the spirit of service and sacrifice.'

'Proved right should be capable of being vindicated by right means as against the rude, i.e. sanguinary means. Man may and should shed his own blood for establishing what he considers to be his right. He may not shed the blood of his opponent who disputes his "right".'

'I look only to the good qualities of men. Not being faultless myself, I won't presume to probe into the faults of others.'

'Everyone who wills can hear the inner voice. It is within everyone.'

'I have been a willing slave to this most exacting Master for more than half a century. His voice has been increasingly audible as years have rolled by. He has never forsaken me even in my darkest hour. He has saved me often against myself and left me not a vestige of independence. The greater the surrender to Him, the greater has been my joy.'

'Evil is, good or truth misplaced.'

'There is no human institution but has its dangers. The greater the institution, the greater the chances of abuse. Democracy is a great institution and therefore it is liable to be greatly abused. The remedy therefore is not avoidance of democracy but reduction of the possibility of abuse to a minimum.'

'I need no inspiration other than Nature's. She has never failed me yet. She mystifies me, bewilders me, sends me into ecstasies. Besides God's handiwork, does not man's fade into insignificance?'

'Man can never be a woman's equal in the spirit of selfless service with which nature has endowed her.'

'A certain degree of physical harmony and comfort is necessary, but above a certain level it becomes a hindrance instead of a help. Therefore the ideal of creating an unlimited number of wants and satisfying them seems to be a delusion and a snare.'

'I believe in the fundamental truth of all great religions of the world.'

'My life is one indivisible whole, and all my activities run into one another, and they all have their rise in my insatiable love of mankind.'

'The real ornament of woman is her character, her purity.'

'To deprive a man of his natural liberty and to deny to him the ordinary amenities of life is worse than starving the body; it is starvation of the soul the dweller in the body.'

'Humility cannot be an observance by itself. For, it does not lend itself to being deliberately practised. It is, however, an indispensable test of "Ahimsa". For one who has "Ahimsa" in him it becomes part of his very nature.'

'God, as Truth, has been for me a treasure beyond price. May He be so to every one of us.'

'Non-violence is the greatest force at the disposal of mankind. It is mightier than the mightiest weapon of destruction devised by the ingenuity of man.'

'Destruction is not the law of humans. Man lives freely only by his readiness to die, if need be, at the hands of his brother, never by killing him. Every murder or other injury, no matter for what cause, committed or inflicted on another is a crime against humanity.'

'The main purpose of life is to live rightly, think rightly, act rightly. The soul must languish when we give all our thought to the body.'

'Unwearied ceaseless effort is the price that must be paid for turning faith into a rich infallible experience.'

'Manliness consists in making circumstances subserve to ourselves.'

'Those who will not heed themselves perish. To understand this principle is not to be impatient, not to reproach fate, not to blame others. He who understands the doctrine of self-help blames himself for failure.'

'Surely conversion is a matter between man and his Maker who alone knows His creatures' hearts. A conversion without a clean heart is, in my opinion, a denial of God and Religion. Conversion without cleanliness of heart can only be a matter of sorrow, not joy, to a godly person.'

'I have not the shadow of a doubt that any man or woman can achieve what I have, if he or she would make the same effort and cultivate the same hope and faith. Work without faith is like an attempt to reach the bottom of a bottomless pit.'

'Ill-digested principles are, if anything, worse than ill-digested food, for the latter harms the body and there is a cure for it, whereas the former ruins the soul and there is no cure for it.'

'The essence of all religions is one. Only their approaches are different.'

'Restraint never ruins one's health. What ruins it, is not restraint but outward suppression. A really self-restrained person grows every day from strength to strength and from peace to more peace. The very first step in self-restraint is the restraint of thoughts.'

'We should meet abuse by forbearance. Human nature is so constituted that if we take absolutely no notice of anger or abuse, the person indulging in it will soon weary of it and stop.'

'True religion is not a narrow dogma. It is not external observance. It is faith in God and living in the presence of God. It means faith in a future life, in truth and Ahimsa. There prevails today a sort of apathy towards these things of the Spirit.'

'Only he can take great resolves who has indomitable faith in God and has fear of God.'

'A small body of determined spirits fired by an unquenchable faith in their mission can alter the course of history.'

'Man's nature is not essentially evil. Brute nature has been known to yield to the influence of love. You must never despair of human nature.'

'I may live without air and water, but not without Him. You may pluck out my eyes, but that cannot kill me. You may chop off my nose but that will not kill me. But blast my belief in God, and I am dead.'

'Freedom is never dear at any price. It is the breath of life. What would a man not pay for living?'

'I know, to banish anger altogether from one's breast is a difficult task. It cannot be achieved through pure personal effort. It can be done only by God's grace.'

'Everyone has faith in God though everyone does not know it. For everyone has faith in himself and that multiplied to the nth degree is God. The sum total of all that lives is God. We may not be God, but we are of God, even as a little drop of water is of the ocean.'

'There is no one without faults, not even men of God. They are men of God not because they are faultless, but because they know their own faults, they strive against them, they do not hide them, and are ever ready to correct themselves.'

'Non-violence and cowardice go ill together. I can imagine a fully armed man to be at heart a coward. Possession of arms implies an element of fear, if not cowardice. But true non-violence is an impossibility without the possession of unadulterated fearlessness.'

'Providence has its appointed hour for everything. We cannot command results, we can only strive.'

'The hardest metal yields to sufficient heat. Even so must the hardest heart melt before sufficiency of the heat of non-violence. And there is no limit to the capacity of non-violence to generate heat.'

'Rights accrue automatically to him who duly performs his duties. In fact the right to perform one's duties is the only right that is worth living for and dying for. It covers all legitimate rights. All the rest is grab under one guise or another and contains in it seed of Himsa.'

'It is good to see ourselves as others see us. Try as we may. We are never able to know ourselves fully as we are, especially the evil side of us. This we can do only if we are not angry with our critics but will take in good heart whatever they might have to say.'

'Far more indispensable than food for the physical body is spiritual nourishment for the soul. One can do without food for a considerable time, but a man of the spirit cannot exist for a single second without spiritual nourishment.'

'A dissolute character is more dissolute in thought than in deed. And the same is true of violence. Our violence in word and deed is but a feeble echo of the surging violence of thought in us.'

'Democracy must in essence, therefore, mean the art and science of mobilising the entire physical, economic and spiritual resources of all the various sections of the people in the service of the common good of all.'

'A principle is a principle and in no case can it be watered down because of our incapacity to live it in practice. We have to strive to achieve it, and the striving should be conscious, deliberate and hard.'

'A nation's culture resides in the hearts and in the soul of its people.'

'Who am I? I have no strength save what God gives me. I have no authority over my countrymen save the pure moral. If He holds me to be a pure instrument for the spread of non-violence in place of the awful violence now ruling the earth, He will give me the strength and show me the way. My greatest weapon is mute prayer. The cause of peace is therefore, in God's good hands.'

'I want to see India free in my life-time. But God may not consider me fit enough to see the dream of my life fulfilled. Then I shall quarrel, not with Him but with myself.'

'All compromise is based on give and take, but there can be no give and take on fundamentals. Any compromise on mere fundamentals is a surrender. For it is all give and no take.'

'Between husband and wife there should be no secrets from one another. I have a very high opinion of the marriage tie. I hold that husband and wife merge in each other. They are one in two or two in one.'

'It is the law of love that rules mankind. Had violence, i.e. hate, ruled us we should have become extinct long ago. And yet, the tragedy of it is that the so-called civilized men and nations conduct themselves as if the basis of society was violence.'

'It is foolish to think that by fleeing one can trick the dread god of death. Let us treat him as a beneficent angel rather than a dread god. We must face and welcome him whenever he comes.'

'The badge of the violent is his weapon, spear, sword or rifle. God is the shield of the non-violent.'

'It is unwise to be too sure of one's own wisdom. It is healthy to be reminded that the strongest might weaken and the wisest might err.'

'It is through truth and non-violence that I can have some glimpse of God. Truth and non-violence are my God. They are the obverse and reverse of the same coin.'

'Before the throne of the Almighty, man will be judged not by his acts but by his intentions. For God alone reads our hearts.'

'I worship God as Truth only. I have not yet found Him, but I am seeking after Him. I am prepared to sacrifice the things dearest to me in pursuit of this quest. Even if the sacrifice demanded my very life, I hope I may be prepared to give it.'

'Morality which depends upon the helplessness of a man or woman has not much to recommend it. Morality is rooted in the purity of our hearts.'

'An opponent is entitled to the same regard for his principles as we would expect others to have for ours. Non-violence demands that we should seek every opportunity to win over opponents.'

'Glory lies in the attempt to reach one's goal and not in reaching it.'

'Just as a man would not cherish living in a body other than his own, so do nations not like to live under other nations, however noble and great the latter may be.'

'No religion which is narrow and which cannot satisfy the test of reason, will survive the coming reconstruction of society in which the values will have changed and character, not possession of wealth, title or birth will be the test of merit.'

'Truth quenches untruth, love quenches anger, self-suffering quenches violence. This eternal rule is a rule not for saints only but for all.'

'How can one be compelled to accept slavery? I simply refuse to do the master's bidding. He may torture me, break my bones to atoms and even kill me. He will then have my dead body, not my obedience. Ultimately, therefore, it is I who am the victor and not he, for he has failed in getting me to do what he wanted done.'

'Power invariably elects to go into the hands of the strong. That strength may be physical or of the heart or, if we do not fight shy of the word, of the spirit. Strength of the heart connotes soul-force. Let it be remembered that physical force is transitory, even as the body is transitory. But the power of the spirit is permanent even as the spirit is everlasting.'

'My work will be finished if I succeed in carrying conviction to the human family, that every man or woman, however weak in body, is the guardian of his or her self-respect and liberty, and that this defence prevails, though the world be against the individual resister.'

'Confession of errors is like a broom which sweeps away the dirt and leaves the surface brighter and clearer. I feel stronger for confession.'

'We do not need to proselytise either by our speech or by our writing. We can only do so really with our lives. Let our lives be open books for all to study.'

'A customer is the most important visitor on our premises. He is not dependent on us. We are dependent on him. He is not an interruption of our work. He is the purpose of it. He is not an outsider to our business. He is part of it. We are not doing him a favour by serving him. He is doing us a favour by giving us the opportunity to do so.'

His Holiness Pope John Paul II

VICAR OF JESUS CHRIST, PATRIARCH OF THE WEST

'When you wonder about the mystery of yourself,
look to Christ, who gives you the meaning of life.'

The Life of Pope John Paul II

1920	18 May: Born in Wadowice Poland.
1942	Commences study for priesthood.
1946	Ordained as priest.
1956	Professor of Ethics at Lublin University.
1958	Auxiliary Bishop of Krakow.
1963	Becomes Archbishop.
1967	Named to the College of Cardinals.
1978	Elected Pope.
1979	Papal visit to homeland.
1981	Wounded by assassin.
1998	5 May: Becomes the longest serving Pontiff of the 20th century.
1998	Meets Castro and celebrates mass in Cuba.
2000	Celebrates Great Jubilee of the Year 2000, St Peter's Square.
	March: Special pilgrimage to the Middle East.
	May: Apostolic visit to Fátima, Portugal.
	October: Canonises 123 Blesseds, including 120 martyrs in
China.	Denounced by Chinese government.
2001	Parkinson's disease confirmed.
	May: First Pope to enter a mosque (1,300-year-old mosque in Damascus).
	16 September: After the 11 September terrorist attack on New York, the Pope is quick to offer prayers, and urges all those affected to show restraint and commit to peace.
2002	March: Addresses the 'grave scandal' of sex abuse in the Catholic Church.
	July: Visit to Toronto, Canada, Guatemala and Mexico.
	August: Visits the Krakow region of Poland.
2003	June: 100th pilgrimage to Croatia.
	September: Visits Slovenia. Aide has to complete his arrival speech as he is too ill – the first time in 102 foreign trips.
2004	*Urbi et Orbi* (city and world) Christmas message, his 27th Christmas as Pontiff.
2005	2 April: Dies at Vatican Apartments, Vatican City.

biography

'Man cannot live without love.'

– POPE JOHN PAUL II

Pope John Paul II is one of the most well-known, widely-loved and most respected people on the planet. He has probably been seen in person, by more people than any other individual in history.

He is the most travelled Pope in history, and a Pope who actively engages with people from all walks of life, all over the world. His call to everyone is to approach life positively, with love, hope and faith, and to proceed through life on the basis that we should 'Be not afraid.' He is a 'witness to hope' for all.

He speaks eight languages fluently and is the author of many scholarly books and dissertations. He has also established a reputation as a staunch defender of religious freedoms, human rights and cultural diversity. His endeavours to build greater bridges of understanding between other faiths and Christianity, including Judaism and Islam, have been widely endorsed.

He has also established himself as a man of ideas and an independent thinker who addresses the hard questions of human existence, and who is not afraid to disagree with popular opinion. His perspective on the human condition is a long-term one – beyond the short term, fickle faddishness of the currently fashionable. No wonder that some of his pronouncements are unpopular, as he seeks to communicate universal truths and wisdoms for the human condition.

His message may be difficult for many, as he asks the hard questions like 'What is good?' 'What is evil?' 'How are we to live?'

He seeks answers about the bigger ideas – and their consequences.

To see this frail old man greeted by adoring teenagers with an almost hysterical and tearful adulation normally reserved for pop stars, is to witness a special event indeed. And there are millions around the world who look to him in this special way, with a love and respect for his constancy of faith, his inspirational leadership and his belief in the teachings of the Church. To have lived his life and still be doing what he does in his advanced years, requires a powerful faith and a considerable wisdom – faith and wisdom informed by a long and rich perspective.

As one would expect, he does have his critics. Some blame him for failing to reform the Catholic Church itself, and for maintaining what some see as controversial teachings on contraception, homosexuality, ordaining women, priestly celibacy, etc, while failing to arrest a decline in both congregations and the relevance of lesser church leaders, not having achieved enough with Vatican II, etc., etc.

Yet at the International World Youth Day in Manila in The Philippines in 1995, he managed to draw a crowd of between five to seven million people, many of whom were young people with whom he engaged in humorous banter!

As the head of one billion Catholics around the world, millions have been touched by this Pope's "luminous" personal presence as he exhorts them to go positively into life and 'be not afraid'. He is the witness to hope for them all, for despite his manifold infirmities, he continues to inspire.

In 1997 His Holiness had guests stay overnight at the Castel Gandolfo outside Rome. They had been allocated a bedroom just under his, and before dawn each morning, they could hear through their ceiling, the noise of his walking cane tapping across the floor above. At breakfast, he asked his guests if the noise of his cane early in the morning may have been disturbing them. They replied that it was not a concern as they were getting up for mass in any case. But they asked him in return why he was awake so early in the morning.

'Because' he replied, 'I like to watch the sun rise.'

Karol Jozef Wojtyla was born on 18 May 1920, at Wadowice, Poland, the youngest of three children of father Karol, a military officer, and Emilia. They had lost their weeks-old infant daughter six years before Karol Junior was even born, and their first child, Karol's brother Edmund, was some 14 years his senior.

It was a loving household, and the young Karol was a healthy, intelligent, active and happy child. But tragedy struck the family again when Karol Jr was just nine years old… his mother died of heart disease. His elder brother was a young doctor, so young Karol became the focus of his father's life. This became even more the case when just three years later, his elder brother died of scarlet fever, contracted from a patient.

His father was a very religious man, and they lived across the street from the church where Karol Jr would often visit several times a day.

The young Karol was a strong, athletic, good-looking lad with a happy and carefree disposition, who participated in a variety of sports, and was also known as "Lolek the goalie".

He grew up in a Poland that was enjoying a short and historically rare period of independent freedom which ended, initially under the Nazis (1939–1944) and then the Communists (1945–1989).

Karol had a long-standing interest in the arts and Polish culture, and after high school, he attended Jagiellonian University, where he exhibited interests in literature, sports, hiking, theatre and acting, as well as religiously inspired poetry. He had always been interested in the Church and it was over a period of many years that Karol became aware that God was calling him to the priesthood.

On Friday 1 September 1939, a young Lolek was assisting at the morning mass in the Cathedral Church of Krakow, high atop the Wawel, the commanding hill which overlooks the ancient capital of Poland, when the sound of attacking German aircraft and retaliatory anti-aircraft fire began. The mass was brought to a prompt conclusion and young Karol ran back to their apartment to check on his father, the only family member he had left in the world. Fortunately he was unharmed.

The Germans took only a few weeks to subjugate Poland. Many Poles fled east, going nowhere in particular, just getting away from the Germans. Among them were young Karol and his father, leaving with just one suitcase. However they were soon to encounter another army heading west – the Russians, and the prevailing opinion was that Krakow even under occupation was better than the Russian alternative. So they walked back some 200 kilometres, arriving back in Krakow many days later.

Some 2,000,000 Poles were shipped out to work camps, and some 5,000 priests were sent to concentration camps, (over 2,000 priests and other religious personnel were killed). Anyone over the age of 16 without a work permit was in considerable peril. Karol managed to find a job as a store messenger for a restaurant which lasted for about a year, and then he found work in a lime quarry as a dynamiter and labourer, which he continued for about four years. It kept him alive and taught him about the dignity of hard work, workers and hardship.

As well as the manual labour, Karol involved himself in underground intellectual and cultural pursuits, as all Polish cultural expression was forbidden.

His father however had been getting weaker, and early in February 1941 when Karol returned home after work one day, he found his father dead. Karol was only 20 years old, and was now an orphan.

His involvement in the cultural resistance group now became an even more important focus, acting and writing in a Rhapsodic Theatre Group. He was contemplating a life in literature and the theatre. Indeed he was undergoing some vocational confusion, not sure in which direction to take his life.

He had been influenced by the mystic Jan Tyranowski, who urged young Karol to 'pray as a means of entering God's presence', and emphasised the need to 'abandon oneself to Christ'. Later, in 1941, Karol did eventually come to the conclusion that he would be a priest and started studying at an underground seminary. One night coming back from work, he was hit by a German military truck and was left for dead, after suffering concussion. Fortunately he was found by a passer-by who rendered assistance. He recovered, and the incident helped convince him that God did indeed have a purpose for his life and his commitment to God became even stronger. In the autumn of 1942, he walked into the residence of the Archbishop of Krakow and asked to be received as a candidate for the priesthood. He was accepted, and young Karol began to lead a secret life.

After the Warsaw uprising in August 1944, Hitler ordered the destruction of the city, and large numbers of Polish youth were rounded up as retribution. It was a lethal environment. Karol made his way across the city, hiding to avoid the German patrols, and eventually made it to the seminary, where he remained hidden with other seminarians, continuing his studies there until the European war was over in May 1945.

Poland has long been a strongly Catholic country, and even though the communists then quickly established themselves in power, the Church still remained strong in Poland. The Church needed men like Karol in the "front line", out among the community, and so he was ordained as a priest on 1 November 1946 and celebrated his first mass the following day.

Over the next few years he wrote doctrinal texts, studied, taught Catholicism and encouraged religious freedom to the extent that he could under the circumstances. He was a very able scholar and priest, and at the age of 26 the Church sent him to Rome to study for his Doctorate in theology, which he earned in 1948 at the Angelicum. His thesis concerned the nature of faith and the nature of human encounter with God.

He was then appointed Assistant Pastor at St Florian's Church in Krakow, in a community that included many intellectuals and students. He was always very interested in people and loved nature, and would often be out in the country with lay friends, both young men and women. He was not by nature didactic, but impressed people as being a good listener and questioner. And he was still interested in scholarship and literature – his first published poem at the time being entitled *Song of the Brightness of Water.*

However, the communist regime was making life hard in Poland. In the 1950s there were some 400,000 people in prisons across Poland.

In 1954 at the age of 34, he accepted a post teaching Ethics in the Philosophy department at Lublin. He was a demanding teacher with high standards that often went over the heads of some of his students. As one student, who became a priest, said in a later interview 'He was a terrible professor... I had no idea what he was talking about... Too difficult.' Nevertheless, he taught there for 24 years, specialising in Ethics. In December 1956 he was appointed Chair of Ethics at Lublin University.

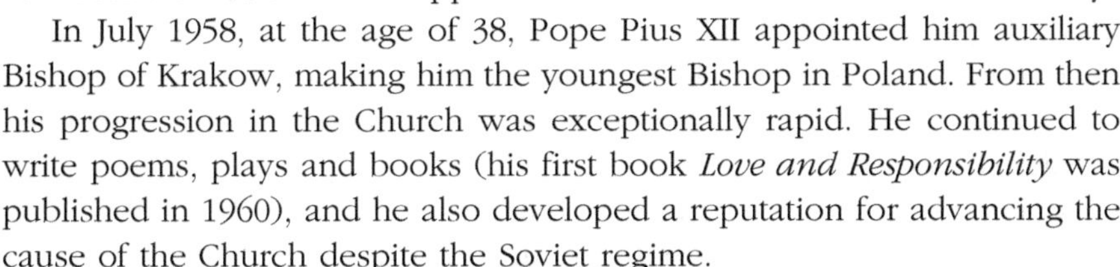

In July 1958, at the age of 38, Pope Pius XII appointed him auxiliary Bishop of Krakow, making him the youngest Bishop in Poland. From then his progression in the Church was exceptionally rapid. He continued to write poems, plays and books (his first book *Love and Responsibility* was published in 1960), and he also developed a reputation for advancing the cause of the Church despite the Soviet regime.

He also contributed significantly and often to The Second Vatican Council, which Pope John XXIII set in motion in 1962. This Council undertook to review and pursue a broad range of possible reforms, and was perhaps the most important move to reform the Catholic Church since the 16th century Ecumenical Council.

Bishop Karol Wojtyla had proven he had a considerable intellect, and he had some significant life experience. He was also renowned as being a very engaged listener – he cared about what people were telling him. Whether they were lay people he met socially, students, politicians, officials, community representatives, artists, scientists, members of the public, or people in his confessionals, he was interested in what they had to say and what they thought.

He gradually came to the conclusion that many of the crises of the modern world were indeed crises of ideas – that the wrong thinking had brought people to these crises. History (what actually happened) was a result of culture and the ideas that formed culture. Flawed ideas produced flawed social results. So ideas mattered – especially about those universal questions of life... about how to live.

Some of the still youngish bishop's conclusions were that as a consequence of being able to formulate ideas, the human person is a moral being. In that situation, he believed that Christ centred hope was the truth of the world.

In December 1963, Pope Paul VI named him Archbishop of Krakow, and he proved himself a very able pastor in the face of communist persecution. During the next few years Wojtyla worked ceaselessly across Poland, gaining concessions from the communist government and widespread support from the public, all the while contributing to Vatican policy. He played a prominent role in the formulation of the Declaration on Religious Freedom (a statement defining how the Vatican saw fundamental rights of religious freedom), and on 26 June 1967 Pope Paul VI appointed him a Cardinal of the Church.

On 16 October 1978, Archbishop Wojtyla was elected by the Cardinals of the Catholic Church as successor to Pope John Paul I, who died from a heart attack after a papacy of only 33 days. Karol Wojtyla became the third Pope during the year of 1978 on 16 October, the first non-Italian to hold the office since Hadrian VI, 455 years earlier (1522-3) and the first Slavic Pope. Wojtyla, comparatively young at 58 years old, was seen as an excellent compromise choice, and adopted his predecessor's name to become John Paul II, partly as a mark of respect, and partly to show a continuation of policy.

One of his most famous exhortations during his first public pronouncement to the world was that God wants us not to fear life; that we are to 'Be not afraid'.

Not even eight months after his inauguration, he returned to Poland as Pope on 2 June 1979, and in so doing, aiding the cause of Solidarity, the first independent labour movement in the Soviet bloc. He celebrated mass out in the open, drawing a crowd of some 3,000,000 people to see him outside Krakow Cathedral. During those days, it was estimated that some 13,000,000 Poles saw him in person.

Thereafter, the pace was unrelenting. In April 1980, he heard the confessions of the faithful for the first time in St Peter's Basilica, on Good Friday.

Then tragedy struck, this time in the form of an assassin's bullet on 13 May 1981, when he was shot in the abdomen and hand by a young Turk, Mehmet Alì Agca, in St Peter's Square.

Just days later, on 17 May, while recovering in hospital, John Paul II forgave his would-be assassin, reciting the *Angelus* at Gemelli Hospital: 'Pray for the brother who shot me, whom I have sincerely forgiven.'

He returned to the Vatican after some 20 days of recovery. But on 20 June, he was back in hospital because of an infection linked to the shooting. It was another nine days before he was able to leave the hospital again.

Thereafter, the work continued apace. In June 1982 he met with Ronald Reagan at the Vatican, and on 15 September 1982 he received Palestine Liberation Organization leader Yasser Arafat, predictably enough provoking criticism from Israel and Jewish groups. However, in 1986 John Paul II became the first Pope to visit a Jewish synagogue, and during the visit, condemned the persecution of Jews.

In 1984 full diplomatic relations were established between the Vatican and the USA.

The Pope's agenda for change was seemingly without end. As well as travelling and meeting international leaders and other people from all over the world, he continued his policy development and writing, including the *Notes on The Correct Way to Present The Jews and Judaism in Preaching and Catechesis in the Roman Catholic Church* (June 1985) and *Mulieris Dignitatem* his apostolic letter on the dignity of women (August 1988).

In September 1989 the first post World War II non-communist leader of Poland was elected, and on 1 December 1989, he held the first meeting ever between a Pope and a Kremlin chief, meeting with Mikhail Gorbachev at the Vatican, where they announced the establishment of diplomatic ties between the Vatican and Moscow.

But in July 1992 he was back in hospital, this time undergoing surgery to remove a benign intestinal tumor, leaving the Gemelli Polyclinic some 11 days later.

The health nightmare continued, when just over a year later in November 1993, he dislocated his right shoulder during a fall at the end of the audience in the Hall of Benediction. Another day in hospital for an operation, and his shoulder was immobilised for a month.

In December 1993, the Pope officiated over the establishment of diplomatic relations between Israel and the Vatican, and in Jerusalem, signed an agreement regulating relations between the Holy See and Israel.

In 1994 he was named *Time Magazine's* Man of the Year and referred to as "John Paul, Superstar." because of his personal magnetism. The question was raised: 'how could this passionate and persuasive defender of human rights, be so doctrinaire when it came to issues like birth control, divorce etc?'.

The magazine's story reflected the opinions of many that 'Christianity is a body of fixed beliefs rather than a faith that ought to be adapted to modern circumstances.' Thus the Pope was the voice of an authoritative tradition – the Pope was not imposing his personal views upon Catholicism. The Church was but the custodian of a body of truths, a 'deposit of faith'.

The Pope did emphasise that there should be no boundaries to the charity with which the Church proposes the truths of which it is the custodian. 'The truth' he said to the bishops in Chicago, 'must always be proposed in love.'

The Pope fell again on 28 April 1994, this time fracturing his right femur. He was taken to hospital where he underwent hip replacement surgery. After a month in hospital, during which time he celebrated his 74th birthday on 18 May, he was released on 27 May.

His extraordinary endeavours continued, however. In September 1994 Israel's first ambassador to the Vatican presented his credentials to the Pope, and in October 1994 the Palestine Liberation Organization established official relations with the Vatican. Earlier in October, the Pope's book *Crossing The Threshold of Hope* was published. This work was an expression of the Pope's core conviction that Jesus Christ is the answer to the question of every human life.

Addressing the UN in 1995, near the end of a "century of wickedness", he famously described himself as a 'Witness to Hope'.

In March 1996 John Paul II made his first visit to a reunified Germany, but on 6 October 1996, he was back in hospital again, this time for surgery to remove an inflamed appendix.

In November his memoir *Gift and Mystery* was published. This memoir was a celebration of the 50th anniversary of his priestly ordination, and its key message was that 'to be an effective priest, meant above all to be a holy priest'.

At the age of 77 he regained his strength sufficiently to stage his own major coup in January 1998, when he went to Cuba to celebrate mass and meet the people and Fidel Castro, who even changed out of his military outfit into a business suit for the occasion!

Seemingly to be continually reviewing the relevance of the Church's teachings across the spectrum of human activity, and experimenting with ways of spreading the word, the Vatican tried a musical experiment on 23 March 1999, releasing a gospel music CD with Sony/Columbia, entitled ABBÀ PATER, recorded by a young people's orchestra at the Church of Santa Caterina d'Alessandria.

The year 2000 was of course a momentous year in the history of the Christian Church, and as part of this Great Jubilee Year, for the first time ever, the Pope celebrated both the midnight mass and the traditional Christmas Urbi et Orbi (City and World) message in St Peter's Square between 24 and 25 December. But even before that, the year had been a particularly busy one.

This was also the year that the Middle East was back on the agenda. Between 20 and 26 March, the Pope met with the leaders of Israel, Jordan and the Palestinian authority, visiting Bethlehem, the Sea of Galilee, Jerusalem, the Jordan River and Nazareth.

A few weeks later, in early May, he made an apostolic visit to Fátima in Portugal.

In China, on 1 October the Pope canonised 123 Blesseds, 120 of whom were martyrs. The Chinese Government responded with considerable displeasure, denouncing the Pope's actions and accusing foreign missionaries and their followers of "notorious crimes" in China.

The extraordinary pressure was inevitably taking its toll however, and in 2001 there was more bad health news – his left hand had been trembling for some time now, he found it difficult to walk quickly, and he had also developed a stoop. It was not a surprise to many when on 3 January 2001, Parkinson's disease was confirmed.

But his work went on. On 21 January 2001 he named 37 new Cardinals.

Then in May he achieved another inter-religious milestone, when he entered a 1,300-year-old mosque in Damascus, and thus became the first Pope ever to enter a mosque.

The 11 September attacks on New York in 2001 were a grave challenge

biography

not only to the Americans, but to the world. The Pope was quick to not only offer prayers, but also to try and reduce the potential for further possible major conflict, by urging all those affected to show restraint and commitment to peaceful means of resolving differences.

And as if that were not enough, the widespread revelations of sex abuse in the Catholic Church had become an issue that demanded addressing. On 21 March 2002, the Pope referred to this as a "grave scandal" and in April he summoned the 12 American cardinals to the Vatican for a special meeting, declaring that there was never a place in the Catholic Church for priests who abuse children.

Just a couple of months later, in July, the Pope then set off for Toronto, Canada, the first part of a journey that would also take him to Guatemala and Mexico. And then astonishingly, the very next month, he began a four-day visit to the Krakow region on 16 August 2002.

His landmark 100th pilgrimage was not until the following year, when he commenced a five-day visit to Croatia on 5 June 2003. But when he visited nearby Slovakia on 11 September later the same year, he was suffering from both Parkinson's disease and hip and knee ailments. For the first time in over 100 foreign trips, he failed to complete his arrival address and one of his aides had to finish his speech for him.

But the spirit was still strong, and despite his infirmities, he continued to travel and appear before the people. In late 1995 the largest crowd in human history gathered to see him in the Philippines.

In 2004 he gave his Urbi et Orbi (city and world) Christmas message, his 27th Christmas as Pontiff. Because of his ailing health his message was his shortest yet, but it was still as powerful as ever. The 84-year-old Pope was still calling 'Men and women of good will, of every people on the earth' to heed God's message of peace: 'You, Prince of Peace, help us to understand that the only way to build peace is to flee in horror from evil, and to pursue goodness with courage and perseverance.'

Courage and perseverance… No longer able to walk, he sat hunched on his wheeled throne at the midnight mass, and spoke his message once again.

It was his second engagement in less than 12 hours.

On 3 April 2004, the news blared from every news source, "Pope John Paul II, who helped topple communism in Europe, is dead".

Amidst a spontaneous global outpouring of grief the news was announced, "Our beloved holy father John Paul has returned to the house of the father. The holy father's final hours were marked by the un-iterrupted prayer of all those who were assisting him in his pious death".

wisdom

Are you a believer? (Is there a God?)

There was not a time in presenting on *Collective Wisdom* to Probus groups (retirees, typically a room full of 100 or more elderly citizens of an average age of 70 or so) that I would not be asked the "God question" – as I came to call it. What was more, young people would find their own way of asking the same question in private after the conclusion of a presentation and a corporate audience would steer completely clear of the topic altogether.

Now, religion is not a topic for polite conversation I had always been taught, and yet it was astounding how many people would raise the "God question" or an answer or view on another question would lead to it.

Some six months after the publication of *Collective Wisdom* I commenced dating a terrific young woman who was a dedicated "Christian". She was intelligent, fun loving, had a laugh that filled a room – and asked "ultimate questions". She challenged me to look at the "God question". Now I had been raised in a Catholic family and school. I accepted the place of God and the Church in my life, was certainly not devout but continued to attend Mass and be interested.

So between dating a girl and being asked at the conclusion of presentations my view of the "God question" I started to seriously examine it for myself. This seeking of wisdom and understanding has been tremendously beneficial to me, my friends and people I have contact with on a day-to-day basis.

In short, when I was about to publish *Collective Wisdom* I had seen an excellent Warren Miller movie on skiing – it showed resorts all around the world – and I will never forget seeing the ski fields of the Dolomite region of Italy. I was sold and vowed to myself that if the book goes alright that I would travel overseas and ski on the Italian ski fields.

Well the rest is history, in the sense that the book did do well – I travelled and went skiing but what was to be more important was that I got to see at close quarters a man whom I had come to respect though not know much about, Pope John Paul II.

When I selected 80 people I would like to interview for *Collective Wisdom* I wrote to the heads of all the major religions in Australia – Anglican, Moslem, Buddhist, Jewish, Uniting Church. As things turned out, only Cardinal Clancy, the most senior cleric of the Catholic Church in Australia responded in the affirmative to my request for an interview. Strange, I thought.

The interview went well and some months later, when contemplating a trip to Italy, I made contact with the Cardinal's office and inquired as to how I would be able to meet the Holy Father, John Paul II. The Cardinal's assistant was very helpful and the Cardinal made available to me a ticket to attend mass on Christmas Eve at St Peter's Basilica in Vatican City.

What this meant was being within five metres of the Pontiff at Midnight Mass.

I include this story as it was a key step to my quest to answer the "God question".

Fundamentally then I came to understand *that a man that stands for nothing may well fall for anything'*. It seemed that resolving for oneself the "God question" had been an imperative part of the life journey of all the people I most admired. And that, most importantly, any particular answer was definitely not as important as the sincere quest to find an answer.

There are countless examples that I come across day-to-day that demonstrate that we all seem to have an innate yearning for our life to have some meaning. It seems that the ways to attempt to satisfy this desire are many – more money, status, power, holidays, clothes, cars, flat screen TVs and the like. Not all of these attempts lead to fulfilment.

In my own search, I have not been able to believe that I am the biggest and best thing going on in the universe, nor anyone I have heard about. It seems extremely unlikely to me that the wind, the rain, the mountains, forests, animals and the like are just random events in a world that seems so ordered. And I have never been able to answer the question of who or what caused the "big bang" that started the world from nothing?

No matter what way one formally expresses their view I came to see that there must be something or someone greater than me. Which, being intimately acquainted with my foibles, was a relief to me. And concluded that the "seeking" had made me a better, less superficial, person.

Pope John Paul II stood for God and Man in staring down the evils of Nazism, took a bullet in the fight against Soviet Communism, endlessly affirmed the inviolable sacredness of human life from conception until a natural death, challenged all regimes to acknowledge religious freedom as a human right, exhorted all people of good will to understand freedom as the opportunity to do good rather than licence to do as one pleases, and begged that we 'be not afraid' to seek wisdom and understanding!

His is an example of standing for something, and particularly for a young person like myself, an inspiration where typically one only encounters people who stand for their own self-interest.

words

Have mercy on me, O God! Psalm 51 [50]

General Audience, Castel Gandolfo – Wednesday, 30 July 2003

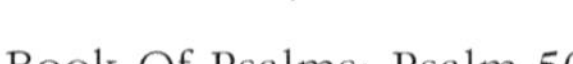

Book Of Psalms: Psalm 50

3 Have mercy on me, O God, according to thy great mercy. And according to the multitude of thy tender mercies blot out my iniquity. 4 Wash me yet more from my iniquity, and cleanse me from my sin. 5 For I know my iniquity, and my sin is always before me.

6 To thee only have I sinned, and have done evil before thee: that thou mayst be justified in thy words and mayst overcome when thou art judged. 7 For behold I was conceived in iniquities; and in sins did my mother conceive me. 8 For behold thou hast loved truth: the uncertain and hidden things of thy wisdom thou hast made manifest to me. 9 Thou shalt sprinkle me with hyssop, and I shall be cleansed: thou shalt wash me, and I shall be made whiter than snow. 10 To my hearing thou shalt give joy and gladness: and the bones that have been humbled shall rejoice.

11 Turn away thy face from my sins, and blot out all my iniquities. 12 Create a clean heart in me, O God: and renew a right spirit within my bowels. 13 Cast me not away from thy face; and take not thy holy spirit from me. 14 Restore unto me the joy of thy salvation, and strengthen me with a perfect spirit. 15 I will teach the unjust thy ways: and the wicked shall be converted to thee.

16 Deliver me from blood, O God, thou God of my salvation: and my tongue shall extol thy justice. 17 O Lord, thou wilt open my lips: and my mouth shall declare thy praise. 18 For if thou hadst desired sacrifice, I would indeed have given it: with burnt offerings thou wilt not be delighted. 19 A sacrifice to God is an afflicted spirit: a contrite and humbled heart, O God, thou wilt not despise. 20 Deal favourably, O Lord, in thy good will with Sion; that the walls of Jerusalem may be built up.

21 Then shalt thou accept the sacrifice of justice, oblations and whole burnt offerings: then shall they lay calves upon thy altar.

Source: http://www.drbo.org

1. For the fourth time during our reflections on the Liturgy of Lauds, we hear proclaimed Psalm 51 [50], the famous Miserere. Indeed, it is presented anew to us on the Friday of every week, so that it may become an oasis of meditation in which we can discover the evil that lurks in the conscience and beg the Lord for purification and forgiveness. Indeed, as the Psalmist confesses in another supplication, 'O Lord... no man living is righteous before you' (Ps 143 [142]: 2). In the Book of Job we read: 'How can man be righteous before God? How can he who is born of woman be clean? Behold, even the moon is not bright, and the stars are not clean in his sight; how much less man, who is a maggot, and the son of man, who is a worm!' (25: 4-6).

These are strong, dramatic words that are intended to portray the full seriousness and gravity of the limitations and frailty of the human creature, his perverse capacity to sow evil and violence, impurity and falsehood. However, the message of hope of the Miserere which the Psalter puts on the lips of David, a converted sinner, is this: God can 'blot out, wash and cleanse' the sin confessed with a contrite heart (cf. Ps 51[50]: 2-3). The Lord says, through the voice of Isaiah, even if 'your sins are scarlet, they shall be as white as snow; though they are red like crimson, they shall become like wool' (Is 1: 18).

2. This time we will reflect briefly on the end of Psalm 51 [50], a finale that is full of hope, for the person praying knows that God has forgiven him (cf. vv. 17-21). On his lips is praise of the Lord, which he is on the point of proclaiming to the world, thereby witnessing to the joy felt by the soul purified from evil, hence, freed from remorse (cf. v. 17).

The person praying witnesses clearly to another conviction, making a link with the teaching reiterated by the prophets (cf. Is 1: 10-17; Am 5: 21-25; Hos 6: 6): the most pleasing sacrifice that rises to the Lord like a fragrance, a pleasant odour (cf. Gn 8: 21), is not the holocaust of bulls and lambs, but rather of 'the broken and contrite heart' (Ps 51 [50]: 19).

The Imitation of Christ, a text so dear to the Christian spiritual tradition, repeats this same recommendation of the Psalmist: 'Humble repentance for sins is the sacrifice that pleases you, its fragrance far sweeter than the smoke of incense... It is there that one is purified and every evil washed away' (cf. III 52, 4).

3. The Psalm ends on an unexpected note in an utterly different perspective that even seems contradictory (cf. vv. 20-21). From the final supplication of a single sinner, it becomes a prayer for the rebuilding of the city of Jerusalem, which takes us from the time of David to that of the city's destruction

centuries later. Moreover, having voiced the divine rejection of animal sacrifices in v. 18, the Psalm proclaims in v. 21 that it is in these same burnt offerings that God will take delight.

It is clear that the last passage is a later addition, made at the time of the Exile and intended, in a certain sense, to correct or at least to complete the perspective of the Davidic Psalm on two points: on the one hand, it was not deemed fit that the entire Psalm be restricted to an individual prayer; it was also necessary to think of the grievous situation of the whole city. On the other hand, there was a desire to give a new dimension to the divine rejection of ritual sacrifices; this rejection could be neither complete nor definitive, for it was a cult that God himself had prescribed in the Torah. The person who completed the Psalm had a valid intuition: he grasped the needy state of sinners, their need for sacrificial mediation. Sinners cannot purify themselves on their own; good intentions are not enough. An effective external mediation is required. The New Testament was to reveal the full significance of this insight, showing that Christ, in giving his life, achieved a perfect sacrificial mediation.

4. In his Homilies on Ezechiel, St Gregory the Great shows a good understanding of the change of outlook that occurs between vv. 19 and 21 of the Miserere. He suggests an interpretation that we too can accept as a conclusion to our reflection. St Gregory applies v. 19, which speaks of a contrite heart, to the earthly life of the Church, and v. 21, which speaks of burnt offerings, to the Church in heaven.

Here are the words of that great Pontiff: 'Holy Church has two lives: one that she lives in time, the other that she receives eternally; one with which she struggles on earth, the other that is rewarded in heaven; one with which she accumulates merits, the other that henceforth enjoys the merits earned. And in both these lives she offers a sacrifice: here below, the sacrifice of compunction, and in heaven above, the sacrifice of praise. Of the former sacrifice it is said: "The sacrifice acceptable to God is a broken spirit." (Ps 51 [50]: 19); of the latter it is written: 'Then will you delight in right sacrifices, in burnt offerings and in whole burnt offerings' (Ps 51 [50]: 21). In both, flesh is offered, since the sacrifice of the flesh is the mortification of the body, up above; the sacrifice of the flesh is the glory of the Resurrection in praise to God. In heaven, flesh will be offered as a burnt holocaust when it is transformed into eternal incorruptibility, and there will be no more conflict for us and nothing that is mortal, for our flesh will endure in everlasting praise, all on fire with love for him.' *(Omelie su Ezechiele/2, Rome 1993, p. 271)*

To the English-speaking pilgrims and visitors

I extend a special welcome to the English-speaking visitors and pilgrims here today, including the groups from Scotland, the Holy Land, Saint Lucia and the United States. May your visit to Castel Gandolfo and Rome bring you peace and hope. Upon all of you I invoke the grace and peace of our Lord Jesus Christ. Happy holidays!

To young people, the sick and newly-weds

Lastly, I greet the young people, the sick and the newly-weds. I invite you, dear young people, to dedicate part of your summer holidays to meaningful experiences of solidarity. I hope that you, dear sick people, will benefit from this time of rest. May you, dear newly-weds, enjoy the serenity of your union during the holidays.

You have the Words of Eternal Life

Message to Young People for the 11th World Youth Day – 1996

'Lord, to whom shall we go? You have the words of eternal life' (Jn 6:68).

Dear Young People,

1. I long to see you, that I may impart to you some spiritual gift to strengthen you, that is, that we may be mutually encouraged by each other's faith, both yours and mine' (Rom 1:11-12).

The Apostle Paul's words to the Christians of Rome summarize the sentiment with which I address you all, as we begin to prepare ourselves for the 11th World Youth Day.

Indeed, I come in spirit to you with this same wish, to meet you in every corner of the earth, wherever you face the intense, daily adventure of life: in your families, where you study or work, in the communities where you gather to hear the word of the Lord and to open your hearts to Him in prayer.

My gaze turns in particular to the young people who are personally involved in too many of the tragedies that still wound humanity: those suffering from war, from violence, from hunger and poverty, thus prolonging the suffering of Christ who, with His Passion, is close to those oppressed by the burden of pain and injustice.

In 1996 World Youth Day will take place in diocesan communities, as usual, in expectation of the new world meeting that will take us to Paris in 1997.

The Future Belongs to the Younger Generation

2. We are journeying towards the Great Jubilee of the Year 2000, an appointment for which in my Apostolic Letter *Tertio millennio adveniente*, I invited the whole Church to prepare with conversion of heart and life.

I also ask you now to undertake this preparation with the same spirit and goals. I entrust to you a plan of action which, based on the words of the Gospel and corresponding to the themes presented to the whole Church for each year, will serve as a guide for the next World Youth Days:

1997: 'Teacher, where are you staying? Come and see' (Jn 1:38-39).
1998: 'The Holy Spirit will teach you all things' (Jn 14:26).

1999: 'The Father loves you' (Jn 16:27).
2000: 'The Word became flesh and dwelt among us' (Jn 1:14).

3. I am appealing especially to you, young people, to look to the epochal threshold of the year 2000, remembering that 'the future of the world and the Church belongs to the younger generation, to those who, born in this century, will reach maturity in the next, the first century of the new millennium... If they succeed in following the road which he points out to them, they will have the joy of making their own contribution to his presence in the next century' (*Tertio millennio adveniente*, n. 58).

As we approach the Great Jubilee, may you be accompanied by the conciliar Constitution, *Gaudium et spes*, which I want to recommend to all of you, as I did to your peers from the European continent in Loreto last September. It is a 'valuable and ever youthful document... Reread it attentively. You will find in it the light to discern your vocation as men and women called to live in this both marvelous and dramatic era, as artisans of brotherhood and builders of peace' (Angelus, 10 September 1995; *L'Osservatore Romano*, English edition, 13 September, p. 2, n. 2).

4. 'Lord, to whom shall we go?' The goal and target of our life is He, the Christ, who awaits us – each one singly and all together – to lead us across the boundaries of time to the eternal embrace of the God who loves us.

But if eternity is our horizon as people starving for truth and thirsting for happiness, history is the setting of our daily commitment. Faith teaches us that man's destiny is written in the heart and mind of God, who directs the course of history. It also teaches us that the Father puts in our hands the task of beginning to build here on earth the "Kingdom of Heaven" which the Son came to announce and which will find its fulfilment at the end of time.

It is our duty then to live in history, side by side with our peers, sharing their worries and hopes, because the Christian is and must be fully a man of his time. He cannot escape into another dimension, ignoring the tragedies of his era, closing his eyes and heart to the anguish that pervades life. On the contrary, it is he who, although not "of" this world, is immersed "in" this world every day, ready to hasten to wherever there is a brother in need of help, a tear to be dried, a request for help to be answered. On this will we be judged!

Charity is the High Road to the Great Jubilee.

5. Remembering the Master's warning: 'I was hungry and you gave me food, I was thirsty and you gave me drink, I was a stranger and you welcomed me, I was naked and you clothed me, I was sick and you visited

me, I was in prison and you came to me' (Mt 25:35-36), we must put the "new commandment" into practice (Jn 13:34).

Thus we will oppose what today seems to be the "disintegration of civilization", in order vigorously to reaffirm the "civilization of love" which alone can open to the men of our time horizons of true peace and lasting justice in lawfulness and solidarity.

Charity is also the high road that must lead us to the goal of the Great Jubilee. To reach this appointment, we need to be able to confront ourselves and undertake a rigorous examination of conscience, the indispensable premise for a radical conversion, which can transform our life and give it an authentic meaning which enables believers to love God with all their heart, with all their soul and with all their strength, and to love their neighbor as themselves (cf. Lk 10:27).

By conforming your daily life to the Gospel of the one Teacher who has "the words of eternal life," you will be able to become genuine workers for justice, following the commandment which makes love the new "frontier" of Christian witness. This is the law for transforming the world (cf. *Gaudium et spes*, n. 38).

6. It is first of all necessary for you young people to give a forceful witness of love for life, God's gift. This love must extend from the beginning to the end of every life and must struggle against every attempt to make man the arbiter of his brother's life, of unborn life, of life that is waning or that of the handicapped and the weak.

I ask you young people, who naturally and instinctively make your "love of life", the horizon of your dreams and the rainbow of your hopes, to become "prophets of life". Be such by your words and deeds, rebelling against the civilization of selfishness that often considers the human person a means rather than an end, sacrificing its dignity and feelings in the name of mere profit. Do so by concretely helping those who need you and who perhaps, without your help, would be tempted to resign themselves to despair.

Life is a talent (cf. Mt 25:14-30) entrusted to us so that we can transform it and increase it, making it a gift to others. No man is an iceberg drifting on the ocean of history. Each one of us belongs to a great family, in which he has his own place and his own role to play. Selfishness makes people deaf and dumb; love opens eyes and hearts, enabling people to make that original and irreplaceable contribution which, together with the thousands of deeds of so many brothers and sisters, often distant and unknown, converges to form the mosaic of charity which can change the tide of history.

Be Prophets of Life, Love and Joy!

7. 'Lord, to whom shall we go? You have the words of eternal life'.

When, considering his language too demanding, many of his disciples left him. Jesus asked the few who had remained: 'Will you also go away?' Peter answered him: 'Lord, to whom shall we go? You have the words of eternal life' (Jn 6:67-68). And they chose to remain with him. They stayed because the master had "the words of eternal life," words which, while promising eternity, gave full meaning to life.

There are times and circumstances when it is necessary to make decisive choices for the whole of life. We are experiencing, and you know it, difficult times in which it is often hard to distinguish good from evil, true teachers from the false. Jesus warned us: 'Take heed that you are not led astray; for many will come in my name, saying, "I am he!" and, "the time is at hand!". Do not go after them' (Lk 21:8). Pray and listen to his words; let yourselves be guided by true pastors; do not ever succumb to the world's flattery and facile illusions which frequently become tragic disappointments.

It is in the difficult moments, in moments of trial, that the quality of decisions is measured. Thus it is in this difficult time that each one of you will be called to have the courage of your decision. There are no short cuts to happiness and light. The torment of all those who, throughout the history of humanity, have tirelessly sought the meaning of life, answers to the fundamental questions written on the heart of every human being, are proof of this.

You know that these questions are no more than the expression of a longing for the infinite, which God himself has planted in each one of us. Thus it is with a sense of duty and sacrifice that you must walk the paths of conversion, commitment, research, work, volunteer service, dialogue, respect for all, without giving up in the face of failure, knowing that your strength lies in the Lord who guides your steps with love and is ready to welcome you like the prodigal son (cf. Lk 15:11-24).

8. Dear young people, I have asked you to be "prophets of life and love". I also ask you to be "prophets of joy": the world must recognize us by our ability to communicate to our peers the sign of a great hope which has already been fulfilled: Jesus, who for our sake died and rose again.

Do not forget that 'the future of humanity is in the hands of those men who are capable of providing the generations to come with reasons for life and optimism' (*Gaudium et spes*, n. 31).

Purified by reconciliation, fruit of divine love and of your sincere repentance, striving for justice and living in thanksgiving to God, you can be creditable and effective prophets of joy in a world so frequently gloomy and sad. You will be heralds of the "fullness of time," whose timeliness is recalled by the Great Jubilee of the Year 2000.

The way Jesus shows you is not easy. Rather, it is like a path winding up a mountain. Do not lose heart! The steeper the road, the faster it rises towards ever wider horizons. May Mary, Star of Evangelization, guide you! Docile like her to the Father's will, take the stages of history as mature and convincing witnesses.

With her and with the Apostles may you repeat at every moment your profession of faith in Jesus Christ's life-giving presence: 'You have the words of eternal life!'.

quotes

'An excuse is worse and more terrible than a lie, for an excuse is a lie guarded.'

'As the family goes, so goes the nation and so goes the whole world in which we live.'

'Do not abandon yourselves to despair. We are the Easter people and hallelujah is our song.'

'From now on it is only through a conscious choice and through a deliberate policy that humanity can survive.'

'Have no fear of moving into the unknown. Simply step out fearlessly knowing that I am with you, therefore no harm can befall you; all is very, very well. Do this in complete faith and confidence.'

'Humanity should question itself, once more, about the absurd and always unfair phenomenon of war, on whose stage of death and pain only remain standing the negotiating table that could and should have prevented it.'

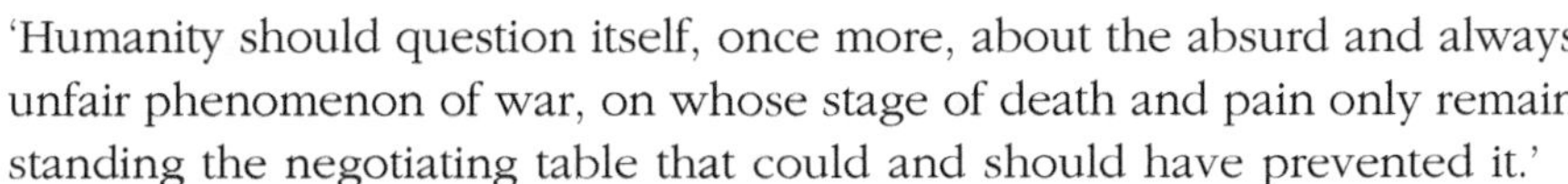

'I have a sweet tooth for song and music. This is my Polish sin.'

'I hope to have communion with the people, that is the most important thing.'

'I kiss the soil as if I placed a kiss on the hands of a mother, for the homeland is our earthly mother. I consider it my duty to be with my compatriots in this sublime and difficult moment.'

'Marriage is an act of will that signifies and involves a mutual gift, which unites the spouses and binds them to their eventual souls, with whom they make up a sole family – a domestic church.'

'Modern society will find no solution to the ecological problem unless it takes a serious look at its lifestyles.'

'The truth is not always the same as the majority decision.'

'Once again, through myself, the Church, in the words of the well-known declaration Nostra Aetate, "deplores the hatred, persecutions and displays of anti-Semitism directed against the Jews at any time and by anyone." I repeat, "By anyone".'

'Pervading nationalism imposes its dominion on man today in many different forms and with an aggressiveness that spares no one. The challenge that is already with us is the temptation to accept as true freedom what in reality is only a new form of slavery.'

'Radical changes in world politics leave America with a heightened responsibility to be, for the world, an example of a genuinely free, democratic, just and humane society.'

'Social justice cannot be attained by violence. Violence kills what it intends to create.'

'The fear of making permanent commitments can change the mutual love of husband and wife into two loves of self – two loves existing side by side, until they end in separation.'

'The great danger for family life, in the midst of any society whose idols are pleasure, comfort and independence, lies in the fact that people close their hearts and become selfish.'

'The historical experience of socialist countries has sadly demonstrated that collectivism does not do away with alienation but rather increases it, adding to it a lack of basic necessities and economic inefficiency.'

'The question confronting the Church today is not any longer whether the man in the street can grasp a religious message, but how to employ the communications media so as to let him have the full impact of the Gospel message.'

'This people draws its origin from Abraham, our father in faith. The very people that received from God the commandment "Thou shalt not kill" itself experienced in a special measure what is meant by killing. It is not permissible for anyone to pass by this inscription with indifference.'

'There are people and nations, Mother, that I would like to say to you by name. I entrust them to you in silence, I entrust them to you in the way that you know best.'

'The cemetery of the victims of human cruelty in our century is extended to include yet another vast cemetery, that of the unborn.'

'The United Nations organization has proclaimed 1979 as the Year of the Child. Are the children to receive the arms race from us as a necessary inheritance?'

'The vow of celibacy is a matter of keeping one's word to Christ and the Church. A duty and a proof of the priest's inner maturity; it is the expression of his personal dignity.'

'To maintain a joyful family requires much from both the parents and the children. Each member of the family has to become, in a special way, the servant of the others.'

'Today, for the first time in history, a Bishop of Rome sets foot on English soil. This fair land, once a distant outpost of the pagan world, has become, through the preaching of the Gospel, a beloved and gifted portion of Christ's vineyard.'

'What we talked about will have to remain a secret between him and me. I spoke to him as a brother whom I have pardoned and who has my complete trust.'

'When freedom does not have a purpose, when it does not wish to know anything about the rule of law engraved in the hearts of men and women, when it does not listen to the voice of conscience, it turns against humanity and society.'

'When you wonder about the mystery of yourself, look to Christ, who gives you the meaning of life. When you wonder what it means to be a mature person, look to Christ, who is the fullness of humanity. And when you wonder about your role in the future of the world look to Christ.'

'Work bears a particular mark of man and of humanity, the mark of a person operating within a community of persons.'

'You are our dearly beloved brothers, and in a certain way, it could be said that you are our elder brothers.'

'Freedom consists not in doing what we like, but in having the right to do what we ought.'

'You are priests, not social or political leaders. Let us not be under the illusion that we are serving the Gospel through an exaggerated interest in the wide field of temporal problems.'

'You will reciprocally promise love, loyalty and matrimonial honesty. We only want for you this day that these words constitute the principle of your entire life and that with the help of divine grace you will observe these solemn vows that today, before God, you formulate.'

'Young people are threatened… by the evil use of advertising techniques that stimulate the natural inclination to avoid hard work by promising the immediate satisfaction of every desire.'

'She had chosen to be not just the least but to be the servant of the least.'

'Where self-interest is suppressed, it is replaced by a burdensome system of bureaucratic control that dries up the wellspring of initiative and creativity.'

'Science can purify religion from error and superstition. Religion can purify science from idolatry and false absolutes.'

'Love is never defeated, and I could add, the history of Ireland proves it.'

'Violence is a lie, for it goes against the truth of our faith, the truth of our humanity, the life, the freedom of human beings. Violence is a crime against humanity, for it destroys the very fabric of society… On my knees I beg you to turn away from the paths of violence and to return to the ways of peace… Let history record that at a difficult moment in the experience of the people of Ireland, the Bishop of Rome set foot in your land, that he was with you and prayed with you for peace and reconciliation, for the victory of justice and love over hatred and violence.'

'It would be simplistic to say that Divine Providence caused the fall of Communism. In a certain sense Communism as a system fell by itself. It fell as a consequence of its own mistakes and abuses. It proved to be a medicine more dangerous than the disease itself. It did not bring about true social reform, yet it did become a powerful threat and challenge to the entire world. But it fell by itself, because of its own inherent weakness.'

Helen Keller

AUTHOR, SPEAKER AND ACTIVIST

*'Many persons have a wrong idea of what constitutes
true happiness. It is not attained through self-gratification but through fidelity to
a worthy purpose.'*

The Life of Helen Keller

1880   27 June: Born in Tuscumbia, Alabama.

1882   At 19 months develops meningitis and becomes deaf and blind.

1887   Anne Sullivan becomes her tutor.

1903   Publishes *Story of My Life*.

1904   Graduates from Radcliffe (women's college at Harvard).

1919-23   Four years of appearances with Anne Sullivan in vaudeville shows.

1936   Anne Sullivan dies.

1958   Publishes *Teacher*, her memoir of Sullivan.

1959   TV show on her life 'The Miracle Worker' broadcast. This was later adapted for stage and cinema.

1968   1 June: Dies in her sleep in Westport Connecticut, aged 87.

biography

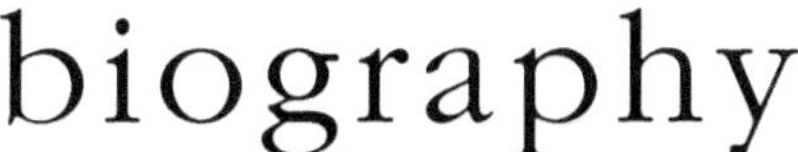

It is 1882. A little town in Alabama, USA…

A spirited, inquisitive and much-loved child is struck down by meningitis at the age of 19 months. She loses consciousness. Mysteriously, the fever vanishes and just as suddenly, she regains consciousness. But she has been rendered blind. And very soon after, deaf as well. The promise of a new young life has suddenly been savagely curtailed.

She cannot see.

She cannot hear.

She knows but the few words of a child…

An incandescent spirit stilled?

Not Helen Keller…

As she later wrote:

I have for many years endeavored to make this vital truth clear; and still people marvel when I tell them that I am happy. They imagine that my limitations weigh heavily upon my spirit, and chain me to the rock of despair. Yet, it seems to me, happiness has very little to do with the senses. If we make up our minds that this is a drab and purposeless universe, it will be that, and nothing else. On the other hand, if we believe that the earth is ours, and that the sun and moon hang in the sky for our delight, there will be joy upon the hills and gladness in the fields because the Artist in our souls glorifies creation. Surely, it gives dignity to life to believe that we are born into this world for noble ends, and that we have a higher destiny than can be accomplished within the narrow limits of this physical life.

Certainly, there is something divine in the art, which some human beings possess to shape life for themselves, no matter what the outward circumstances may be. That is the power of the Celestial Artist, the Will, to find life worth living, despite the handicap imposed.

The story of Helen Keller is more than a person with a range of exceptional personal qualities overcoming extreme personal handicap. It is the story of a person who pushed well beyond overcoming those handi-caps to live a life much fuller than most. In so doing, she enriched the lives of millions of others, inspiring them to engage in all the glory of life with passion and enthusiasm, courage and perseverance, and above all, hope.

She led by example, inspiring others not only with her optimism and determination, but also with her compassion, concern for others, and strong moral principles. She was a tireless speaker, writer and campaigner for the disabled as well as those disadvantaged for a variety of reasons, including the underprivileged.

The drive of this outspoken woman was extraordinary. Even at the age of 10 she had achieved considerable international fame – and this would increase as she became a household name around the world. Indeed, she considered herself a citizen of the world, and travelled extensively, appearing in 35 countries in five continents between 1939 and 1957. She also managed to author at least 14 books, and met hundreds of leading figures from around the world, including all twelve American presidents from Calvin Coolidge to J F Kennedy.

Winston Churchill called her, 'the greatest woman of our age', and she was described in 1968 by USA Senator Lister Hill as 'one of the few persons not born to die', a woman who will forever be known as, 'the first lady of courage'.

Alexander Graham Bell said about her: 'I have seen more of the divine than has been manifest in anyone I met before,' and Samuel Clemens (Mark Twain) described her as the most remarkable woman he ever met, and probably the most remarkable woman since Joan of Arc.

She was certainly an outstanding example of what hope, courage, determination – and the love of other good people – can achieve. She became an icon of overcoming handicaps to achieve the highest in mental, moral and spiritual development.

Helen Adams Keller was born to Kate Adams Keller and Captain Arthur Keller in Tuscumbia, Alabama, on 27 June 1880. He had been a Confederate officer and is now the publisher of *The North Alabamian* newspaper. Helen is a spirited, inquisitive and independent child until her second winter, when she is stricken with a disease called by the doctors of the time "brain fever" (meningitis). She is not expected to live. When she does survive, it is some days later that the parents notice that things are not as they were before… there is something strangely amiss with their little daughter… to their horror, her sight and then her hearing are lost.

The child could no longer learn to talk because she could not hear. Understandably frustrated by her "imprisonment" she would throw wild temper tantrums, and refuse to let anyone comb her hair or order her clothes. She was often frightened to walk unless holding her mother's skirts.

At the time, there appeared to be little that could be done, and the family was advised to have her institutionalised. However her dedicated parents continued loving the little girl. One could speculate that together with the innate qualities of the child herself, the love and commitment of her parents were very formative in what Helen Keller was to become.

Her parents researched far and wide for any remedies or assistance, in the meantime dedicating themselves to helping their little girl as best they could, as well as caring for two older half brothers, and soon after, a little sister.

'My mother moreover, succeeded in making me understand a good deal. I always knew when she wished me to bring her something, and I would run upstairs or anywhere else she indicated. Indeed, I owe to her loving wisdom all that was bright and good in my long night,' she wrote in her first book *The Story of My Life* which was published in 1903 when she was just 23. 'She is so near to me that it almost seems indelicate to speak of her.'

The family was fortunate that the household had a nurse for Helen, as well as a cook.

In the same book, she described her father as 'most loving and indulgent, devoted to his home, seldom leaving us, except in the hunting season.' He was a hospitable man who also loved his dogs and his garden. He would bring her 'the first ripe grapes and the choicest berries. I remember his caressing touch as he led me from tree to tree, from vine to vine, and his eager delight in whatever pleased me.' He died in 1896 after a brief illness when she was away up north. It was her 'first great sorrow – my first personal experience with death.'

An article in the book *American Notes* by Charles Dickens gave them some hope. Although it had been written some 40 years before, it mentioned a breakthrough with Laura Bridgman, a blind and deaf student of the Perkins Institution for the Blind. Her teachers had been able to get through to her and teach her how to communicate with the outside world.

At the time, as well as inventing prolifically and building up a significant business, Dr Alexander Graham Bell was, among many other things, interested in deafness, and had become somewhat of an advocate for the deaf. He believed that the deaf should learn to speak in order to become participating members of the wider community. The Keller family was eventually referred to him. He happened to know a Dr Johnson, the founder of Alabama Institute for Deaf and Blind, but the Institute did not have a program for people who were both deaf and blind. Bell also advised them of the Perkins Institution in Boston, which was the only school they could find in the USA with experience in helping people that were both deaf and blind.

After some negotiation, it was arranged for 21-year-old Anne Sullivan (1866-1936), a teacher from the Perkins Institution, to be sent to Tuscumbia, and she duly arrived by train on the 3 March 1887, some three months before Helen's 7th birthday. Anne Sullivan had studied the finger-spelling techniques used to teach Laura Bridgman, and was a recent graduate of the Institution. She was herself visually impaired.

Little Helen was stubborn and used to having her own way. She had grown up being able to help a little around the house, but she was often very frustrated at being closed off from the world. Some time later she wrote: 'sometimes I stood between two persons who were conversing and touched their lips. I could not understand, and was vexed. I moved my lips and gesticulated frantically without result. This made me so angry at times that I kicked and screamed until I was exhausted.'

But her teacher Anne was very strict as well as being quite resilient and also very strong-willed. She described little Helen as being both without language and in an ethical sense, a "tyrant" with a violent temper, impossible for her family to control, and whose 'untaught, unsatisfied hands destroy whatever they touch.'

She described her first impression of little Helen in the first letter she wrote three days after arriving… Helen knew someone was arriving, and when Anne appeared, the little girl threw herself at Anne, nearly knocking her over, feeling her face, her dress and her bag, which she then took from Anne and tried to open.

'There is nothing pale or delicate about Helen,' she wrote, 'she is large, strong and ruddy and as unrestrained in her movements as a young colt… She has none of the nervous habits that are so noticeable and so distressing in blind children. Her body is well formed and vigorous, and… she has not been ill a day since the illness that deprived her… you see at a glance that she is blind… one eye is larger than the other and protrudes noticeably… she is very quick tempered and willful, and nobody except her brother James has attempted to control her…The greatest problem I shall have to solve is how to discipline and control her without breaking her spirit. I shall go rather slowly at first and try to win her love… One thing that impresses everybody is Helen's tireless activity… She is here, there and everywhere… her restless spirit gropes in the dark. Her untaught, unsatisfied hands destroy whatever they touch because they do not know what else to do with things.'

When the little tyrant found out about the function of keys, she locked her mother in the pantry, where she remained trapped for three hours. And when Anne Sullivan arrived, she could not wait to inflict some mischief on her as well… and locked her in an upstairs room! Little Helen did not produce that key for some months afterwards, despite the family's entreaties. Her father was forced to free poor Anne by using a ladder to get to the upstairs window!

Anne stood her ground and soon some measure of discipline was

biography

seen to be developing. As Anne wrote on 20 March 1887, 'The wild little creature of two weeks ago has been transformed into a gentle child. She is sitting by me as I write, her face serene and happy, crocheting... she learned the stitch this week... when she is in a particularly gentle mood she will sit on my lap for a minute or two... The little savage has learned her first lesson in obedience, and finds the yoke easy. It now remains my pleasant task to direct and mould the beautiful intelligence that is beginning to stir in the child soul.'

Anne had engaged the little girl in the adventure of learning and communicating. Within a few days she had taught Helen how to spell words with her hands, using the manual alphabet. Little Helen was immediately trying to teach the dog how to spell.

However Helen didn't really quite understand what these "words" truly meant, until one morning on the 5 April that year, at the water pump, a major breakthrough occurred...

Anne had Helen put her hand in the water. Then Anne spelled out the word "water" on Helen's other hand. Helen immediately got the idea – she tapped the ground and Anne spelled the word "earth" for her. Suddenly these "words" actually represented something real in the outside world – here was a way to find out about the world and communicate back. The adventure of learning and exploring had begun!

Thirty words were learned that day. And there was no stopping them... She was on her way, and many of her frustrations could now be overcome. She was quick to master Braille, and began to read voraciously and widely. She also learned to write and began developing a talent for learning and communication that would make her name famous around the world. Books became a window to a new universe. She started writing letters at the age of eight, and asking questions such as 'where did I come from?' and 'where will I go when I die?'.

'Literature is my Utopia. Here I am not disenfranchised,' she would later write, 'No barrier of the senses shuts me out from the sweet gracious discourse of my book friends.' Even so, it could be a frustrating and slow process – not nearly fast enough for her quick and eager young mind. By October 1893 she had read the histories of Greece, Rome and the United States, and had even acquired enough French to read various works by La Fontaine. As well as her books she loved the outdoors, and enjoyed swimming and rowing.

In 1890, by the time she was ten, she had learned to speak by feeling her teacher's mouth when she talked. This was no easy task, even for someone as driven as Helen. But she would not be deterred, and although she took many lessons in speaking and elocution, she was never satisfied with her speech. Unfortunately, many people found it hard to understand her, even in adult life. Regardless, she learned to read French, German, Greek, and Latin in Braille, and could speak in French and German as well as English! Her German pronunciation was particularly good.

She was an international celebrity, being the first blind and deaf person to effectively communicate with the rest of the world.

She was particularly bright and excited by life. And she was very fortunate indeed to have the assistance of her parents, as well as the very dedicated Anne Sullivan and other supporters to help her on her way in such a committed fashion. It was the 'investment' by these people that would provide inspirational returns for millions around the world for years.

The story of Helen Keller is also the story of the remarkable Anne Sullivan… she was the daughter of impoverished Irish immigrants, and her mother died when she was eight. When she and her two siblings were abandoned by her alcoholic and abusive father two years later, she and her younger brother were sent to the poorhouse. The boy was dead within three months and Anne's eyesight was badly impaired by trachoma. Remarkably, after four years, she managed to get a scholarship to go to the Perkins Institution for The Blind in Boston. She was a keen student, but was ever angry at having been abandoned, and at the difference in social class she perceived between herself and others more fortunate.

Nevertheless, she bravely took on the responsibility of Helen Keller, writing in May 1887: 'I know that the education of this child will be the distinguishing event of my life, if I have the brains and perseverance to achieve it.'

One month later she wrote: 'something within me tells me that I shall succeed beyond my dreams… I know that she has remarkable powers, and I believe that I shall be able to develop and mould them. I cannot tell how I know these things. I had no idea a short time ago how to go to work; I was feeling about in the dark; but somehow I know now, and I know that I know.'

In 1899 Helen Keller passed her entry exams for Radcliffe, the Women's College at Harvard University, having met the same admission require-ments as for sighted applicants (subjects included Elementary Greek, Advanced Latin, Geometry, Algebra and Advanced Greek). She deferred entry for a year before entering Radcliffe and graduating with honours in 1904 at the age of 24. Despite her disabilities, she studied the same subjects as the other students, and she also had the additional difficulty of obtaining learning materials in Braille, or finding someone to read the material to her.

Education was a fundamental and liberating part of her life – it was her window to the rest of the world. In 1891, at the age of just eleven she wrote to her father: 'I cannot believe that parents would keep their deaf or blind children at home to grow up in silence and darkness if they knew there was a good school at Talladega where they would be kindly and wisely treated. Little deaf and blind children love to learn… and God means that they shall be taught. He has given them minds that can understand and hands with sensitive fingertips that are almost as good as eyes. I cannot see or hear, and yet I have been taught to do nearly everything that other girls do. I am happy all the day long because education has brought light and music to my soul…'

Even at Radcliffe, Helen had a vision of a greater and out-of-the-ordinary purpose for her life. Indeed, it was during Radcliffe that she wrote her first book, *The Story of My Life*. It was a bestseller overnight, and reprinted many times in the first year.

That first book was translated into 50 languages, and made her even more of a household name around the world. She lectured all over America as well as in Europe and Asia, raising funds for the blind as well as promoting various social causes such as civil and women's rights. She wrote many more books, including *The World I Live In* (1908), and *Helen Keller's Journal*, using two typewriters, one regular, and one Braille.

She was not only the epitome of hope in the face of adversity; she was also an outstanding example of compassion and concern for others. She was cognisant of how much support she had received from so many people, and in the concluding chapter of her first book she wrote: 'Thus it is my friends have made the story of my life. In a thousand ways they have turned my limitations into beautiful privileges, and enabled me to walk serenely and happy in the shadow cast by my deprivation.'

All this from a woman who could not hear, could not see and who could never speak very clearly. But she had an incisive mind, a gift for language and energy and enthusiasm in abundance – as well as a compassionate heart.

No matter how independent-minded she may have been however, she was always dependent upon others to guide her and interpret the visual world onto her hand. Anne Sullivan accompanied her to Boston and the Perkins Institution, to Radcliffe College, and indeed all over the world. She became a friend, adviser and confidante as well as never-ceasing helper. Anne's devotion to Helen was an extraordinary act of love and commitment in itself.

However, while Helen was writing her first book *Story Of My Life*, a young man was prevailed upon to assist with the book, and take some of the pressure off Anne, who was herself visually impaired. The extra reading was proving difficult for her. After some time, the young man, John Albert Macy, married Anne Sullivan. However the marriage was short-lived.

Getting through college with honours was in itself a major achievement, however this was only the start for an ambitious Helen. People around the world were fascinated by her valiant and optimistic approach to life, as well as her concern for others. Upon graduation, she had the objective to support herself and her teacher as an author. While people were genuinely interested in her battle against her disabilities, they were less interested in her writing about other diverse matters that were important to her, so financial independence was always a bit of a struggle. Although she often had to rely on the help of wealthy patrons she nevertheless pressed on indomitably.

She was a forceful campaigner for her beliefs, having learned that taking a position, setting her objectives, and then applying herself assiduously, was a way that worked for her. Because she cared for others, she had opinions across a diversity of issues, and she championed many of the more liberal and progressive causes of her time, even if they were not always universally popular. Having been born in a time when women could not vote in the USA, she was a vigorous fighter for women's issues, civil rights and world peace, and kept a busy schedule of writing and speaking around the world. She also supported reforms in workplace conditions called for by the Socialist Party. No wonder her outspoken opinions even resulted in the FBI having a file on her.

After graduating in 1904, she announced that her life would be dedicated to the amelioration of blindness. But she then went on to address a diversity of what she saw as injustices. She wrote 'My work for the blind has never occupied a center in my personality. My sympathies are with all those who struggle for justice.' She was a complex character... her nominations for the most important people of the century were Charlie Chaplin, Thomas Alva Edison and Lenin!

She had been greatly moved by H G Wells' case for socialism in his book *New World for Old,* and from there moved on to Marx and Engels, joining the Socialist Party in 1909 and the more militant Workers of the World in 1911. For over a decade thereafter, most of her work was focused on social causes. Rather than literature, she advocated that women study 'Industrial Economics', society and politics, so that they could play a more powerful role right across everyday society.

She was particularly strongly influenced by the eighteenth-century Swedish philosopher, scientist and theologian, Emanuel Swedenborg, and this is particularly apparent in her book *My Religion.* Her religious beliefs were a fundamental part of her value set.

Not many things got in her way... she wrote, travelled and spoke at fund raising and promotional activities throughout the country and around the world. Anne Sullivan was always at her side to introduce her and interpret her remarks to the audience if required.

Her outspokenness on social issues antagonised many people, and she found by the end of World War I, that her speaking engagements were drying up – people were more interested in her as a handicapped heroine rather than a firebrand social reformer, and consequently her finances were affected.

From 1919 to 1923 she and Anne even did the vaudeville circuit, educating people about her condition, as well as trying to earn a living. It was a tough, relentless and demanding life, with constant travel, but even though it was frowned upon by many people at the time, it was one of the best ways they had of earning a living. And it did get her message out to the public!

She was always restlessly busy, and in many ways she was an indefatigable entrepreneur. Because of the widespread interest in her story, a movie based on her life was produced. She had high hopes that this would provide some financial salvation, but this proved not to be nearly enough. No matter, there was always so much more to be done.

Despite the diversity of her causes, she was indeed a constant advocate for the blind, and in 1923 became associated with the American Foundation for the Blind (AFB), and began to work with the Foundation in 1924. She was a highly visible and effective spokesperson and ambassador for the Foundation until her death in 1968.

She was also a passionate campaigner for the American Foundation for the Overseas Blind, which is now called Helen Keller Worldwide.

When her great friend and aide Anne Sullivan died in 1936, Helen Keller was forced to take on another challenge – that of now living independently, which she did for another 32 years. And in so doing she set the standard and provided further inspiration for the disabled around the world.

It is perhaps difficult to truly understand just how well-known and appreciated she was around the world – her name was an international byword for the power of hope and courage. She inspired works of art, including two Oscar-winning movies, and received an astonishing variety of gifts, diplomas and awards from around the world. She herself was presented with an Oscar award in 1955 for the documentary film *Helen Keller in Her Story*. She was feted around the world, receiving the Presidential Medal of Freedom (the highest American civilian honor), a key to the City of Tokyo, a boomerang from Australian Aborigines, and an inscribed photograph from Mark Twain.

Despite all her difficulties, she was able to touch people around the world.

A strong and courageous voice, she had conviction and passion which sustained her on her very own distinctive way. It was a long and inspirational life that showed many people, disabled and otherwise, that with hope, love, faith and courage, there is a way forward – a way that shows us all a path beyond the constraints of hardship, timidity and convention.

wisdom

Why do you think my son (brother) killed himself?

There are three things that quotes from Helen Keller said to me that come straight to my mind when asked this sort of question.

The first is, 'People do not like to think. If one thinks, one must reach conclusions. Conclusions are not always pleasant'. And the second, 'One can never consent to creep when one feels an impulse to soar' and finally, 'Many persons have a wrong idea of what constitutes true happiness. It is not attained through self-gratification but through fidelity to a worthy purpose.'

You see after writing *Collective Wisdom* and making presentation after presentation, I became aware of the terrible suicide statistics for young men in Australia. It is not an area we would like to think of ourselves as competing for world's best at! But there we are right near the top of the list.

So as I went from place to place, the strange phenomenon occurred on a number of occasions where after my presentation, after Questions and Answers, after the function itself, generally someone would quietly approach me and ask about my thoughts on suicide generally and/or of the suicide of a son, friend or relative.

I was staggered at this phenomenon, and before anyone points out my lack of qualifications to answer such a question, let me point them out myself. I am not a psychologist, doctor, Pope or any other type of expert. Rather, what I offer, are my own reasonings worked out at the depth of my own struggle in losing my job, sorting through some of life's challenges and meeting so many people during the course of presenting *Collective Wisdom* and since.

The uncomfortable conclusion I have reached is that it is important what you hope for in life. Not revolutionary. But let me explain.

When I was down and struggling, I hoped in a better future and could not let suicide be an option. I had been taught by my parents and Church that it was ungrateful and cowardly as it was a refusal to live. What's more, it was a heinous act of pride to take the gift of life God had given me and throw it back into His face. And further, that it was hurtful to others.

So I had to fight on – attack my own faults and try to become a better person.

Now while these ideas might seem offensive to some – I did not kill myself.

Many young people who do kill themselves today, do so influenced by a mental illness. This is a great tragedy. But the numbers killing themselves suggest either that our society is producing an extraordinary amount of mental illness in its young or that there are other causes.

It is the examination of these other causes where Helen Keller comes to mind. Consideration of her thinking leads us towards, 'Conclusions (that) are not always pleasant.'

In my case, what I had been taught to hope in stopped me pursuing the path of killing myself. What are other young people being taught to hope in? Would different ideas reap different outcomes?

Keller went on to say to me in a quote: 'One can never consent to creep when one feels an impulse to soar.' And it was this quote that helped me examine something I had observed time and time again.

Parents ask me, 'why do you think my friend's son killed himself? Why are so many young people killing themselves?'

Short answer: Because they are hope-less. That is, without hope in a better tomorrow or any tomorrow at all.

The father who asks me is clearly distressed and I would say to him, 'when you have a really critical life-changing decision to make, who do you ask about it or consult with?' All too often the father answers, 'I work it out for myself.' 'Why do you ask?' the father normally enquires.

I would answer, 'Your son/friend's son probably just did what you had shown him to do. Work it out for himself. Upon realising he did not have any answers he killed himself. Maybe he could not work out how to work it out. But he certainly ran out of ideas to solve his problems.'

The father would normally quietly agree.

The exhaustion of ideas is front of the mind when one considers Helen Keller – deaf and blind, what hope for a good life for her? She answers her own question when she says, *Many persons have a wrong idea of what constitutes true happiness. It is not attained through self-gratification but through fidelity to a worthy purpose.'*

Are we giving our young people examples of fidelity to worthy purpose(s)? Reasons why life is worth living? And sources of good ideas when things become tough?

The statistics say, "no". An uncomfortable conclusion.

words

The dreams that come true

*'When One who Can neither See nor Hear Finds Joy in a Flower Garden'
by Helen Keller. 'Dreams That Come True' – as published in Personality,
December 1927*

Swedenborg says that 'many arts in this world derive their laws and
harmonies from Heaven.'

Certainly, there is something divine in the art which some human
beings possess to shape life for themselves, no matter what the outward
circumstances may be. That is the power of the Celestial Artist, the Will,
to find life worth living, despite the handicap imposed.

I have for many years endeavored to make this vital truth clear; and
still people marvel when I tell them that I am happy. They imagine that
my limitations weigh heavily upon my spirit, and chain me to the rock
of despair. Yet, it seems to me, happiness has very little to do with the
senses. If we make up our minds that this is a drab and purposeless
universe, it will be that, and nothing else. On the other hand, if we believe
that the earth is ours, and that the sun and moon hang in the sky for our
delight, there will be joy upon the hills and gladness in the fields because
the Artist in our souls glorifies creation. Surely, it gives dignity to life to
believe that we are born into this world for noble ends, and that we have
a higher destiny than can be accomplished within the narrow limits of this
physical life.

'I can understand,' I hear some one interrupting me, 'that you enjoy
flowers and sunshine and that sort of thing; but when you sit by yourself
in that little study on the top of the house all day, aren't you dreadfully
bored? You can't see a bit of color from the window, or hear a sound!
Don't you get tired of the – well, the sameness of the objects you touch
when you can't see the play of light and shadow upon them? Aren't the
days and the hours all alike to you?'.

Never! My days are all different, and no hour is quite like another.

Through my sense of touch I am keenly alive to all changes and
movements of the atmosphere, and I am sure the days vary for me as
much as they do for my friend who observes the skies – often not caring

about their beauty, but only to see if it is going to rain. There are days when the sun pours into my study, and I feel all of life's joys crowded into each beam. There are rainy days when a sort of shade clings about me and lays a cool hand upon my face, and the smell of the moist earth and damp objects lingers everywhere. There are days really "dark" for me when I feel the ten windows in the study shudder and sob with the winter blast. Then glad days that feel like light come when the sonorous west wind booms its message of spring into my hand as I lay it against the pane, and I am eager to be away in the woods.

> *Where the soul need not repress*
> *Its music, Lest it should not find*
> *An echo in another's mind.*

This is a drowsy day when the summer breeze comes languidly to my cheek, tempting me to go out to my little screened tent, stretch out and dream with the irises and bee-haunted pinks.

There is the hour when the morning sun kisses me awake, and the hour when the burden of material things drops from my shoulder, and I drift to Slumberland. There are hours of breathless haste to catch up with the letters that cover my desk, hours of glad expectancy when a beautiful dream seems about to come true, hours fragrant with tender memories; and always there are the endlessly varied hours I spend with the thinkers and poets and philosophers of all times! How can there be a dull moment when my books are all about me!

I live in a thought-filled world. Those who have all their faculties have no idea what wonderful gardens lie hidden behind the dark silent walls. The very silence vibrates to my every mood and to every consciousness I have of others' existence!

Because silence is such a sublime kind of poetry, it puts soul and meaning into all the vibrations which find their way to me through the channels of touch. There are footsteps of those I love in the house passing and repassing, there is the sudden bark of my beautiful long-eared Great Dane. Every now and then huge trucks filled with material for the new boulevard that is being built not far from this street rumble by, shaking the house and sending little showers of dust down upon the furniture, and instantly I feel astir with the fierce, splendid, never-resting activity of New York. Some time ago I had a breathless moment when twenty aeroplanes rushed by on their way to the Lindbergh parade, and several of them came so near the house I distinctly perceived the roar of the motor through the walls of my study. What a crowd of admiring, far-gazing thoughts that vibration started on the wing. As the birds follow summer, so my mind again followed in the vision, the dauntless youth who had crossed the

Atlantic alone. Out there, on trackless levels of the night, I again saw him. In my own soul I recreated that agony of solitude, the lurking herd of fears and doubts, the awful abysmal dark. I tried to imagine his thoughts as he drove on and on, sensing the primal mystery – darkness as inaccessible as God's light. In the world's market, where they sell all things, he had bought a dream, and carried it on dewy wings into the shining east, his plane swaying with the winds and curving with the clouds! My spirit seemed to stand still as I imagined him losing the celestial trail and leaping into the unmeasured void, with a million white-faced deaths blowing across his path! Because I know the dark so deeply, I had peculiar sympathy with him guiding his plane that like a lamp grimly burned in ice – now rising above the treachery of fog and sleet, now swooping seaward, hunting an unseen course as a blind man feels his way in the dark! But at last, fluttering down the golden bar of dawn, he glimpsed the dim rim of earth, and all the glory of a mighty day shone upon him! All this the Artist within brought thrillingly to my consciousness as I felt the sonorous roar of those planes speeding over Long Island to do him honor. And what other marvelous pictures he conjured up for my delight! They come fast, they come fast – the Fliers crossing the Pacific, fliers who seek to read the baffling secrets of mist and snow and airy heights, fliers who overtake the swiftest fires and quench them, fliers who shall charm shut clouds to pour bounty upon thirsty fields, fliers who shall bear messages weaving a chain of friendship to encircle the world – peacebringers who shall outspeed strife and hate, and dare and dare, and yet again dare until all men walk the earth unafraid, brothers one to another!

I have other sensations which bring me warm, human contacts with the outer world. The sense of smell is most precious and important in my everyday world. It brings within my reach a multitude of little joys which take the place of color and light. The atmosphere is charged with countless odors, from which I learn much about places and objects. I recognize many flowers by their graceful shapes and fragrance, and it is amazing how many kinds of sweetness there are in leaves, fruits, and seeds! Even the same plant gives forth a different scent in sunshine and in rainy weather. In spring and autumn there are qualities which I can describe only approximately, as I have not found anything like a satisfactory vocabulary of smell terms – or touch terms either. There are tender odors like the lilac. The honeysuckle seems to lavish its fragrance upon one with something like affection. The odor of the lily when once captured is a precious satisfaction, but how shy and elusive it can be even though one stands close to the flower! There are sunshine and calm for me in the smell of a new-mown hayfield, the woods and mountains are full of quiet, eternal odors that make me want to worship. There are many beautiful odors that seem to reach out to me like friendly greetings each time I pass, and this is a sweet compensation for the void I feel when I cannot see loved objects unless I stretch my hand and touch them. Smell is like a friend who gossips with me about little everyday things as well as the Spirit of Beauty. It tells me when it rains, when the grass is cut, when automobiles pass in the street, what new houses are going up in this growing town – and when it is mealtime. It is the thousand scents I perceive which differentiate one house or a street from another, and always I prefer to be as near the country as possible.

I should like the city pretty well if it were not for my exacting touch and odor perception. But the avalanche of noises and the turmoil of New York weary me, and the heavy smells of crowded shops and sultry streets and air congested with gasoline oppress me. Give me the noiseless little noises of growing things and the morning and evening odors of my tiny garden, and I am content in a world flooded with the harmony and the brilliance of the spirit. Imagination gives eyes and ears to those who lack a sense or two, builds a satisfying whole out of the fragmentary and often unrelated details which drift into one's consciousness out of a dark silent chaos. I had an experience recently which I should like to relate because it brought out in a most happy manner the delightful sensations and the witchery of the soul which render my life as full and liveable as that of any one with all his powers intact.

I was sitting at my typewriter the other day, waiting rather impatiently for an idea which I desperately needed to finish a chapter in my auto-biography, when I received an invitation from Mr Doubleday to come and smell the roses in his garden. 'Bless my soul,' I said to myself, 'this welcome interruption has saved my life! It has put to flight the recalcitrant thoughts that were destroying me utterly. What better thing could I do than go out there to smell roses!'

The drive to Garden City was beautiful. Long Island is always beautiful under the touch of June. The caressing air makes one realize the useless-ness of toilsome effort when all out-of-doors breathes an irresistible invitation to come and be a child again, when even the most diligent finds work irksome, when every live boy dreams of playing "hookey". I thought, 'Perish the task that would keep one indoors on such a day!' They are rare enough as one grows older. Running away like the boy with the circus is our only chance of being young again.

Are you amazed, O reader, that I should sympathize with the boy's enthusiasm for the circus? Well, I have a perennial desire myself to get under a circus-tent, and be a part of the riotous pageant – the segregated wonders of the world. I remember that when I was a little girl, not quite seven years old, my teacher took me to the circus. It was the greatest object-lesson of my childhood. My vocabulary was very limited. Miss Sullivan had been teaching me only two months; but I had learned enough words to understand that I was going to touch 'very tall, very large, very strong animals.' The phaeton came around to the front door, and I touched Charlie, the old horse. He had been in the family longer than I had. I asked if the "animals" were as tall as Charlie. When Miss Sullivan told me that one of them, the elephant, was as high as the phaeton itself, I became so excited I could hardly sit still. Charlie was very slow. I had observed that when the whip was applied to his fat sides, he went a little faster. I seized the whip, and before Miss Sullivan could stop me, I had given the poor old fellow a terrible whack which made him rear, and nearly upset the phaeton. My teacher quieted Charlie, and delayed our progress long enough to make me understand that if I did that again, I should go right home and never, never, never see the huge elephant.

The first thing of which I was conscious when we finally got inside the tent was a strange, terrifying smell. I clutched Miss Sullivan's skirt, and for a moment my impulse to run away was stronger than my curiosity. But, her hand on one side and the big hand of the circus man on the other side reassured me. They gave me a bag of peanuts and took me at once to see the elephant. I felt his huge forelegs, and the circus man lifted me up on his shoulder, so that I could touch the creature's head and fan-like ears and his broad back, on which there was an Oriental silk covering with tassels and bells. (Someone was going to ride him later.) I was told to give him some peanuts, and perhaps he would let me touch his "long nose" and put it into his mouth. I was amazed, and a little angry; for I liked peanuts, and I had intended to eat some myself. But my disappointment was only for a second or two. Someone gave me another bag of peanuts, and I was allowed to feel my benefactress's beautiful, slim body. She was a trapeze performer, and wore only pink tights. She laughed with pretty confusion at my scrutiny, and kissed me.

I also made the acquaintance of the Arabian marvels and their gorgeous riders, and felt the splendid chariots. I was allowed to sit in one of them like a gypsy princess. The camel was made to kneel, and let me climb up on his queer, humpy back. But oh, the smell of him! At last the wonderful hour came to an end, and we had to leave. My dejection was a little lightened by my teacher's assurance that the circus would came (sic) back after days and days, and I should be taken there again. Of course all the details of this strange nomadic caravan are intensely interesting to any child, and to one who had almost no contact with the outer world they were overwhelmingly fascinating.

What a far cry it is from the automobile which bore me along at the rate of twenty miles in half an hour to that slow horse plodding a mile in the same period of time and an old-fashioned circus in an out-of-the-way village! But it is one way to illustrate the magical changes I have witnessed in the past forty years, and the piled up interest and novelty of my present experiences. When my friends and I arrived at the great publishing house, Mr Doubleday received us with cordial kindness, and from his personality and conversation I judged he was a lover of nature as well as a collector and distributor of books.

After a few minutes' chat we went out into the gardens, and smell roses I did! Multitudes of them. There seemed to be as many kinds and scents and ways of growing as there were roses. Gorgeous ramblers climbed up with insatiate desire and tossed great clusters in the breeze. Long-petalled, curly-headed roses romped and spread themselves out like active, eager children seeking adventure. Delicate roses with single petals and slender stems trembled in my hand, while large, full roses exacted tribute with stately grace. All roses that are most fondly twined with memories of home and simple joys grew there, and my fingers thrilled as I recognized the moss-rose of my childhood. Some of the roses were so high and large that they seemed like cascades dancing softly down from the sky.

But I did much more than smell roses. For there were quantities of peonies, in all their splendor and stateliness, all kinds of lilies and pinks and larkspur and masses of honeysuckle. Every breath was a delight, and every flower touched glowed with tints of inexhaustible beauty which no mortal eye may behold.

There was another world of beauty for me in those gardens in the evergreens. There is plenty of room for them, and consequently they have a chance to grow unhampered. Every kind of conifer which will make friends with our climate has been brought there, and planted where it shows to the best advantage. My fingers revelled in many new forms from a superb giant pine with thick, bright green needles to an exquisite small white pine with thin, soft foliage, almost like a silk fringe. A light breeze followed us as we passed from one to the other, and I listened to them as they played the invisible violins of the air – an inexpressibly restful music. Then there were the firs and spruces John Ruskin had so enthusiastically described with their branches extending in magnificent ridge upon ridge and the sunbeams dancing in and out, offsetting the darker greens. I have always loved evergreens with a deep love. There is nothing in nature which has such a potent, deep-rooted appeal for me. They seem human, and at the same time they symbolize whatever is imperishable and up-lifting in life – hope, courage, and serene faith. Their unfading greenness and fragrance breathe immortality, and are a blessing to me amid the grim monotony of winter. It may be imagined how gratified I was when Mr Doubleday said that he also found peculiar happiness in the companion-ship of pines and firs, and had worked for many years to have that wonderful retreat of evergreens made possible right in the heart of a restrictive, machine-driven civilization. He also told me how several men who had visited him, among them John Burroughs and John Muir, had planted a tree in that garden.

Truly, I left those gardens immensely refreshed, with a crowd of bright thoughts tumbling out of their hidden nests and burrows to put me in the right mood for my work again.

Such is the world I live in, and yet how few people understand the simplest truths about it! I have learned many things which stand out boldly in my mind, and when I think of some of them, I wonder, and say to myself, 'Do other people have similar thoughts and emotions? Are they as conscious as I am of the life of the spirit?' From what the people tell me I must needs (sic) conclude that physical limitations somehow strengthen and clarify intellectual processes. I confess, it appears paradoxical that weakness should develop strength. Still, there is scriptural authority for this belief. St Paul says, 'When I am weak, then am I strong' – which is an exceedingly comforting thought to those who are physically damaged.

The explanation undoubtedly is that limitations drive one inward for diversion, with the result that one's own thoughts become absorbingly interesting. The small events of daily life take on extraordinary importance when Celestial Artist combines them with spiritual elements in the Laboratory of Mind. It is a miracle how an incident of no particular value comes out of the mental crucible beautiful and precious. Little by little the transformation and classification of ideas take place in the brain, where are registered the beings and the events which give delight to circumscribed lives. Stored in the memory, they furnish plentiful entertainment for solitary hours; and that is why I never feel "deaf blind". I left that horrible abyss of hopelessness long, long ago.

My life has been happy because I have had wonderful friends and plenty of interesting work to do. I seldom think about my limitations, and they never make me sad. Perhaps there is just a touch of yearning at times; but it is vague, like a breeze among the flowers. The wind passes, and the flowers are content. But into the sweet night of my individual blindness has come the call – the urge of others' need. It is as persistent as the love-note which the mother-bird hears when her nestlings are in trouble, and I know that it will never cease until I have done the utmost of which I am capable to help others break down the walls of darkness and pour the sweet waters of joy into the deserts of silence.

quotes

'Although the world is full of suffering, it is full also of the overcoming of it.'

'Character cannot be developed in ease and quiet. Only through experience of trial and suffering can the soul be strengthened, ambition inspired, and success achieved.'

'College isn't the place to go for ideas.'

'Life is either a daring adventure or nothing. Security does not exist in nature, nor do the children of men as a whole experience it. Avoiding danger is no safer in the long run than exposure.'

'Many persons have a wrong idea of what constitutes true happiness. It is not attained through self-gratification but through fidelity to a worthy purpose.'

'No pessimist ever discovered the secret of the stars or sailed an uncharted land, or opened a new doorway for the human spirit.'

'One can never consent to creep when one feels an impulse to soar.'

'People do not like to think. If one thinks, one must reach conclusions. Conclusions are not always pleasant.'

'Self-pity is our worst enemy and if we yield to it, we can never do anything good in the world.'

'Smell is a potent wizard that transports you across thousands of miles and all the years you have lived.'

'The best and most beautiful things in the world cannot be seen or even touched. They must be felt within the heart.'

'We could never learn to be brave and patient, if there were only joy in the world.'

'When one door of happiness closes, another opens; but often we look so long at the closed door that we do not see the one which has been opened for us.'

'When we do the best that we can, we never know what miracle is wrought in our life, or in the life of another.'

'The highest result of education is tolerance.'

'Science may have found a cure for most evils; but it has found no remedy for the worst of them all – the apathy of human beings.'

'When indeed shall we learn that we are all related one to the other, that we are all members of one body?'

'Keep your face to the sunshine and you cannot see the shadow.'

'I long to accomplish a great and noble task, but it is my chief duty to accomplish small tasks as if they were great and noble.'

'I seldom think of my limitations, and they never make me sad. Perhaps there is just a touch of yearning at times; but it is vague, like a breeze among flowers.'

'What we have once enjoyed we can never lose. All that we love deeply becomes a part of us.'

'Everything has its wonders, even darkness and silence, and I learn, whatever state I may be in, therein to be content.'

'Be of good cheer. Do not think of today's failures, but of the success that may come tomorrow. You have set yourself a difficult task, but you will succeed if you persevere; and you will find a joy in overcoming obstacles.'

'Avoiding danger is no safer in the long run than outright exposure. The fearful are caught as often as the bold.'
'Faith is the strength by which a shattered world shall emerge into the light.'

'To keep our faces toward change, and behave like free spirits in the presence of fate, is strength undefeatable.'

'Knowledge is love and light and vision.'

'As selfishness and complaint pervert the mind, so love with its joy clears and sharpens the vision.'

'We can do anything we want to if we stick to it long enough.'

'Optimism is the faith that leads to achievement. Nothing can be done without hope or confidence.'

'While they were saying among themselves it cannot be done, it was done.'

'Life is an exciting business, and most exciting when it is lived for others.'

'It is wonderful how much time good people spend fighting the devil. If they would only expend the same amount of energy loving their fellow men, the devil would die in his own tracks of ennui.'

'It is hard to interest those who have everything in those who have nothing.'

'Until the great mass of the people shall be filled with the sense of responsibility for each other's welfare, social justice can never be attained.'

'I have often been asked, "do not people bore you?" I do not understand quite what that means. I suppose the calls of the stupid and curious, especially of newspaper reporters, are always inopportune. I also dislike people who try to talk down to my understanding. They are like people who when walking with you try to shorten their steps to suit yours; the hypocrisy in both cases is equally exasperating.'

'It gives me a deep comforting sense that "things seen are temporal and things unseen are eternal".'

'I sometimes wonder if the hand is not more sensitive to the beauties of sculpture than the eye. I should think the wonderful rhythmical flow of lines and curves could be more subtly felt than seen. Be this as it may, I know that I can feel the heart-throbs of the ancient Greeks in their marble gods and goddesses.'

'The problems of deafness are deeper and more complex, if not more important, than those of blindness. Deafness is a much worse misfortune. For it means the loss of the most vital stimulus – the sound of the voice that brings language, sets thoughts astir and keeps us in the intellectual company of man.'

'Have you ever been at sea in a dense fog, when it seemed as if a tangible white darkness shut you in and the great ship, tense and anxious, groped her way toward the shore with plummet and sounding-line, and you waited with beating heart for something to happen? I was like that ship before my education began, only I was without compass or sounding line, and no way of knowing how near the harbor was. 'Light! Give me light!' was the wordless cry of my soul, and the light of love shone on me in that very hour.'

'A child must feel the flush of victory and the heart-sinking of disappointment before he takes with a will to the tasks distasteful to him and resolves to dance his way through a dull routine of textbooks.'

'It is a terrible thing to see and have no vision.'

'Literature is my Utopia. Here I am not disenfranchised. No barrier of the senses shuts me out from the sweet, gracious discourses of my book friends. They talk to me without embarrassment or awkwardness.'

'I do not want the peace that passeth understanding. I want the understanding which bringeth peace.'

'It is not possible for civilization to flow backward while there is youth in the world.'

'Youth may be headstrong, but it will advance its allotted length.'

'What a blind person needs is not a teacher but another self.'

'It is for us to pray not for tasks equal to our powers, but for powers equal to our tasks, to go forward with a great desire forever beating at the door of our hearts as we travel toward our distant goal.'

'As the eagle was killed by the arrow winged with his own feather, so the hand of the world is wounded by its own skill.'
'Walking with a friend in the dark is better than walking alone in the light.'

'Toleration is the greatest gift of mind, it requires the same effort of the brain that it takes to balance oneself on a bicycle.'

'My share of the work may be limited, but the fact that it is work makes it precious.'

'The world is moved along, not only by the mighty shoves of its heroes, but also by the aggregate of tiny pushes of each honest worker.'

'The heresy of one age becomes the orthodoxy of the next.'

'Unless we form the habit of going to the Bible in bright moments as well as in trouble, we cannot fully respond to its consolations because we lack equilibrium between light and darkness.'

'There is much in the Bible against which every instinct of my being rebels, so much that I regret the necessity which has compelled me to read it through from beginning to end. I do not think that the knowledge which I have gained of its history and sources compensates me for the unpleasant details it has forced upon my attention.'

'Death is no more than passing from one room into another. But there's a difference for me, you know. Because in that other room I shall be able to see.'

Mother Teresa of Calcutta

FOUNDER, MISSIONARIES OF CHARITY

'True love does not count the cost, it just loves.'

The Life of Mother Teresa

1910   26 August: Born in Shkup (now Skopje in Macedonia), then part of the Ottoman Empire. Baptised on 27 August as Agnes Gonxha Bojaxhiu.

1928   Joins Irish Loreto convent, takes name Sister Teresa.

1929   Sent to Darjeeling India.

1929   Arrives in Calcutta to teach at St Mary's High School.

1931   Teaching at Calcutta Girls' School.

1937   Takes final vows as a nun.

1946   Receives "call" to work among the poor.

1947   Permitted to leave her order and moves to Calcutta's slums to set up her first school.

1950   Pope sanctions her order, The Missionaries of Charity.

1962   Awarded India's Padma Shri for services to the people of India.

1979   Awarded Nobel Peace Prize.

1983   Heart attack while visiting Pope John Paul II in Rome.

1985   Awarded Medal of Freedom, the highest US civilian award.

1989   Has a second and nearly fatal attack. Doctors implant a pacemaker.

1991   Suffers pneumonia in Tijuana, Mexico, leading to congestive heart failure, and is hospitalised in La Jolla, California.

1996   16 November: Made an honorary US citizen.

1997   13 March: Steps down as head of her order.

1997   5 September: Dies in Calcutta, at the age of 87.

biography

'I will never tire of repeating this: what the poor need most is not pity but love. They need to feel respect for their human dignity, which is neither less nor different from the dignity of any other human being.

Do not wait for leaders; do it alone, person to person.'

– MOTHER TERESA

How many resources are consumed by the wealthy and powerful around the globe, in just "analyzing the problem" and setting up organisations to "address the issues" of poverty and the poor?

They could all learn something from a tiny nun who, with Christian love as her guiding inspiration, just went and did it – practised without even preaching!

And in the process she touched the hearts and changed the lives of millions around the world...

A particularly single-minded and focused individual with an enormous drive and a monumental faith in her cause, she had a simple and fundamental message – it was touching people with a Christian love.

If our work were to just wash and feed and give medicines to the sick, the center would have closed a long time ago. The most important thing in our centers is the opportunity we are offered to reach souls.

A nun who prayed hard and worked hard, she saw herself as the pencil, with God doing the writing.

Agnes Gonxha Bojaxhiu was born on 26 August 1910, in Shkup (what is now Skopje in Macedonia), into a devout Catholic family, the youngest of three children of an Albanian building contractor and importer. However, she considered her real birthday to be 27 August, the day of her baptism, which was more important to her than the actual day of her birth.

'By blood and origin I am all Albanian,' she described herself. 'My citizenship is Indian. I am a Catholic Nun. As to my calling, I belong to the whole world. As to my heart, I belong entirely to the heart of Jesus.'

Even as a child she was very religious, and piety was an important part of her life from very early on. Her father was killed when she was but

7 years old, and her mother supported the family with a clothing and embroidery business.

In an answer to the British journalist and writer, Malcolm Muggeridge's question about 'where did all this begin with you?' she replied: 'Many years ago when I was at home with my people... in Skopje in Yugoslavia. I was only twelve years old then... we children used to go to a non-Catholic school, but we also had very good priests who were helping the boys and girls with their vocation according to the call of God. It was then that I first knew I had a vocation to the poor... in 1922.' At the age of twelve!

In an environment dominated by Orthodox Christians and Muslims, she held steadfastly to her Catholic faith, regularly reading *Catholic Missions Magazine*, a publication distributed by a charismatic movement of Catholic Yugoslav priests. Over these years she became particularly interested in missionary work.

When she was in her late 50s, she was able to recall of her teenage years, 'at the beginning, between 12 and 18, I didn't want to become a nun. We were a very happy family. But when I was 18, I decided to leave my home and become a nun, and since then, some 40 years, I've never doubted even for a second that I've done the right thing; it was the will of God. It was His choice.'

So at the age of 18 in 1928, she joined the Sisters of Loreto convent in Ireland. Included in the instruction was the study of English. She spent just 3 months there before being sent to India.

She arrived in Calcutta on 6 January 1929, and stayed there nearly a week before being sent to Darjeeling near the Himalayas, to begin her novitiate. She was then sent back to Calcutta to teach geography and catechism at St Mary's High School for well-to-do girls. She spoke only broken English and had not even taken her vows. She was also learning Hindi and Bengali.

She took her vows as a Sister of Loreto on 24 May 1937, choosing the name Sister Teresa after St Teresa of Lisieux, also known as the Little Flower of Jesus.

In the region, 1942 was a time of famine and hardship. While Mother Teresa particularly liked teaching and enjoyed her time cloistered behind the walls of St Mary's, she was aware that life was a lot harder for the poor on the streets. She became increasingly concerned about the plight of these poor in the streets, and gradually became convinced that her calling was with the poorest of the poor.

In 1944 she was made principal of the school. With a lifelong respect for authority, she was very strict and efficient. It is interesting to consider how often during the course of her life, however, she boldly confronted so many established authorities both in India and around the world.

When she appeared to contract tuberculosis in 1946, she was sent off to Darjeeling on a retreat to recuperate, and it was on that train to Darjeeling that she recalled receiving a calling from God 'to serve Him among the poorest of the poor'. In a moment of prayer, she felt 'aware of a calling in the midst of my vocation. I had to leave the convent (Loreto) and consecrate myself to the poor, living among them.' Her decision was made, and her life was about to change – she decided to leave St Mary's and work among the poorest of Calcutta.

However, it was not just a matter of walking out into the street... first she had to apply to the Archbishop of Calcutta, and then only after his approval did Mother General of the Loreto nuns give her permission to write to Rome. She was a nun who had taken final vows, and could not just up and leave the convent. Finally she was able to write to Pope Pius XII, and by return post she received a positive answer on 12 April 1948, some two years after the Darjeeling train trip. She was then able to go out into the wider world, still living the religious life, and still under obedience to the Archbishop of Calcutta.

So after 19 years in the relative security and comfort of Loreto, at the age of nearly 38, she headed out to the streets with nothing but love, faith and commitment.

First she went briefly to the Sisters in Patna to get some basic medical training, and then she started "operations" in the compound of a family in the slums. Total capital for this bold project was the grand sum of 5 rupees. But people quickly became aware of what she was doing and she never had to ask for money. Gifts, aid and money just started flowing in.

She started working with those she found first – abandoned children, teaching them hygiene, the rudiments of reading, giving them love and helping them survive. 'In determining which work would be done,' she later recounted, 'there was no planning at all. I headed the work in accordance with how I felt called by the people's sufferings. God made me see what He wanted me to do.'

She was doing God's work. Teaching the poor how to look after themselves, setting up little schools for children and taking in the sick and dying. She was where she wanted to be... out in the world in her trademark blue and white sari. She became an Indian citizen in 1949.

In 1950, she founded a religious order in Calcutta called the Missionaries of Charity. The order now provides food for the needy and operates hospitals, schools, orphanages, youth centres, and shelters for lepers and the dying poor. It now includes thousands of nuns, in over 500 missions in more than 100 countries around the world.

At the time of founding the Missionaries, the poor were left to die in the streets. Mother Teresa describes how she took in her first dying person...

The first woman I saw, I myself picked up from the street. She had been half-eaten by the rats and ants. I took her to the hospital but they could not do anything for her. They only took her in because I refused to move until they accepted her. From there I went to the municipality and asked them to give me a place where I could bring these people, because on the same day I found other people dying in the streets. The Health Officer... took me to the Kali Temple, and showed me the Dormashalah where the people used to rest after worshipping the Kali goddess. It was an empty building. I was very happy to have that place for many reasons, but especially knowing that it was a centre of worship and devotion for the Hindus. Within 24 hours we had our patients there and we started the work of the home for the sick and dying who are destitutes.

So in 1952, the first Nirmal Hriday, or "Pure Heart", home was in operation, followed next year by her first orphanage, the Shishu Bhavan.

One of her greatest aims was to "make the unwanted feel wanted." Love was always the answer to overcoming that awful loneliness of not being wanted.

'In the West there is loneliness, which I call the leprosy of the West. It is worse than our poor in Calcutta,' she would say. 'The poor do not need our condescending attitude or our pity,' she would say, 'They only need our love and our tenderness.'

As her good work became more widely known, so did her reputation around the world. Of course there were always the suspicions about what a Catholic nun was doing in a predominantly Hindu country with a high proportion of Muslims. Was she taking in the poor and needy to convert them? And her views on the sanctity of life and anti-abortion stance sat rather oddly with the Hindu ideas of reincarnation. 'What was she really up to?' many would think.

But she doggedly maintained her regime, and through her actions rather than preaching, she popularised Christian teaching in India and around the world. She demonstrated the good that could be done. It was more important to do good before fighting evil.

When she set up the leprosarium it was yet another strong signal that this nun was practising rather than preaching. Many saw her close physical contact with lepers as bordering upon the suicidal. In a 1974 interview she said: 'I see God in every human being. When I wash the leper's wounds, I feel I am nursing the Lord himself. Is it not a beautiful experience?'

She was no mere Christian proselytiser, and increasing numbers of volunteers came forward from the local Calcutta community to help, inspired by the good deeds she was actually doing.

Many saw her as a tiny, and very high-powered oddity, but everyone recognised her as a woman on a powerful mission. And her way of going about it was to simply persevere and persevere and persevere... She seemed to have superhuman stamina, and would rarely get to bed until after midnight, yet she was up at 4.30 am to pray.

Gradually her work began to be more widely recognised, and in 1962 she was awarded her first prize for her humanitarian work, the Padma Shri award for distinguished service. As more awards and prizes followed, she was able to use the money from such prizes, as well as various donations and bequests, to expand her work, and found dozens of new homes.

In those early days there were no speeches and political initiatives... just a simple message of love for thy fellow and the action to prove it. She was not going out to preach, she was out there doing what mattered to people on the streets. While some in India were prospering, there were still millions who were doomed to an abject poverty which they could do nothing about.

Where were the jobs, she would ask, where was the large-scale investment in human development? Where were the dreams of Mahatma Gandhi and Jawaharlal Nehru, for an India that provided justice and prosperity for all?

Her diminutive size never seemed to stop her, there was an inner spiritual resolve which was extraordinarily intense.

And she had an uncanny knack for publicity. Mother Teresa knew how to use her increasingly iconic status to generate interest for her cause and get some good media coverage as well.

She became a spokesman for the poor and repressed everywhere, far beyond India – helping them in their local communities, as well as articulating their hopes and needs to the powerful.

It was only in the 1960s when she was already in her fifties, that she started travelling widely, and her message and her work began to have a truly global reach. By 1960 she had established 25 homes around India. More followed... Rome and Tanzania in 1968, Australia in 1969, and USA in 1971.

In 1966 The Missionary Brothers of Charity was formed. She soon had many thousands of sisters and brothers working for the cause around the world.

She received many awards for her work with the needy, including the 1971 Pope John XXIII Peace Prize and India's Jawaharlal Nehru Award for International Understanding in 1972. In 1979 Mother Teresa was awarded the Nobel Peace Prize. She reflected:

The reason I was given the Nobel Peace Prize, was because of the poor. However the prize went beyond appearances. In fact it awakened consciences all over the world. It became a sort of reminder that the poor are our brothers and sisters and that we have the duty to treat them with love.

She was not a conventional politician but she had a politician's sense of issues and timing: she knew how to lead by example and do symbolic works that would resonate with the consciences of millions around the world. So she was a constant and visible critic of overweight bureaucracies that consumed so much of what was supposed to get to the end recipients.

She was extremely popular wherever she went, and would easily draw large crowds. She always appeared modest, accessible and humble, even though she was now an international icon recognised around the world.

And she appeared in many places in the world, both with some of the best known leaders and public figures around the globe, as well as the most wretched.

For example, she appeared in the Middle East in 1982, intervening between warring Israelis and Palestinians to stop the shooting, long enough to rescue 37 disabled children from a besieged hospital in Beirut. Once again her ability to do something practical but also highly symbolic and iconic, had been made manifest.

Mother Teresa was driven by a strong sense of who she was and what her values were. She had decided what was important and what mattered. The way she saw it was the way she told it. And that was not always what people wanted to hear. Her address to the United Nations in 1985 made it very clear that she was against abortion and contraception – at a time when population control was very much on the international agenda.

As a Catholic true to the teachings of her Church, she opposed abortion, which was permitted in India. Many politicians, bureaucrats, health and social policy professionals, as well as many others around the world, saw Mother Teresa as one of the most significant impediments to the international population control movement – perhaps even more so than America's "right-to-lifers".

What people found it hard to argue against however, was that her work in Calcutta's slums illustrated the value of direct, one-to-one assistance "on the ground" – help where it was needed, not blocked in some remote bureaucracy.

Love, compassion and determination could help people take that first step, that first and fundamental step of regaining some measure of being worth something, that step of self-esteem through being loved. Doing little practical things sooner, rather than making grand plans for a far off future was very much her preferred modus operandi.

It was an approach that worked and struck an appreciative chord around the world. In an age of mass media, celebrity and self-promotion, Mother Teresa did not set out to be a star, yet there she was on the cover of *Time Magazine* in 1975.

She dealt with this in the same way she dealt with everything else… from the viewpoint of her principles, in her practical, humble, down–to-earth fashion.

But she also developed a very worldly wisdom about how the world worked as a consequence of her dealing with so many people from all walks of life. She became an adept political operator at the highest international level, shrewd enough in the ways of the world to use her skills to the advantage of her cause as required. So in 1988, she was more than up to the task of lobbying even people like Maggie Thatcher.

Although she had commenced her order in one of the poorer communities on earth, she was only too aware that her work needed to be done not only in the poorest countries of the world, but in certain areas of even the wealthiest nations. Accordingly, her missions were established even in some of the richest cities of the world, such as New York.

Although Mother Teresa's life was generally regarded as exceptional, being as visible as she was, it was inevitable that she would be the target of criticism from time to time.

There were always her religious opponents who were suspicious of her motivations and methods, and accused her of forcing conversions upon the defenceless. There were those too, who criticised her stance on abortion. In 1994, a British television documentary entitled *Hell's Angel: Mother Teresa of Calcutta*, accused her of taking donations without questioning the sources. Mother Teresa was undeterred by this sort of criticism, stating, 'No matter who says what, you should accept it with a smile and do your own work.'

She had also received criticism for allegedly over-emphasising the problems of Calcutta, for using those she helped to further her own cause, and for offering limited real medical assistance. Her simple response to such assertions was along the lines of 'God does not demand that I be successful. God demands that I be faithful. When facing God, results are not important. Faithfulness is what is important.'

Life as a working international icon was not without its demands…

'We are not social workers,' she would respond. 'We may be doing social work in the eyes of some people, but we must be contemplatives in the heart of the world. For we must bring that presence of God into your family, for the family that prays together, stays together. There is so much hatred, so much misery, and we with our prayer, with our sacrifice, are beginning at home. Love begins at home, and it is not how much we do, but how much love we put into what we do.'

It was only a matter of time before her years of hard work and dedication would inevitably start to exact a personal toll. In 1989 she visited Albania, saddened that she had not been able to get back to see her mother and sister before they died. (The Government denied her access).

She was a small person and had not always enjoyed the best of health, and in the same year, at the age of 79 she had a second and nearly fatal heart attack, which resulted in the implantation of a pacemaker.

In 1990 she announced her intention to resign as head of the organisation, and a meeting of sisters was arranged to select her successor. A secret ballot was held, and when the results were revealed, Mother Teresa had been re-elected with only one dissenting vote – her own. So she was back in charge.

However in 1991 she was stricken with pneumonia whilst in Mexico, and this resulted in congestive heart failure, requiring hospitalisation in California. This was followed by a fall in Rome in 1993 that left her with three broken ribs. She was hospitalised again in August for malaria, and then again in September in Calcutta, for surgery on a blocked blood vessel.

Thereafter, illnesses came thick and fast... another fall and a broken collarbone in April 1996, malarial fever and failure of the left heart ventricle in August, chest infection and recurring heart problems in September, followed by re-admission to hospital with chest pains and breathing problems in November.

In the midst of all this misfortune, she was made an honorary US citizen on 16 November of that year.

By 1997 the inevitable had to happen at last, and she finally stepped down as head of her order on 13 March. Just a few months later on 5 September, she died in Calcutta at the age of 87 – a life's work done.

There is no denying that an exceptional person had departed this earth – an exceptional person with an exceptional approach to the very experience of being truly alive. She had been a rare spirit full of love and compassion, living a life of considerable and valuable wisdom.

The prayer of St Francis of Assisi, which the Missionaries of Charity repeated every day, was one of her favourites. She would always find the time and silence to pray: 'The first requirement for prayer is silence. People of prayer are people of silence,' she would say. Her prayer was:

> Lord make me an instrument of your peace:
> where there is hatred let me sow love;
> where there is injury, pardon;
> where there is doubt, faith;
> where there is despair, hope;

where there is darkness, light;
where there is sadness, joy.
Lord, may I not so much seek
to be consoled as to console;
to be understood as to understand;
to be loved as to love.
Because it is in giving that we receive,
In pardoning that we are pardoned.

French President Jacques Chirac most elegantly summed up her legacy when upon her death he offered: 'This evening, there is less love, less compassion, less light in the world.'

For one who said about herself: 'As far as I am concerned, the greatest suffering is to feel alone, unwanted, unloved', she at least could now take her leave, knowing that she was not alone, that she was widely welcomed and certainly much loved.

wisdom

Are you married? (What is love?)

You have to laugh, as a young man, when a grandmother, mother or young woman herself puckers up with this question. And it certainly was flattering to be considered in this light from time to time by members of the groups I addressed.

What was a special privilege in my travels with the book was to meet couples who had been married for very long periods of time. I do remember, at one function, sitting at a table with three couples who had all been in their respective marriages for more than 60 years – and were delighted by the fact.

I mention this story to highlight a part of the question of love that seemed so often to occur to me – how long does love last? As I had been one of those young people who found it hard to say, 'I love you' willy nilly because I thought love meant forever. But all around it had seemed from time to time, there were people proposing that that need not necessarily be the case.

The answer to the question is, yes I am very newly and happily married to Rebecca.

But the question was much deeper than simply this; it would come in other forms depending on the forum such as, 'how do I know if my girlfriend / boyfriend loves me / is the one for me?' in youth groups.

It is an ultimate and daily question of life, what is love? What is the loving way in any particular situation? How do I know if someone loves me? How should I love someone else?

It is in search of answers to these questions that Mother Teresa of Calcutta entered my life with proposals such as:

'True love does not count the cost, it just loves.'

'If we really want to love we must learn how to forgive.'

'The fruit of faith is love.'

'The greatest disease in the West today is not TB or leprosy; it is being unwanted, unloved and uncared for. We can cure physical diseases with medicine, but the only cure for loneliness, despair and hopelessness is love. There are many in the world who are dying for a piece of bread but there are many more who are dying for a little love.

The poverty of the West is a different kind of poverty – it is not only a poverty of loneliness but also of spirituality. There's a hunger for love, as there is a hunger for God.'

'It is not how much you do but how much love you put into the doing and sharing with others that is important.'

'We must grow in love and to do this we must go on loving and loving and giving and giving until it hurts – the way Jesus did. Do ordinary things with extraordinary love: little things like caring for the homeless, the lonely and the unwanted, washing and cleaning for them. You must give what will cost you something.'

'There is no greater love than to lay down one's life for another.'

You can see how there is nowhere to hide with this sort of standard of love – not only in the power and simplicity of the words but in considering the witness of her life. However I did not have a definition and thus a way of knowing whether I was in fact, executing this desire to love in my own life.

In coming to understand and try to better comprehend what this love, that even John Lennon agreed was all we needed, actually is and should be manifested in my life, I came across the following checklist view of a thousand-year-old scripture:

1. Love is patient
2. Love is kind
3. Love is not jealous
4. Love is not boastful
5. Love is not arrogant
6. Love is not rude
7. Love does not insist on its own way
8. Love is not irritable
9. Love is not resentful
10. Love does not rejoice at wrong
11. Love does rejoice in the good
12. Love bears
13. Love believes
14. Love hopes
15. Love endures forever

This list has given me a definitive standard of love to apply in my life. And when someone now asks the question, 'What is love?', I feel better pre-pared to offer the best answer I have found to date for their consideration – a simple, easy-to-use, yet profound checklist!

Now innocuously placed at the end of this list is a small but earth shattering revelation – you see the love I promised when I recently married Rebecca, if it is to be love under the above definition, it must endure forever! A noble and worthy challenge.

words

I will not forget you

Nobel prize acceptance speech in Oslo, Norway – 1979

*'See! I will not forget you… I have carved you on the palm of My hand…
I have called you by your name… You are Mine… You are precious to Me…
I love you.'*

– ISAIAH

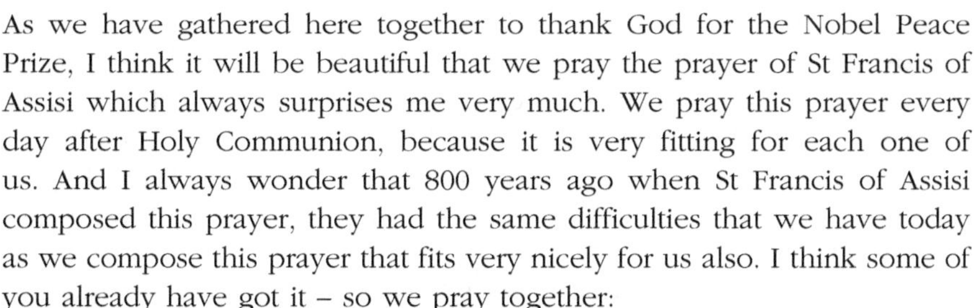

As we have gathered here together to thank God for the Nobel Peace
Prize, I think it will be beautiful that we pray the prayer of St Francis of
Assisi which always surprises me very much. We pray this prayer every
day after Holy Communion, because it is very fitting for each one of
us. And I always wonder that 800 years ago when St Francis of Assisi
composed this prayer, they had the same difficulties that we have today
as we compose this prayer that fits very nicely for us also. I think some of
you already have got it – so we pray together:

> Lord, make me an instrument of your peace:
> Where there is hatred, let me sow love;
> Where there is injury, pardon;
> Where there is doubt, faith;
> Where there is despair, hope;
> Where there is darkness, light;
> Where there is sadness, joy;
> O divine Master, grant that I may not so much seek
> To be consoled as to console,
> To be understood as to understand,
> To be loved as to love.
> For it is in giving that we receive,
> It is in pardoning that we are pardoned,
> It is in dying that we are born to eternal life.
> Amen.

Let us thank God for the opportunity that we all have together today,
for this gift of peace that reminds us that we have been created to live that

peace, and that Jesus became man to bring that good news to the poor. He, being God, became man in all things like us except in sin, and he proclaimed very clearly that he had come to give the good news.

The news was peace to all of good will and this is something that we all want – the peace of heart. And God loved the world so much that He gave His son – it was a giving: it is as much as if to say it hurt God to give, because He loved the world so much that He gave his son. He gave him to the Virgin Mary, and what did she do with Him?

As soon as He came into her life, immediately she went in haste to give that good news, and as she came into the house of her cousin, the child – the child in the womb of Elizabeth, leapt with joy. He was, that little unborn child was, the first messenger of peace. He recognized the Prince of Peace, he recognized that Christ had come to bring the good news for you and for me. And as if that was not enough – it was not enough to become a man – He died on the cross to show that greater love, and He died for you and for me and for that leper and for that man dying of hunger and that naked person lying in the street not only of Calcutta, but of Africa, and New York, and London, and Oslo – and insisted that we love one another as He loves each one of us. And we read that in the Gospel very clearly: 'love as I have loved you; as I love you; as the Father has loved me, I love you.' And the harder the Father loved Him, He gave Him to us, and how much we love one another, we too must give to each other until it hurts.

It is not enough for us to say: 'I love God, but I do not love my neighbor.' Saint John says that you are a liar if you say you love God and you don't love your neighbor. How can you love God whom you do not see, if you do not love your neighbor whom you see, whom you touch, with whom you live? And so this is very important for us to realize that love, to be true, has to hurt.

It hurt Jesus to love us. It hurt Him. And to make sure we remember His great love, He made Himself the bread of life to satisfy our hunger for His love – our hunger for God – because we have been created for that love. We have been created in His image. We have been created to love and to be loved, and He has become man to make it possible for us to love as He loved us. He makes Himself the hungry one, the naked one, the homeless one, and He says: 'You did it to me'. He is hungry for our love, and this is the hunger that you and I must find. It may be in our own home.

I never forget an opportunity I had in visiting a home where they had all these old parents of sons and daughters who had just put them in an institution and forgotten, maybe. And I went there, and I saw in that home they had everything, beautiful things, but everybody was looking towards the door. And I did not see a single one with a smile on their face. And I turned to the sister and I asked: 'How is that? How is that these people who have everything here, why are they all looking towards the door? Why are they not smiling?'

I am so used to seeing the smiles on our people, even the dying ones smile. And she said: 'This is nearly every day. They are expecting, they are hoping that a son or daughter will come to visit them. They are hurt because they are forgotten.' And see – this is where love comes. That poverty comes right there in our own home, even neglect to love. Maybe in our own family we have somebody who is feeling lonely, who is feeling sick, who is feeling worried, and there are difficult days for everybody. Are we there? Are we there to receive them? Is the mother there to receive the child?

I was surprised in the West to see so many young boys and girls given into drugs. And I tried to find out why. Why is it like that? And the answer was: 'Because there is no one in the family to receive them.' Father and mother are so busy they have no time. Young parents are in some institution and the child goes back to the street and gets involved in something. We are talking of peace. These are things that break peace.

But I feel the greatest destroyer of peace today is abortion, because it is a direct war, a direct killing, direct murder by the mother herself. And we read in the scripture, for God says very clearly: 'Even if a mother could forget her child, I will not forget you. I have carved you in the palm of My hand.' We are carved in the palm of His hand; so close to Him, that unborn child has been carved in the hand of God. And that is what strikes me most, the beginning of that sentence, that even if a mother could forget, something impossible – but even if she could forget – I will not forget you.

And today the greatest means, the greatest destroyer of peace is abortion. And we who are standing here – our parents wanted us. We would not be here if our parents would do that to us.

Our children, we want them, we love them. But what of the other millions. Many people are very, very concerned with the children of India, with the children of Africa where quite a number die, maybe of malnutrition, of hunger and so on, but millions are dying deliberately by the will of the mother. And this is what is the greatest destroyer of peace today. Because if a mother can kill her own child, what is left for me to kill you and you to kill me? There is nothing between.

And this I appeal in India, I appeal everywhere – 'Let us bring the child back' – and this year being the child's year: What have we done for the child? At the beginning of the year I told, I spoke everywhere and I said: Let us ensure this year that we make every single child born, and unborn, wanted. And today is the end of the year. Have we really made the children wanted?

I will tell you something terrifying. We are fighting abortion by adoption. We have saved thousands of lives. We have sent word to all the clinics, to the hospitals, police stations: 'Please don't destroy the child; we will take the child.' So every hour of the day and night there is always somebody – we have quite a number of unwedded mothers – tell them: 'Come, we will take care of you, we will take care of the child from you, and we will get a home for the child.' And we have a tremendous demand for families who have no children, that is the blessing of God for us. And also, we are doing another thing which is very beautiful. We are teaching our beggars, our leprosy patients, our slum dwellers, our people of the street, natural family planning.

And in Calcutta alone in six years – it is all in Calcutta – we have had 61,273 babies less from the families who would have had them because they practice this natural way of abstaining, of self-control, out of love for each other. We teach them the temperature method which is very beautiful, very simple. And our poor people understand. And you know what they have told me? 'Our family is healthy, our family is united, and we can have a baby whenever we want.' So clear – those people in the street, those beggars – and I think that if our people can do like that how much more you and all the others who can know the ways and means without destroying the life that God has created in us.

The poor people are very great people. They can teach us so many beautiful things. The other day one of them came to thank us and said: 'You people who have vowed chastity; you are the best people to teach us family planning because it is nothing more than self-control out of love for each other.' And I think they said a beautiful sentence. And these are people who maybe have nothing to eat, maybe they have not a home where to live, but they are great people.

The poor are very wonderful people. One evening we went out and we picked up four people from the street. And one of them was in a most terrible condition. And I told the Sisters: 'You take care of the other three; I will take care of this one that looks worse.' So I did for her all that my love can do. I put her in bed, and there was such a beautiful smile on her face. She took hold of my hand, as she said one word only: 'thankyou' – and she died.

I could not help but examine my conscience before her. And I asked: 'What would I say if I was in her place?' And my answer was very simple. I would have tried to draw a little attention to myself. I would have said: 'I am hungry, I am dying, I am cold, I am in pain', or something. But she gave me much more – she gave me her grateful love. And she died with a smile on her face – like that man who we picked up from the drain, half eaten with worms, and we brought him to the home – 'I have lived like an animal in the street, but I am going to die like an angel, loved and cared for.' And it was so wonderful to see the greatness of that man who could speak like that, who could die like that without blaming, without cursing anybody, without comparing anything. Like an angel – this is the greatness of our people.

And this is why we believe what Jesus has said: 'I was hungry; I was naked, I was homeless; I was unwanted, unloved, uncared for – and you did it to me.'

I believe that we are not really social workers. We may be doing social work in the eyes of people. But we are really contemplatives in the heart of the world. For we are touching the body of Christ twenty-four hours. We have twenty-four hours in His presence, and so do you and I. You too must try to bring that presence of God into your family, for the family that prays together stays together. And I think that we in our family, we don't need bombs and guns, to destroy or to bring peace – just get together, love one another, bring that peace, that joy, that strength of presence of each other in the home. And we will be able to overcome all the evil that is in the world. There is so much suffering, so much hatred, so much misery, and we with our prayer, with our sacrifice are beginning at home. Love begins at home, and it is not how much we do, but how much love we put in the action that we do. It is to God Almighty – how much we do does not matter, because He is infinite, but how much love we put in action. How much we do to Him in the person that we are serving.

Some time ago in Calcutta we had great difficulty in getting sugar. And I don't know how the word got around to the children, and a little boy of four years old, a Hindu boy, went home and told his parents: 'I will not eat sugar for three days. I will give my sugar to Mother Teresa for her children.' After these three days his father and mother brought him to our house. I had never met them before, and this little one could scarcely pronounce my name. But he knew exactly what he had come to do. He knew that he wanted to share his love.

And this is why I have received such a lot of love from all. From the time that I have come here I have simply been surrounded with love, and with real, real understanding love. It could feel as if everyone in India, everyone in Africa is somebody very special to you. And I felt quite at home, I was telling Sister today. I feel in the convent with the Sisters as if I am in Calcutta with my own Sisters. So completely at home here, right here.

And so here I am talking with you. I want you to find the poor here, right in your own home first. And begin love there. Be that good news to your own people. And find out about your next-door neighbor. Do you know who they are?

I had the most extraordinary experience with a Hindu family who had eight children. A gentleman came to our house and said: 'Mother Teresa, there is a family with eight children; they have not eaten for so long; do something.' So I took some rice and I went there immediately. And I saw the children – their eyes shining with hunger. I don't know if you have ever seen hunger. But I have seen it very often. And she took the rice, she divided the rice, and she went out. When she came back I asked her: 'Where did you go, what did you do?' And she gave me a very simple answer: 'They are hungry also.' What struck me most was that she knew – and who are they? a Muslim family – and she knew. I didn't bring more rice that evening because I wanted them to enjoy the joy of sharing.

But there were those children radiating joy, sharing the joy with their mother because she had the love to give. And you see this is where love begins – at home. And I want you – and I am very grateful for what I have received. It has been a tremendous experience and I go back to India – I will be back by next week, the 15th I hope, and I will be able to bring your love.

And I know well that you have not given from your abundance, but you have given until it has hurt you. Today the little children, they gave – I was so surprised – there is so much joy for the children that are hungry. That the children like themselves will need love and get so much from their parents.

So let us thank God that we have had this opportunity to come to know each other, and that this knowledge of each other has brought us very close. And we will be able to help the children of the whole world, because as you know our Sisters are all over the world. And with this prize that I have received as a prize of peace, I am going to try to make the home for many people that have no home. Because I believe that love begins at home, and if we can create a home for the poor, I think that more and more love will spread. And we will be able through this understanding love to bring peace, bring the good news to the poor. The poor in our own family first, in our country and in the world.

To be able to do this, our Sisters, our lives have to be woven with prayer. They have to be woven with Christ to be able to understand, to be able to share. Today, there is so much suffering and I feel that the passion of Christ is being relived all over again. We are there to share that passion, to share that suffering of people – around the world, not only in poor countries. But I found the poverty of the West so much more difficult to remove.

When I pick up a person from the street, hungry, I give him a plate of rice, a piece of bread, I have satisfied. I have removed that hunger. But a person that is shut out, that feels unwanted, unloved, terrified, the person that has been thrown out from society – that poverty is so hurtful and so much, and I find that very difficult. Our Sisters are working amongst that kind of people in the West.

So you must pray for us that we may be able to be that good news. We cannot do that without you. You have to do that here in your country. You must come to know the poor. Maybe our people here have material things, everything, but I think that if we all look into our own homes, how difficult we find it sometimes to smile at each other, and that the smile is the beginning of love.

And so let us always meet each other with a smile, for the smile is the beginning of love, and once we begin to love each other, naturally we want to do something. So you pray for our Sisters and for me and for our Brothers, and for our Co-Workers that are around the world. Pray that we may remain faithful to the gift of God, to love Him and serve Him in the poor together with you. What we have done we would not have been able to do if you did not share with your prayers, with your gifts, this continual giving. But I don't want you to give me from your abundance. I want you to give me until it hurts.

The other day I received $15 from a man who has been on his back for 20 years and the only part that he can move is his right hand. And the only companion that he enjoys is smoking. And he said to me: 'I do not smoke for one week, and I send you this money.' It must have been a terrible sacrifice for him but see how beautiful, how he shared. And with that money I bought bread and I gave to those who are hungry with a joy on both sides. He was giving and the poor were receiving.

This is something you and I can do – it is a gift of God to us to be able to share our love with others. And let it be able to share our love with others. And let it be as it was for Jesus. Let us love one another as He loved us. Let us love Him with undivided love. And the joy of loving Him and each other – let us give now that Christmas is coming so close.

Let us keep that joy of loving Jesus in our hearts, and share that joy with all that we come in touch with. That radiating joy with all that we come in touch with. That radiating joy is real, for we have no reason not to be happy because we have Christ with us. Christ in our hearts, Christ in the poor that we meet, Christ in the smile that we give and the smile that we receive. Let us make that one point – that no child will be unwanted and also that we meet each other always with a smile, especially when it is difficult to smile.

I never forget some time ago about 14 professors came from the United States from different universities. And they came to Calcutta to our house. Then we were talking about the fact that they had been to the home for the dying. (We have a home for the dying in Calcutta, where we have picked up more than 36,000 people from the street and of that number more than 18,000 have died a beautiful death. They have just gone home to God). And they came to our house and we talked of love, of compassion. And then one of them asked me: 'Say, Mother, please tell us something that we will remember.' And I said to them: 'Smile at each other, make time for each other in your family. Smile at each other.'

And then another one asked me: 'Are you married?' and I said: 'Yes, and I find it sometimes very difficult to smile at Jesus because He can be very demanding sometimes.' This is really something true. And there is where love comes – when it is demanding, and yet we can give it to Him with joy.

Just as I have said today, I have said that if I don't go to heaven for anything else I will be going to heaven for all the publicity because it has purified me and sacrificed me and made me really ready to go to heaven.

I think that this is something, that we must live life beautifully, we have Jesus with us and He loves us. If we could only remember that God loves us, and we have an opportunity to love others as He loves us, not in big things, but in small things with great love, then Norway becomes a nest of love. And how beautiful it will be that from here a center for peace from war has been given. That from here the joy of life of the unborn child comes out. If you become a burning light of peace in the world, then really the Nobel Peace Prize is a gift of the Norwegian people. God bless you!

quotes

'Keep the joy of loving God in your heart and share this joy with all you meet especially your family. Be holy – let us pray.'

'I once picked up a woman from a garbage dump and she was burning with fever; she was in her last days and her only lament was: 'My son did this to me.' I begged her: You must forgive your son. In a moment of madness, when he was not himself, he did a thing he regrets. Be a mother to him, forgive him. It took me a long time to make her say: "I forgive my son." Just before she died in my arms, she was able to say that with a real forgiveness. She was not concerned that she was dying. The breaking of the heart was that her son did not want her. This is something you and I can understand.'

'When once a chairman of a multinational company came to see me, to offer me a property in Bombay, he first asked: "Mother, how do you manage your budget?" I asked him who had sent him here. He replied: "I felt an urge inside me." I said: "Other people like you come to see me and say the same. It was clear God sent you, Mr A, as He sends Mr X, Mrs Y, Miss Z, and they provide the material means we need for our work. The grace of God is what moved you. You are my budget. God sees to our needs, as Jesus promised". I accepted the property he gave and named it Asha Dan (Gift of Hope).'

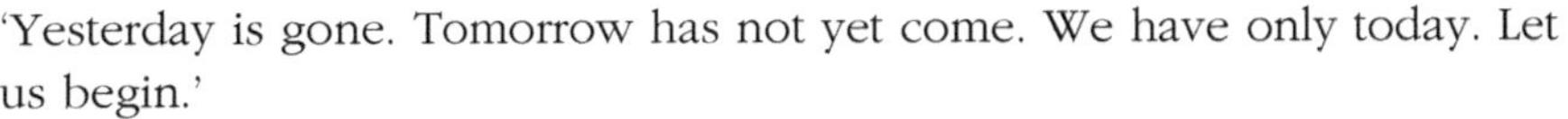

'Yesterday is gone. Tomorrow has not yet come. We have only today. Let us begin.'

'Like Jesus we belong to the world living not for ourselves but for others. The joy of the Lord is our strength.'

'There is only one God and He is God to all; therefore it is important that everyone is seen as equal before God. I've always said we should help a Hindu become a better Hindu, a Muslim become a better Muslim, a Catholic become a better Catholic. We believe our work should be our example to people. We have among us 475 souls – 30 families are Catholics and the rest are all Hindus, Muslims, Sikhs – all different religions. But they all come to our prayers.'

'There are so many religions and each one has its different ways of following God. I follow Christ:
Jesus is my God,
Jesus is my Spouse,
Jesus is my Life,
Jesus is my only Love,
Jesus is my All in All;
Jesus is my Everything.'

'Make us worthy, Lord, to serve those people throughout the world who live and die in poverty and hunger. Give them through our hands, this day, their daily bread, and by our understanding love, give them peace and joy.
I heard the call to give up all and follow Christ into the slums to serve Him among the poorest of the poor. It was an order. I was to leave the convent and help the poor while living among them.'

'When a poor person dies of hunger, it has not happened because God did not take care of him or her. It has happened because neither you nor I wanted to give that person what he or she needed.'

'You and I, we are the Church, no? We have to share with our people. Suffering today is because people are hoarding, not giving, not sharing. Jesus made it very clear. Whatever you do to the least of my brethren, you do it to me. Give a glass of water, you give it to me. Receive a little child, you receive me.'

'Everybody today seems to be in such a terrible rush, anxious for greater developments and greater riches and so on, so that children have very little time for their parents. Parents have very little time for each other, and in the home begins the disruption of peace of the world.'

'If we really want to love we must learn how to forgive.'

Epilogue

An Epilogue was included in the planned format of this book, not because I had anything at the time particularly to say, but rather because I wanted the book to have a clear point of ending.

Now in setting myself to write an Epilogue, surrounded by headlines such as that of the *Sydney Morning Herald* of Saturday 9 April 2005 which reads, 'The Greatest Farewell in History, Pope's funeral brings more than 100 nations to Rome', what I want to say has been so well said.

It has been said in the incredible outpouring of respect on the death of Pope John Paul II, a funeral with 5 million attendees including more than 200 dignitaries from more than 11 nations. His inclusion in *Universal Wisdom* was the most controversial as people seemed to have mixed views of the man. But then, on his death, so much of the story of his life that so few had previously appreciated, came to light.

The message to my mind was best summed up by Mark Steyn when he wrote following the death of the Holy Father, 'The root of the Pope's thinking – that there are eternal truths no one can change even if one wanted to – is completely incomprehensible to the progressivist mindset.' One could as easily write, 'The root of Warren Buffett's thinking – that there are investing rules no one can change even if one wanted to – is completely incomprehensible to the finance academe mindset.'

Universal Wisdom uncovers the source of the certainty that powers the lives of the truly great.

BRETT KELLY
August 2005

APPENDIX

Appendix A – Worksheets

These Worksheets have been included following a comment from my childhood mate, Brad. He observed that so many books are 'theory that is hard to put into practice'. Hopefully, I offer these pages as a place to start in considering the possibilities for application of the ideas offered in *Universal Wisdom*.

1. WISE CHOICES

What is the biggest lesson you learned from your experiences with *Collective Wisdom*?

'If principles date over time, they are not principles.'

a. List 20 principles that you have been taught or learned along life's journey to date.

b. Decide if you think they are "universal wisdoms". And consider why.

1. ____ ☐ ☐
2. ____ ☐ ☐
3. ____ ☐ ☐
4. ____ ☐ ☐
5. ____ ☐ ☐
6. ____ ☐ ☐
7. ____ ☐ ☐
8. ____ ☐ ☐
9. ____ ☐ ☐
10. ____ ☐ ☐
11. ____ ☐ ☐
12. ____ ☐ ☐
13. ____ ☐ ☐
14. ____ ☐ ☐
15. ____ ☐ ☐
16. ____ ☐ ☐
17. ____ ☐ ☐
18. ____ ☐ ☐
19. ____ ☐ ☐
20. ____ ☐ ☐

2. JUSTICE

'What are you doing for others?'

List those people that you have offended or that have helped you and say:

'I have realised how I did not do the right thing by you and I am very sorry about that. Can you forgive me?'
or
'I just wanted to phone and thank you for being a good friend to me and encouraging me to be the best I can be.'

1. □

2. □

3. □

4. □

5. □

6. □

7. □

8. □

9. □

10. □

1. □

2. □

3. □

4. □

5. □

6. □

7. □

8. □

9. □

10. □

3. COURAGE

What do you live for?

'Seek wisdom, get understanding.'

a. List seven people that you admire.

b. Consider what it is that you admire about them.

c. Do some research and try to discover the motivating theme of their lives – the thing that they have been, or were, "prepared to die for".

1. ____

2. ____

3. ____

4. ____

5. ____

6. ____

7. ____

Notes ____

____

____

____

____

____

____

____

____

____

4. FREEDOM

How did you just pick yourself up and write a book, after being sacked?

'Be the change you wish to see in the world.'

a. Are there any of the following that you are not "free" from worry about, or dependence on?

	Free	Not free
• Money	☐	☐
• Status	☐	☐
• Power	☐	☐
• Alcohol	☐	☐
• Drugs	☐	☐
• Gambling	☐	☐
• Sex	☐	☐
• Always being right	☐	☐
• Never asking for forgiveness	☐	☐
• Debt	☐	☐

5. FAITH

Are you a believer?

'That a man that stands for nothing may well fall for anything.'

a. Take time to consider the experience of faith outlined by some of the greatest thinkers in the history of Western Civilisation as follows:

Read

- *Confessions* by St Augustine ☐
- The *Rule of St Benedict* ☐
- *The Divine Comedy* by Dante Alighieri ☐
- *Mere Christianity* by C. S. Lewis ☐

6. HOPE

Why do you think my son killed himself?

'Many persons have a wrong idea of what constitutes true happiness. It is not attained through self-gratification but through fidelity to a worthy purpose.'

a. Make a list of the ideas/things/people that you have hope in and/or for.

b. Consider ranking these ideas/things/people in order of most importance.

c. Write a 200 word Eulogy for your own funeral describing the character of the life you would hope to have led.

Ideas	Most-to-least important
1. _______	1. _______
2. _______	2. _______
3. _______	3. _______
4. _______	4. _______
5. _______	5. _______
Things	6. _______
1. _______	7. _______
2. _______	8. _______
3. _______	9. _______
4. _______	10. _______
5. _______	11. _______
People	12. _______
1. _______	13. _______
2. _______	14. _______
3. _______	15. _______
4. _______
5. _______

Eulogy *(200 words)*

7. LOVE

Are you married? (What is love?)

'True love does not count the cost, it just loves.'

Review some significant current and former relationships from your life and rate (1 to 10) them against the listed qualities below:

	Name 1		Name 2	
Tick if 'Yes' or 'No'	Y	N	Y	N
1. Love is patient	☐	☐	☐	☐
2. Love is kind	☐	☐	☐	☐
3. Love is not jealous	☐	☐	☐	☐
4. Love is not boastful	☐	☐	☐	☐
5. Love is not arrogant	☐	☐	☐	☐
6. Love is not rude	☐	☐	☐	☐
7. Love does not insist on its own way	☐	☐	☐	☐
8. Love is not irritable	☐	☐	☐	☐
9. Love is not resentful	☐	☐	☐	☐
10. Love does not rejoice at wrong	☐	☐	☐	☐
11. Love does rejoice in the good	☐	☐	☐	☐
12. Love bears	☐	☐	☐	☐
13. Love believes	☐	☐	☐	☐
14. Love hopes	☐	☐	☐	☐
15. Love endures forever	☐	☐	☐	☐

Total Score   __________   __________

Appendix B

INTRODUCTION TO *COLLECTIVE WISDOM*

'We have decided to terminate your employment.'

It's not a great start to the day, and it's one that I've got in common with many Australians. And for me, like anyone else, it was a shock, it was depressing, and it made me question just what the hell I was doing.

It was not until later, after months of to-ing and fro-ing when one contributor finally agreed to an interview, that I understood what it was I had been getting so wrong. The process of getting the interview – and others on *Collective Wisdom* – revealed some important things that I'd overlooked in my life so far, things that were so important they have changed my life direction. It was just a pity that I had to lose my job to be able to have the time to work them out.

When I was sacked – and there's no other way to put it – it was the first time that anything had ever gone wrong for me. And it went wrong in a big way. The boss called me in and let me know my work wasn't good enough, that I was different, and that I didn't fit in with the others. That was fairly in-your-face for a 22-year-old who'd always played by the rules, and who was working hard at being a success.

When you've never had things go really wrong, the first time they do it's a real catastrophe. I'd had a good run. I was good at sport and at study. I'd talked my way into a prestigious merchant bank before I'd even finished my studies. I'd worked hard, but things seemed to work out for me too. It's not so difficult when all you do is follow a path seen as desirable by your workmates, parents and friends.

When things come that easy you don't think about them. You don't think about what's truly important to you, what success really is, or what you want your life to be. You just keep running along the same path, letting people assume that you want the life that they have. I'd swallowed the whole deal – that success is the fast car, the big house, lots of money, the "important" job.

So when I lost my job I felt as though the worst thing that could happen in life had happened. Now I know it isn't such a big deal, but then, when I thought my career was a disaster, when screwing up my priorities had killed off a personal relationship, and a back injury had stopped my sporting efforts, it seemed things could not get much worse.

They could.

I thought about the managers I'd worked for, who thought nothing of working 16 hours a day, who didn't know their kids, who had beer guts and who were seen as successful and who appeared not to have much joy for life. That was where I was headed until I lost my job. With that model of success gone, I didn't know what to do.

Without a job my confidence was challenged. So I did nothing, my attitude stank and I had no idea where I was going. What I needed was to find some sense of satisfaction and passion in my life. And I can tell you, that wasn't going to happen the way I was.

I slipped into a routine of getting up late, reading the paper, watching *The Midday Show*, and wasting the afternoon. Without direction it's an easy thing to do. But after a while I started to notice something special about *The Midday Show*, The host, Kerri-Anne Kennerley, has a tremendous talent – her passion for her job. You can see her enjoying her work and it's this that makes her a great performer. I wanted that passion and energy for my life. The problem was I had no idea where to find it.

I asked all the classic 'What am I here for?' questions. It's no surprise that I couldn't answer them, because no one else has been able to either. So, a little more humbly, I tried to work out my purpose for the next year. And it was then that some things started to happen. My mates had been planning to go skiing, and I had decided not to go. At the last minute I changed my mind and went with them. I had committed to taking more risks, to be open to change, to live more for today and to just have a go.

I'd never been skiing before, so I was a bit clueless on the slopes. But because I wanted to improve I took extra lessons and eventually got my skiing together. What made a real difference though, was observing the Austrian ski instructor up close. I learnt to ski by being right behind him and doing exactly what he did – I just copied how he skied and suddenly I could ski.

Of course it was only skiing, but it started me thinking. I still didn't know what success was, I was still directionless. But I knew there were lots of successful people. It then became clear to me that you might be able to learn success just like you can learn skiing. You can watch the experts, copy the basics and make the rest your own.

That's the real birthplace of this series of interviews – on the ski slopes just as I'd learnt from the expert skier, I wanted to get a glimpse of what made successful people successful. I wanted to learn what I could from them, and to find a few clues on how they tick.

I had suddenly found a passion. I started making lists of names of people to interview. I was almost obsessive, writing down names wher-ever they came to me. I imagined I could meet anyone I wanted to, any-one famous and/or interesting, anyone whose qualities, experience or achievements I could learn from. My mum despaired somewhat and would ask me when I'd go back to a normal life and get a proper job.

I made lists and lists of people. But I hadn't contacted anyone because I didn't know what to say. Why would they want to talk to me? I was young, "between jobs", and that was about it. There are plenty of young people without jobs, so how was I going to get their interest?

It took a while, but eventually I came up with the idea of a book. I realised I could learn from the successful while helping others to learn from them as well by putting my interviews in a book.

It's intense at the best of times, so once I identified what project I wanted, I scared myself with how focused I was. In five days I read eight books on publishing and wrote letters to every person I wanted to meet. I thought it would be that easy.

It wasn't. Everywhere I turned I was told how and why I would fail. That I should get a sensible job and "just get on with life". Every time I heard something like that (and it was often) it nibbled away at my confidence. It also made me more determined.

People in publishing tried to discourage me by saying, 'Books of interviews don't sell; you are not Ray Martin or Phillip Adams so who will buy your book? And anyway, you are not going to get the interviews you think you are!' A leading trade union official, who agreed to an interview, decided during the interview time, I would benefit more from a 20-minute lecture on why the book would never be published.

So, people in the book business were saying I couldn't do it. Some of the people I was interviewing seemed a bit sceptical. And worse, some of my "friends" made a point of letting me know I was unemployed and that I should stop dreaming and start thinking about my future.

All I had was a see-sawing confidence in me: confidence in someone with no contacts, no experience, no job, no publisher and no money. It's odd, but as the pressure grew, my resolve strengthened, and I decided *Collective Wisdom* would just have to happen.

But there were physical as well as emotional barriers to cross. To put together 34 interviews I had to make more than 3,000 phone calls, send hundreds of letters and pass six months without earning an income. What's more, successful people are busy, with many demands on their time and energy, and you have to prove you're not wasting their time, because they get a lot of time-wasters. I had to jump through hoops for media minders, managers and personal assistants. I changed my diary so many times I could hardly read it. I called back over and over to make it easier for people to speak to me. I did everything I could to make the interview happen – and the most important thing was the fact to stay calm, pleasant, and always, always, flexible.

Surprisingly, I managed to get twelve interviews done in the first seven weeks. After those first few interviews I thought things would gradually become easier. Was I wrong! The first interviewees had agreed almost immediately, and then there was a period of more than a month without a single success. Every call I made or letter I sent led to a dead end. It was looking pretty grim.

But the breakthrough came with Bob Hawke. Not only did he contribute, he encouraged me at a time when I needed it. His interview then built a momentum that carried over into more interviews. By persisting through that five- or six-week period, I had got the project off the ground. And by persisting further the remaining interviews came through in waves of two or three at a time.

Then Peter Garrett set a major hurdle. When I contacted him, he asked for some sort of evidence that the book was going to happen. And fair enough too, because he was so busy. I could only give him my personal commitment. That was enough for him to agree "in principle". I knew that to get an interview with him I had to come back with something solid, to show that I was going to follow through. With that hurdle set, I moved on to prove myself, and to Peter, that I could do it.

I was lucky too. Some people who had no time for an interview helped in other ways. Thomas Kenneally was too busy, but offered to write review notes for the back cover. Kim Beazley made every effort to contribute, but fell sick at the last minute – while his media adviser spent a lot of time giving me tips and advice on how to get the book done. People were willing to accept constant follow-up calls, rescheduled appointments, re-confirmations and reorganisation. I was fortunate that such considerations were given.

However, I had a lot of trouble getting female contributors for the book. For this edition there are only seven out of 34, even though around half the people I approached were women. Sadly, they either didn't want to talk on the record about the issues in the book, or they didn't want to contribute to someone without a publisher and to a project as uncertain as mine.

And then there were the practicalities. How will I get it published? Do I know what I am doing? Above all else, how would I pay for it? These were basic problems, and I was surprised to discover that my confidence and commitment helped give me a solution.

I talked to everyone I could about the project, I rang an author of books on publishing, who took the time to advise me. I called the creator of a great tape series to ask for his tapes. And the more I talked to people, the more opportunities came my way. I met a publisher, who recommended an editor that was, and is, a total gem. Through her I found a book designer who was not only encouraging, but who offered to do the work at half price. Publicists and marketeers offered support. This help from people who had been around for a while in the industry made it clear I was onto something. And all of them gave me help I had no right to expect, some without even charging for it. Suddenly, I had behind me a professional team with more than 100 years experience between them. I was learning fast.

The interviews themselves also came through people. Contributors introduced me to contributors I couldn't have reached otherwise. Gerry Harvey introduced me to John Singleton, who unfortunately didn't have time. Peter Fitzsimons put in a word for me with Kim Beazley. The list goes on and on. And once things started to happen, luck runs your way as well. After I had interviewed Jeff Kennett, I was walking down Collins Street in Melbourne when I bumped into Malcolm Fraser. I interviewed him the next day.

Within six months I had done 34 face-to-face interviews, and had a great time doing it. Even now I can see myself talking to H G Nelson in a café in Bondi, doubled over with laughter for three hours. My cheeks are still sore. But even the less outrageous interviews gave me a lot. Putting the interviews together, and talking to the contributors them-selves, showed me a lot of things I wouldn't have seen otherwise: from Edmund Capon's self-deprecating humour (and awesome secretary) to John Elliott's commitment to doing something rather than just going to meetings. To the need for persistence and honesty in achieving anything. In the process I ate Macca's with Peter Ritchie, chairman of McDonald's, discussed morality with Cardinal Edward Clancy, and politics with Cheryl Kernot. These are the sorts of learning opportunities people would kill for.

All this was possible due to one very important group of people, the personal assistants of the contributors. A lesson I quickly learnt was that unless I could quickly establish some kind of rapport with the assistants to the contributors then my request for an interview was never going to see the light of day. I tried hard to make helping me as easy as possible and I remained pleasant, completely flexible and respectful of their position.

But despite all this, the problem of how to publish the book remained. After talking to lots of people about the difficulties I was having, and how little support publishers seemed to offer, I decided to self-publish the book. In the end I didn't want to give control of my work to a company who hadn't helped make the project happen, or had even discouraged me. I called myself Clown Publishing – because the serious players thought I was kidding about the book, and because I like the light tough clowns bring to their lives.

I needed a large amount of money to make my book a reality. But being out of work for six months meant I had absolutely none. I'd come to the end of my resources even though the book was ready to go. The money had to come from somewhere, and since no publisher would give it to me, I had to get a sponsor.

While I was trying to get sponsorship together, I managed to find a great job. That was a winning move. With the help of my new boss, we put together a list of ten people who could act as patrons of the book. I approached six of them, and told them the story of the book, why I had done it and my need for funding. Oh, and I guaranteed I would pay it back no matter what, no matter how long it would take.

All six agreed to put up the money. I was stunned, relieved, overjoyed. I knew then the project could happen!

Through all the interviews I really had to learn some difficult truths about myself. When I was sacked, my boss said I needed to learn to listen – so for these interviews I really had to learn. I bought books on listening, particularly Hugh Mackay's book *Why Don't People Listen?* I worked on my listening skills in each of the interviews, trying to improve more each time, watching and copying others, until I had the pleasure of listening to Hugh himself a couple of months later. Funnily enough, our education system concentrates on teaching us to talk but rarely spends much time on listening skills. That personal development was one of the toughest aspects of this project.

This leads us back to Peter Garrett and that hurdle. And to the key things that I have learnt from this whole exercise. Peter was eventually convinced that the book was a reality, not by me, but when my photographer brother Nathan sent him a letter with a photo taken at a Midnight Oil concert. The letter outlined the people I had already interviewed, and explained how the book was going to happen. That was enough to convince him. A letter and a photo, distributed by someone else, was what made the difference. It was what convinced Peter to do the interview.

That's the real gain I've made from the whole series of interviews. I wanted to learn what made successful people successful. Foolishly, I thought it would be something external, some skill or talent. But it doesn't seem to be like that. What seems to make people successful is exactly the same as what made my book a reality – the support, the help, the goodwill and the skills of people.

When I look at the people I've interviewed, one of the things they have in common is a great skill at building relationships. They build rapport and relate to people with little effort. Not once did I feel ill-at-ease in an interview, nor did I walk away without feeling I had got to know them in some way. They were friendly, generous and encouraging, much more so than I would ever have expected. In the main, they are people – people who can understand, relate to and work with others. Small touches come naturally to most of them. For example, Bob Hawke made a friend for life when he gave Nathan a Cuban cigar as a reminder of our visit.

They certainly have enormous reserves of energy and enthusiasm for what they do. And they are different and enjoy difference. If they weren't different they wouldn't be in this book. I am sure many of them weren't popular with their teachers at school. I'm sure many of them never fitted the mould school and work made for them. But merely being energetic and different doesn't seem to be enough without relationship skills.

The realisation that relationships make success has changed my view of success, and has changed my way of living. I had chased qualifications, skills, experience… and let personal relationships flounder. I had some vision of being self-made, where I would be the total of my own efforts. Yet now I know all I can ever do is supply the energy and attitude to projects that coordinate peoples' abilities, ideas and enthusiasm. Everything is done with people.

That's the shift in my life – one that's happened through writing this book. You can't be successful unless relationships are the primary part of that success. With those relationships, you achieve more, your life is richer and more interesting, and you have a lot more fun. The differences between people, and their unique experiences, add an extra dimension to your life. Putting this book together is a classic example. Not only have I succeeded because of others, my life and vision is richer for all the people I have met and all the help given to me.

Everything worth achieving is achieved with people. This may be obvious to a lot of you… it certainly wasn't to me. No one is truly self-made – after all, we start as the product of a few minutes joint effort. By seeing through the eyes of those who have contributed to *Collective Wisdom'*, I hope you will be able to see how important others are to your success. No individual can solve the difficult issues we face as a society, but people working together in harmony have shown that anything is possible!

BRETT KELLY
April 1998

ORDER FORM PLEASE PRINT ORDER BY FAX NOW ON 02 9763 5049

For your copy of *Collective Wisdom* and/or *Universal Wisdom* please fill in details:

Name: ____

Address: ____

Tel: _________________________________ Fax: ________________________

Email: ____

PAYMENT METHOD *(Please tick one. Make cheques payable to 'Clown Publishing')*

☐ Personal Cheque   ☐ Bank Cheque   ☐ Bankcard   ☐ Visa   ☐ Mastercard

Cardholder's Name: ____

Card Number: |__|__|__|__| |__|__|__|__| |__|__|__|__| |__|__|__|__| Expiry Date: __________ / __________

Signature: ____

Number of Books: ☐ 'Collective Wisdom' *(soft cover)* at $29.95 each $ _______________

☐ Universal Wisdom *(hard back)* at $44.95 each $ _______________

Postage at $5.00 per book $ _______________

Total Cost $ _______________

☐ Please tick if you would like your book signed to you *(your name)* by the Author.

SEND TO Clown Publishing, PO Box 1764, North Sydney NSW 2059, Australia *(Allow 21 days for delivery)*
Tel: 02 9763 5050 *Fax:* 02 9763 5049 *Website:* www.brettkelly.com.au

www.ingramcontent.com/pod-product-compliance
Lightning Source LLC
Chambersburg PA
CBHW051441050726

47593CB00005B/1873